"If I was President…

My Blueprint for America"

By Marty Piatt, Architect

This book is dedicated

to the 99% of us living

on Main Street that

proudly occupy America.

While every effort has been made to provide dependable and reliable information, the publisher and author cannot be held responsible or liable for any errors or omissions whether direct or indirect, including consequential, incidental, special or punitive damages, caused directly or indirectly by any error or omission, or arising out of, or in connection with, the information contained herein.

Please excuse any spelling or grammatical errors you may find. I have attempted to do my very best in the writing and formatting of this book. I have had no help in doing so, and this book is the exclusive result of my personal and individual effort.

Information contained herein is and shall remain the exclusive personal Intellectual Property (IP) of the author. Under intellectual property law of the United States, the author is granted exclusive rights to intangible assets including: literary, artistic works, discoveries, inventions, and words, phrases, and designs including but not limited to the following:

"Unicameral Congress, A Committee of States, 12 Supreme Court Justices (6 men, 6 women), non-religious Patriotic National Tithe, 10% Gross Income Tax (GIT), Americare, 28th Amendment to the Constitution, 2013 (and 2017) Articles of Federation, Equal Rights Proclamation, Equal Rights Article, Saturn 2.0, Saturn C8 "Supernova", Saturn C5/C8 INT-21, Libra Colony, Libra Station, Lunar Orbital Outpost, Peary Lunar Outpost, Mars Orbital Outpost, and Martius Colony."

The views and opinions expressed herein may not reflect or represent the views and opinions of the United States Government, the Department of Defense, or the Department of the Navy. None are explicitly implied nor stated.

AuthorHouse™
1663 Liberty Drive
Bloomington, IN 47403
www.authorhouse.com
Phone: 1-800-839-8640

Published by AuthorHouse 05/07/2012
Revised by AuthorHouse 10/02/2015

ISBN: 978-1-4685-9520-8 (sc)
ISBN: 978-1-4685-9515-4 (hc)
ISBN: 978-1-4685-9519-2 (e)

Library of Congress Control Number: 2012907204

Print information available on the last page.

Any people depicted in stock imagery provided by Thinkstock are models,
and such images are being used for illustrative purposes only.
Certain stock imagery © *Thinkstock.*

This book is printed on acid-free paper.

Because of the dynamic nature of the Internet, any web addresses or links contained in this book may have changed
since publication and may no longer be valid. The views expressed in this work are solely those of the author and
do not necessarily reflect the views of the publisher, and the publisher hereby disclaims any responsibility for them.

authorHOUSE®

INTRODUCTION

I am not a writer. I am an Architect in Federal service to the United States Department of Defense as a civilian employee proudly serving my country at Naval Facilities Engineering Command (NAVFAC), SW region.

My writing style has structure, as you might expect from an Architect, rather than a professional writer. No ghostwriter was used in the preparation of this book. Every word was written and typed by myself. Each chapter is built with a supporting foundation, that being historical fact, making opposing debate certainly more difficult. The chapters contained in this book stand alone, each becoming an individual structural column together supporting the content covering my political ideals.

There has been discussion regarding the title of my book. Some in the literary community would suggest that the book's title should have been: "If I were President...", rather than: "If I was President...". I actually debated the difference on a personal level for quite a long time and finally decided against the use of the word "were", which seemed in my opinion to imply a past tense rather than the grammatically correct "conditional present tense" as most literary scholars would prefer. The use of "was" appeared to be more in the present tense. Although both uses are generally accepted as correct, I believe that common Americans would understand the book title meaning in spite of the literary critics preference. My intension was to use title version in a more spoken form. Because I am not a writer, you will discover that my writing style is more in the context of written speech dictated as to what I would actually have spoken.

I wrote this book because of my personal sense of being absolutely powerless as a citizen of this great country to make a significant difference in American politics. Not unlike most Americans, I have grown tired of the politics of politics. The lies and corruption of our Senate and House of Representatives that form our United States Congress, including our Presidency, have finally become totally unacceptable.

The first version of this book was published in early 2012 prior to the November Presidential election, less than six months before Americans went to the ballot box to elect a new President. I was unfortunately unable to spend the amount of time necessary to write a more comprehensive book, which still required more than six months to complete. Since then, I have had the opportunity to revise and update the content of the book. This book's original Forward of has become the INTRODUCTION, and the final chapter now titled LEADERSHIP has become the most important chapter, which superseded the original Conclusion. While this version is not really considered a Second Edition of the book printing, I would however consider it a 2016 EDITION. This newer version contains the same relevant political content, only updated. With the improvements including the addition of the leadership material, the information contained herein is still very important to the 2016 Presidential election.

The coming political campaigns of our Congressional and Presidential candidates will have them telling all Americans they have all the answers, yet providing no details or specific plans to make our country the great nation it once was, and can be. The solutions to the many challenges facing our country are really quite simple, certainly not rocket science; which is also one of my more favorite topics in this book having an entire chapter dedicated to NASA and our future explorations of the universe.

I believe my plans to replace our corrupt Congress, stalled economy, high unemployment and under unemployment, skyrocketing budget deficit, outdated electoral college, and our lack of Federal Democracy are really not as complicated as one might think. I question whether our Congress and President really understand the many courses of action necessary to greatly improve the unacceptable circumstances impacting all Americans today. Within the following pages this book, "If I was President…" I intend to propose, hopefully with all Americans in agreement, the paths to recovery and road to prosperity "We The People" of the United States of America will hope to achieve together, which is… "My Blueprint for America".

TABLE OF CONTENTS

"If I was President..."

By Marty Piatt, Architect

UNITED STATES GOVERNMENT

The history of America begins nearly two hundred years prior to the former British colonies becoming what is now the United States of America in 1776. The original thirteen colonies were: Connecticut, Delaware, Georgia, Massachusetts, Maryland, New Hampshire, New Jersey, New York, North Carolina, Pennsylvania, Rhode Island, South Carolina, and Virginia.

On March 25, 1584, Sir Walter Raleigh was granted a charter by Queen Elizabeth I for the colonization of the North American area known as Virginia. According to the charter, Raleigh had only seven years to establish a settlement in North America or lose his charter to colonize the area. The expedition was financed and organized by Raleigh and carried out by Ralph Lane and Raleigh's distant cousin, Richard Grenville. The intentions of Raleigh and the Queen would be that the venture could provide riches from the New World.

On April 27, 1584, Raleigh dispatched Phillip Amadas and Arthur Barlowe to lead an expedition to explore the North American Eastern coast. Arriving on Roanoke Island on July 4, 1584, they soon established relations with the local native Indians known as the Croatans and the Secotans. Located in what is now present-day Roanoke Island in Dare County, North Carolina, the Roanoke Colony was the very first, yet unsuccessful, attempt to establish a permanent English settlement. Three years after the last shipment of supplies arrived from England, the final group of Roanoke colonists disappeared during the Anglo-Spanish War. The settlement, known as "The Lost Colony", vanished in 1590 with the ultimate fate of the colonists remaining unknown to this day.

On May 14, 1607, the Virginia Company of London founded James Fort. As it would later be referred, Jamestown became the first permanent settlement of the thirteen British Colonies to become successful in what would become the Colony of Virginia. To help improve the settlement, the Virginia Company brought Dutch and Polish colonists within one year of its founding. In 1619 the first documented Africans were brought to Jamestown; although the modern concept of forced slavery in the future United States would not occur in Virginia until later in 1660. The Virginia Colony would serve as the Capital from 1616 until 1699, nearly 83 years.

1

During that early colonial time, the Dutch Republic had also settled what was known as New Netherland. After the surrender of Fort Amsterdam by the Dutch in 1664, the settlement of New Netherland would later be ceded to the English in 1674 and become the Province of New York.

On April 17, 1702 the east and west portions of the New York settlement located between the Hudson River and the Delaware River would later unite and become the Province of New Jersey, which was named after the British Isle of Jersey. Many French Huguenots, who were Protestants that had fled France wishing to escape religious persecution from the Catholic nation and Vatican, settled in colonial New Jersey.

In 1712, my sixth great grandfather John Hull Piatt was born in the Province of New Jersey; believed to have French Aristocratic family ancestry. He would take the maiden name of his mother Mary Hull as his middle name. He and his wife Francis would have five sons, all born in New Jersey. John was born in 1740, Abraham in 1741, William in 1743, Daniel (who was my fifth great grandfather) in 1745, and Jacob in 1747. All five sons of John Hull Piatt would enlist and become military officers commissioned in the Continental Army during the American Revolution in support of the leadership of General George Washington. Their military ranks were: Captain John, Major Abraham, Captain William, Major Daniel, and Colonel Jacob Piatt. The five Piatt brothers would later become famously known as the "Fighting Five Piatts" during the American Revolutionary War, fighting for our freedom and independence from the British crown. Many major and decisive battles were fought in New Jersey during our Revolution. Playing a very important role, the Province of New Jersey would rightfully earn the title of the "Crossroads of the Revolution" and "Capitol of the Revolution".

The British levied the first direct tax known as the 1765 Stamp Act, which General George Washington was opposed, becoming a leading role in the growing colonial resistance early in our American Revolution. With the resistance in dire need of financing and capitol for our Revolution, it is believed that Major Daniel Piatt would then sail to France, to meet with wealthy Piatt family members of the French Aristocracy who had remained in France during the exodus of the French Huguenots in the late sixteenth century. Many of those that would flee France and immigrate to colonial America, would settle in the Province of New Jersey, and nearby regions.

By Marty Piatt, Architect

Upon arrival in France, Major Daniel Piatt would meet Gilbert du Motier Marquis de Lafayette, presumably a French family relative. Born on September 6, 1757, he was a French Aristocrat and would become a Lieutenant General serving in the French Army. Following in his family's long line of proud military heritage, he became a commissioned officer at the age of 13. He would later become famously known just simply as "Lafayette" in what would become the future United States of America.

It is my understanding that Major Daniel Piatt and Lafayette were believed to be distant French cousins having a common Aristocratic heritage. They became close and often discussed details of the burgeoning Revolution in colonial America. Historians suggest that Lafayette hated the British for killing his father in 1759, which encouraged him even greater wanting to assist General George Washington in defeating the British, whose sole intent was to crush the American resistance. Convinced the Revolution was a noble cause, Lafayette would eventually sail to America to join the colonial resistance to fight the British invasion.

The French ancestry of the Piatt family linage and the Lafayette family linage had presumably intersected in some maternal fashion, where they possibly shared a related family Aunt, or Great Aunt, who was also an extremely wealthy French Aristocrat. After discussions of the American Revolution and the dire need for financial support with the wealthy family Aristocrat, Major Daniel Piatt is believed to have been successfully able to secure $7 million dollars to assist in the financing of our American Revolutionary War. This substantial sum of money was an incredibly huge amount for the eighteenth century time period, estimated to have a current value well over $212 million dollars, when adjusted for 2015 dollars. This American revolutionary wartime debt has never been repaid to any of the living Piatt Family descendants. We believe the historical accounts of our Piatt family's ancestors financing a substantial portion of our American Revolutionary War was researched and published in the Los Angeles Times newspaper in the late 1950's according to Piatt family sources and legend.

On September 5, 1774 the First Continental Congress was convened at Carpenters' Hall in Philadelphia in response to the passage of the Coercive Acts by the British Parliament, which was meant to punish Bostonians for the Boston Tea Party. The Congress was attended by 56 members appointed by the legislatures of twelve of the thirteen colonies. The Colony of Georgia, considered a convict state, did not send any delegates.

The First Continental Congress would also create the Continental Association to establish a coordinated protest of the Coercive Acts. The Congress would meet briefly to consider petitioning King George III for redress of their grievances.

Peyton Randolph would be elected as the first President of the First Continental Congress. The Presidents of Congress were the lesser-known, yet no less important, leaders of the American Revolution because of the limited role they played in the office. The President was a member of Congress elected by other delegates to serve as an impartial moderator during meetings of Congress, and was the presiding officer of the Continental Congress. Fearful of concentrating political power in one individual, the position had little authority by design and was largely a ceremonial position with little influence. The First Continental Congress agreed that a Second Continental Congress should reconvene to plan and implement future responses in their defense if the British did not repeal or modify the Coercive Act, or if Congress' petition to the British Crown to halt enforcement became unsuccessful. The American colonists would actually refer the British retribution as the "Intolerable Acts".

On May 11, 1775, when the petition to the British Crown ultimately failed, the Second Continental Congress convened to organize the defense of the Colonies at the beginning of the American Revolution. Georgia who had not participated in the First Continental Congress did not initially send delegates to the Second Continental Congress. Delegates would urge each Colony to establish and train its own military militia. During that time, the American Revolutionary War had already begun and was well underway. General George Washington had sadly been defeated battling the British in New York, placing the Province of New Jersey in danger of invasion.

On May 4, 1776, Rhode Island became the first colony to declare independence from British rule, two months prior to the other colonies.

On June 11, 1776, the Second Continental Congress appointed a committee to draft what would become our Declaration of Independence, and was instructed to present the results of their efforts the following day.

On June 12, 1776, the Second Continental Congress appointed another committee having 13 colony members to prepare a draft of a potential constitution, which was intended to create a "union" of the colonial states.

By Marty Piatt, Architect

On July 2, 1776, the Province of New Jersey adopted their first Constitution, having taken only seven days to both draft and ratify. New Jersey became the first of the 13 colonies to do so in American history. The prompt actions of New Jersey were in support of the patriotic leadership of General George Washington, and to establish a temporary Colonial government in the region preventing not only the collapse of the colony of New York, but to avert the potential descent into anarchy of the entire colonial region. The New Jersey Constitution also contained the first of civil rights provisions in American history, which granted the right to vote to unmarried women, and blacks that met property requirements.

On July 4, 1776, members of the Second Continental Congress would, in one of the most historical events of the American Revolution, formally adopt and sign our "Declaration of Independence", and thereafter the new nation was officially referred to as the "United States of America".

On July 31, 1777, after arriving in America and offering his service to General George Washington and the Continental Army without pay, Gilbert du Motier Marquis de Lafayette, was commissioned by the Second Continental Congress as a military officer and given the extraordinary rank of Major General at the age of only 19 years old. Lafayette would finally meet with General George Washington for the first time over dinner on August 5, 1777, and the two would bond almost immediately. Lafayette would express his strong desire to share in the military glory of defeating the British, who killed his father 18 years earlier. He would also become close friends with Alexander Hamilton and Thomas Jefferson. Lafayette would later have a son and name him George Washington de La Fayette.

On November 15, 1777, the final draft of Articles of Confederation, officially known as the "Articles of Confederation and Perpetual Union" was adopted by the Second Continental Congress, and sent to the colonial States for ratification. It was an agreement among the thirteen colonies that was meant to formally establish a national government, or "union". Samuel Huntington, became the last Congressman elected as President of the United States Continental Congress on September 25, 1779

On April 16, 1780, Major Daniel Piatt, my fifth great grandfather, sadly died at the early age of only 34 years in New Jersey, the place of his birth. Two sons, brothers Robert Piatt and John Piatt, my fourth great grandfather, who would continue his paternal family legacy, survived him.

I am honored and grateful he was able to pass on the American patriotism of the "Fighting Five Piatts" to all that have descended him and his brothers, who fought for our nation's freedom and liberty.

Major Daniel Piatt proudly served his country and our great nation during an important and critical period in the rich history of the United States of America. Regretfully, he did not live to see the fruits of his labors that helped create the United States of America. He did however live to see the independence declared fighting for our freedom and liberty

He was a true American Patriot, and I am very proud to be a recipient of the paternal Piatt family lineage and ancestry he was able to give me. His dedication to America and our founding fathers shall not be forgotten.

On March 1, 1781, after receiving the very last remaining ratification by the State of Maryland, the Articles of Confederation were enacted into use, which then created our very "first" United States government. The new government was established as a "Confederation of Sovereign States" and served as our country's very first Constitution. A "Confederation" type of union permitted the voluntary participation in the government of the United States.

The Articles of Confederation gave legitimacy to the Second Continental Congress, which enabled them to direct the American Revolutionary War, and assume control of the "Continental Navy" that was previously established on October 13, 1775.

There were many debates on issues such as sovereignty, and the precise powers given to the government. The States were to retain sovereignty over all functions not specifically relinquished to the Confederate government. The Articles of Confederation also created a "unicameral" Congress having no Senate. The Confederate Congress gave States equal representation and each had veto power on most decisions.

I truly believe the creation of a "unicameral" Congress having only a House of Representatives would become the single most significant and important political event in the entire history of the United States.

The Articles of Confederation, which consisted of a Preamble, Articles I through XIII, and a Conclusion, contained the following 13 Articles:

By Marty Piatt, Architect

Article I created the Confederacy of the "United States of America";

Article II stated that each state retains its sovereignty, freedom, and independence, and every power, jurisdiction, and right, which is not by the confederation expressly delegated to the United States.

Article III, bearing an uncanny resemblance to the Preamble our current Constitution stated:

"The said States hereby severally enter into a firm league of friendship with each other, for their common defense, the security of their liberties, and their mutual and general welfare, binding themselves to assist each other, against all force offered to, or attacks made upon them, or any of them, on account of religion, sovereignty, trade, or any other pretense whatever."

Articles IV through XII gave greater detail to the organization of the newly formed Confederate government.

Article IX, the most extensive of all the Articles of Confederation, detailed what would the rudimentary basis for the Executive and Judiciary Branches of the Confederate government, without clearly defining those portions as precisely as they are defined in our present Constitution.

With the several State legislatures having their own Judiciary Branch of government, the new Congress was given the authority and power as the last resort of Appeal in all disputes and differences subsisting or arising between two or more of the States, acting much in the same capacity as our Supreme Court does today.

Under the Articles of Confederation, if the disputing State parties could not agree to "…appoint by joint consent, commissioners or judges to constitute a court for hearing and determining the matter in question", Congress would establish an alternate appellate court to hear the dispute.

These commissioners or judges, drawn out by lot, would become what we now know as the first type of supreme appellate judiciary within the United States government.

Article XIII, the last of the thirteen Articles stated:

"Every State shall abide by the determination of the united States in congress assembled, on all questions which by this confederation are submitted to them. And the Articles of this confederation shall be inviolably observed by every State, and the union shall be perpetual; nor shall any alteration at any time hereafter be made in any of them; unless such alteration be agreed to in a congress of the united States, and be afterwards confirmed by the legislatures of every State."

Unlike our present Constitution, Article XIII required 100% of the colony States to ratify any changes to the Articles of Confederation to ultimately ensure the timeless and perpetual integrity of the agreement. The new Confederate Congress was given authority to appoint an executive committee to sit in the recess of Congress.

A Committee of the States consisted of one delegate from each of the 13 colonial States. The executive committee would appoint other committees and civil officers as necessary to manage the general affairs of the government under their direction, and would appoint one of their members to the Office of President.

In 1783, the American Revolutionary War ended in "Garden State" of New Jersey. Historical accounts suggest the American Revolution ended in Virginia during the Battle of Yorktown on October 19, 1781, where both General George Washington and Major General Lafayette would play vital roles commanding our Continental Army. However, the entire State of New Jersey was actually a battleground from 1776 through 1783.

On February 21, 1787, six years after ratifying the Articles of Confederation, the "First Constitutional Convention" convened in Philadelphia, Pennsylvania to address various problems in governing the United States. The delegates would appoint General George Washington to preside over the convention after having received the majority of votes cast by the convention delegates. Possessing little legitimacy, the unicameral Congress, having only about fifty members, lacked the authority to lay and collect taxes, regulate commerce among the States, or enforce laws it had attempted to enact. Only the thirteen colonial States had voting privileges in the Confederate Congress.

By Marty Piatt, Architect

Although the First Constitutional Convention delegates wanted to revise the Articles of Confederation, the real intention all along was to create a new government rather than try to fix the old one. I believe abandoning the Articles of Confederation would become our founding fathers "first" greatest mistake in our nation's history.

During the First Constitutional Convention, the "Garden State" would submit the "New Jersey Plan" on June 15, 1787 that once again would propose a unicameral Congress consisting of a House of Representatives, which was supported by the old Patriots, or "Anti-Federalists". The New Jersey Plan proposal consisted of the following revisions:

1. The Articles of Confederation would be amended;

2. Under the Articles of Confederation, Congress would gain authority to raise taxes via tariffs and other measures, and was able to regulate interstate commerce and commerce with other nations. Cases involving these powers would still be heard by state courts unless appealed to the federal judiciary;

3. Congress would have the authority to collect taxes from the states based on the number of free residents including 3/5ths of slaves in that state. This authority would however require the consent of some proportion of the states;

4. Congress would elect a federal executive, consisting of multiple people, who could not be re-elected and could be recalled by Congress when requested by the majority of the states;

5. A Supreme Tribunal, appointed by the federal executive having authority in federal impeachment cases, would represent the federal judiciary and become the appeal of last resort in cases dealing with national matters, including international treaties;

6. The Articles of Confederation and treaties would become the supreme law of the land. The federal executive would be able to use force to compel non-compliant states to observe the law;

7. A policy of admission of new states would be established;

8. A single policy for naturalization would be established;

9. A citizen of one state could be prosecuted under the laws of another state where the crime was committed.

The delegates of the First Constitutional Convention would unfortunately dismiss the "New Jersey Plan" proposal having a unicameral Congress in favor of the Virginia Plan, which proposed the structure of government we have today. In terms of rejecting a unicameral Congress, this would become our founding fathers "second" greatest mistake in our nation's history.

On July 24, 1787 during the First Constitutional Convention, a Committee of Detail was appointed by the delegates to produce the first draft of our Constitution. In the preparation the draft, the Committee would refer to the State's constitutions, the existing Articles of Confederation, and other pertinent documents. The Committee of Detail, consisting of five members chaired by John Rutledge, included Edmund Randolph who wrote the preamble of the Committee's Report citing:

"In the draught of a fundamental constitution, two things deserve attention:

1. To insert essential principles only; lest the operations of government should be clogged by rendering those provisions permanent and unalterable, which ought to be accommodated to times and events: and,

2. To use simple and precise language, and general propositions, according to the example of the constitutions of the several states."

After more discussion and refinement, a second committee, the Committee of Style and Arrangement was appointed to produce the final version of what would become our Constitution on September 8, 1787. The final version of our United States Constitution, closely resembling the first draft, was subsequently submitted to the several States for ratification on September 28, 1787. Only twelve of the original thirteen colony States would sign the Constitution.

On September 13, 1788, the United States of America was once again established with the signing and ratification of our Constitution. It would become our county's "second" national government having a "Republican" form of Federal government. This would become our founding fathers "third" greatest mistake of our nation's history.

On November 15, 1788, Cyrus Griffin became the tenth and last President of the United States under the Articles of Confederation after the Confederate government was subsequently abandoned being deemed bankrupt and impotent.

On March 4, 1789, the "Confederation of Sovereign States" government was officially dissolved by the Confederate Congress and replaced by adoption with the "Republican" form of Federal government that exists today. The United States of America continued to exist, yet under a new United States Constitution, and the new Federal government officially began operations as it is today.

Contrary to popular belief, General George Washington was not the first President of United States.

Samuel Huntington presided as President representing the United States during the final ratification of the Articles of Confederation on March 1, 1781, which officially created the United States first Confederate government. He would serve in the Office of the President until July 9, 1781. Some would argue that Samuel Huntington was actually the first President of the United States of America.

1. Samuel Huntington – 1779
2. Thomas McKean – 1781
3. John Hanson – 1782
4. Elias Boudinot – 1783
5. Thomas Mifflin – 1784
6. Richard Henry Lee – 1785
7. John Hancock – 1786
8. Nathaniel Gorham – 1786
9. Arthur St. Clair – 1787
10. Cyrus Griffin – 1788
11. George Washington – 1789
55. Marty Eugene Piatt – 2017

On May 29, 1790, the State legislature of Rhode Island finally ratified the Constitution, after a failed popular referendum on March 24, 1788, becoming the very last of the colony States to do so. The State of Rhode Island is the only State not to sign the original Constitution document.

Having three very important and definitive branches of government established, they would share power with checks and balances to provide uniform and separate governance. To protect our country against the abuse of power, each branch of government had a separate sphere of interest and authority and could check the other branches according to what is now known as the "Separation of Powers" principle.

The check and balance within our government's bicameral Congress, would become our founding fathers "fourth" greatest mistake in our nation's history.

I believe our present Constitution, was unfortunately, yet deliberately written to be broad and flexible accommodating future social or technological change, is often cited as the "genius" of the Constitutional framers having one of the timeless arguments for the framework of a living Constitution. Two centuries worth of amendments and changes by a power-hungry and corrupt bi-cameral Unites States Congress would later prove contrary.

On April 23, 1843, Amos Daniel Piatt, my second great grandfather, was born in the State of Kentucky. He was the son of Henry William Harrison Piatt and Caroline Piatt. At the age of 18 years old, Amos Daniel joined the Union Army and fought for our American civil rights and the equality of all men, both black and white, against the tyranny of slavery and oppression during our American Civil War. From about 1861 to 1865, Amos Daniel Piatt proudly served our great country, as did all American Civil War soldiers, irrespective of whether they served for the North or the South. Our country lost more than 620,000 precious American lives during our country's American Civil War, which is nearly equal to all wars and conflicts the United States has fought in our nation's history since combined. As an American Civil War veteran, Amos Daniel survived the greatest tragedy that had divided our nation, which unfortunately became a very dark and devastating period unprecedented in our American history.

On August 11, 1912 Amos Daniel Piatt died an American Patriot in Frankfort, Marshall County, KY at the age of 69. Fortunately for those that are his descendants, he was able to pass on his patriotism and that of the "Fighting Five Piatts" ancestry to his son Joseph Wesley Piatt, my great grandfather, continuing the paternal Piatt lineage of my proud American family's heritage.

Now in the present, the vast number of unemployed and under-employed American citizens roughly equals the 12 million illegal foreign nationals unlawfully residing in our country.

Our nation's senior citizens, Veterans, and American children are not receiving the proper care they deserve, while illegal aliens and their anchor babies are receiving treasonous aid and comfort at the expense of hard-working American taxpayers.

We have no real energy policy, relying in part on foreign oil from countries that despise America, many whose religious Islamic beliefs appear entirely incompatible with Western ideological freedoms. We are at the mercy of Oil Companies and their greedy Wall Street managers and speculative futures markets.

Our national debt is roughly equal to our Gross Domestic Product. Our national banking system, with the complicit assistance of the Federal Reserve, has robbed the wealth and future prosperity of our country. Our Federal government sold-out Main Street, and bailed-out Wall Street.

After only sixteen years, and two Presidential administrations, the Republican Party and Democratic Party have equally brought our county to near destruction. The Republican National Committee (RNC) and the Democratic National Committee (DNC) are running and ruining America.

President George W. Bush and the Republican Party had destroyed America's economy, driving our nation into financial crisis unseen since the Great Depression, which still remains unprecedented in the twenty-first century. President Bush started two Middle-eastern wars, which shed the precious blood of our proud American warfighters and peacekeepers for crude oil in one. The Iraqi War, which was entirely unnecessary, has actually destabilized the region much greater than when Saddam Hussein was in power, which should be considered for international war crimes.

President Barack Hussein Obama, our nation's first black President, and the Democratic Party have destroyed America's social fabric with racial unrest not seen since American Civil War and the Civil Rights Era of the early- to mid-twentieth century. President Obama has personally directed our United States Attorney General which Federal laws he has chosen to enforce, and those he has chosen not to enforce.

13

President Obama has ignored nearly all of our nation's immigration laws and has flooded our country with unwanted illegal aliens from the Middle East and Latin America having absolutely no alliance whatsoever to our nation, while having utter disregard for securing our country's borders.

Our country is divided, now more than ever before; by wealth and poverty; by haves and have-nots; by the majority and the minority; by blacks and whites; by the left and the right; by Democrats and Republicans; by race and gender; by believers and non-believers; by American citizens and non-citizens; by Bi-lingual languages; by Bi-partisan duopoly political parties; and by the Bi-cameral corrupt-redden Congress.

Bi-, prefix, origin: Latin meaning: number denoting two; two parts, divided in half.

Uni-, prefix, origin: Latin meaning: one; having or consisting of one only, a single entity.

Our country needs unity, to be unified and united; a nation undivided; a nation having wealth and prosperity for all; a nation with equality having no majority or minority; a nation gathered towards the center; a nation sharing common interests and beliefs; a nation having one national English language; a nation with non-partisan politics; a national government with a unicameral Congress; and the time is now. America can wait no longer.

It is very important that I also describe the Presidential candidate we don't need during our national general election in November 2016.

We don't need a Republican candidate;
We don't need a Democrat candidate;
We don't need a Socialist candidate;
We don't need a Conservative candidate;
We don't need a Liberal candidate;
We don't need a Religious or non-religious candidate,
We don't need a Divisive candidate;
We don't need a Celebrity candidate;
We don't need a Dynasty candidate;
We don't need a Wealthy candidate;
We don't need a Career Politician candidate;
We don't need a Lawyer or Attorney candidate.

14

By Marty Piatt, Architect

Our country needs a Presidential candidate who is an American Patriot. We need a candidate that is an independent thinker who will empower and inspire all Americans to achieve great success. We need a candidate who has a blueprint to unite our divided country and fix the three broken and flawed branches of our United States government.

I hear so often the saying: "Washington is broken". Washington is not broken. Washington it is just a place, a point on the map, the center and Capitol of our government. What makes up Washington is truly broken. And yet, I believe it can be fixed.

The Executive Branch of government, our Presidency, is not broken. The process in which our President is elected is broken and greatly flawed. And yet, it too can be fixed.

The Judicial Branch of government, our Federal Courts and Justice System is not broken. The process organizing our court system and interpretation of our laws are greatly flawed.
And yet, it too can be fixed.

The Legislative Branch of government, our Congress is irreparably broken, and cannot be fixed without great change. I truly believe Congress is the ultimate source of all political greed and government corruption. The fox can no longer guard the hen house. Our Congress, as it currently exists today, must now be abandoned and replaced by "We the People".

By Marty Piatt, Architect

LEGISLATIVE BRANCH

The Legislative Branch of our government was formally established by Article I, Sections 1 through 10 of our U.S. Constitution and created as a bicameral Congress consisting of two chambers, the Senate and House of Representatives; or collectively referred to as the United States Congress. It was established within the Constitution to enact law, not to enforce or interpret law. The term Congress can also refer to a particular meeting of the Senate and House of Representatives. A Congress covers a two-year period. The current one, which is the 114th Congress, began on January 3, 2015 and will end on January 3, 2017. Both Senators and Representatives are chosen through direct election by each of the States citizens. The Senate and House of Representative are meant to be equal partners in the Legislative Branch of government. Our Constitution does however grant each chamber or house of Congress very unique powers. Legislation cannot be enacted without the consent of both chambers of Congress.

The Senate now consisting of one hundred (100) members total, two Senators from each the several States now totaling fifty. The original un-amended U.S. Constitution dictated that Senators were to be selected by the several State legislatures, and later unfortunately changed by the vote and elected by the People thereof, with the ratification of the seventeenth (XVII) amendment to the U.S. Constitution. Each of the several States, regardless of its population, has two senators, who serve six-year terms. The terms are staggered, so every two years, approximately one-third of the Senate is up for election. The Senate ratifies treaties and approves top presidential appointments. The Senate decides impeachment cases and a two-thirds vote of the Senate is required before an impeached person can be forcibly removed from their office.

The House of Representatives now consisting of four hundred and thirty-five (435) members total, was originally based upon no greater than one Representative for each of the thirty thousand citizen residents of the now fifty United States, and apportioned among the several States by population elected by the people and electors of several States. The Apportionment Act of 1911 set the number of House representatives at 435. Each of the 435 members of the House of Representatives represents a district and serves only a two-year term. The House initiates revenue-generating bills, and initiates impeachment cases.

When the Constitution was finally ratified in 1787, the Connecticut Compromise gave every state, large or small, an equal vote in the United States Senate. Residents of smaller states have more clout in the Senate than residents of larger states since each state has two senators. At that time the ratio of the populations of large states to small states was roughly twelve to one. But since 1787, the population disparity between large and small states has grown. Back in 2006, California had more than nearly seventy times the population of Wyoming. Some critics of the current Senate chamber of Congress have suggested that the population disparity works against residents of large states and causes a steady redistribution of resources from larger states to smaller states. However, others argue that the Connecticut Compromise was the deliberate intent by the Framers of the Constitution to construct the Senate so that each State had equal representation that was not based on population. This vital concern of the sovereign States can however be achieved in much greater manner to be addressed later in this chapter.

Congress has authority over financial and budgetary policy through the enumerated power to lay and collect taxes, duties, imposts and excises, to pay the debts and provide for the common defense and general welfare of the United States of America. In the nearly two hundred and forty years since the signing of our Declaration of Independence, the beliefs and goals of our founding forefathers has been lost to the greed and corruption of Congressional politics. Our country's second government of the United States of America was formed as a representative and "Republican" form of government, not to be confused with the Republican Party.

Our current government is not a true Democracy, as some would believe it to be. In the quest for power, our Congressional representative members have ceased to represent the constituents and citizens they represent, in favor of representing their political campaign donors, deep-pocket lobbyists, and special interests groups having their own agenda that fuel the Congress member's individual ambitions for wealth, political power, and re-election. The unbridled authority of Congress over budgets and spending has today brought not only our government, but also our country to the brink of financial collapse. According to analyst Eric Patashnik, it has been suggested that much of our Congress's authority to manage the government's budget has been lost when the welfare state expanded since "entitlements were institutionally detached from Congress's ordinary legislative routine and rhythm".

By Marty Piatt, Architect

The Keynesian belief that a balanced budget is unnecessary is another crucial factor resulting in our unprecedented national debt. Keynesian economics, based on the ideas of 20th-century English economist John Maynard Keynes, advocates active policy responses by the public sector, monetary policy initiated by the central bank, and fiscal policy actions by the government stabilizing output over the business cycle. One could argue the private sector decisions lead to more inefficient macroeconomic results.

Our United States Congress has become a corrupt gang of criminal racketeers in need of immediate replacement in its entirety. The Federal definition of a gang as used today by our Department of Justice and the Department of Homeland Security is described as follows:

1. An association of three or more individuals;

2. Whose members collectively identify themselves by adopting a group identity, which they use to create an atmosphere of fear or intimidation, frequently by employing one or more of the following: a common name, slogan, identifying sign, symbol, tattoo or other physical marking (i.e. political party);

3. Whose purpose in part is to engage in criminal activity and which uses violence or intimidation to further its criminal objectives;

4. Whose members engage in criminal activity or acts of juvenile delinquency that if committed by an adult would be crimes with the intent to enhance or preserve the association's power, reputation or economic resources;

5. The association may also possess some of the following characteristics:

    a. The members may employ rules for joining and operating within the association;
    b. The members may meet on a recurring basis;
    c. The association may provide physical protection of its members from others;
    d. The association may seek to exercise control over a particular geographic location or region, or it may simply defend its perceived interests against rivals;
    e. The association may have an identifiable structure.

19

Generally speaking, the word "racketeer" is used to describe a business or syndicate that is based on a belief that it is engaged in the sale of a solution to a problem that the institution itself creates, and perpetuates, with the specific intent to engender continual patronage by the customer. Racketeers are exactly what our Legislative Branch of government has become. If these descriptions of our corrupt gang of criminal racketeers are not the epitome of our current government's Congress, nothing is. The three branches of our government consist of the Legislative, Executive, and Judicial. All branches being separate and distinct, yet all branches share one indisputable commonality. All three branches consist for the most part of attorneys, which I undoubtedly believe is the major source of all political greed and corruption within this country and government today. Granted, attorneys are a necessary evil required to assist our Judicial Branch of government, and certainly not all are evil. However, having the attorneys both create and interpret our nation's laws is, as stated previously, a lot like having the fox guard the hen house. And let us not forget that our country's Judges are just attorneys wearing black gowns.

Our bicameral Legislature consisting of the Senate and the House of Representative has become much too powerful and destructive and I believe is solely responsible for the gradual decay and decline of the United States of America in the past two centuries. Our founding fathers first realized a single-chamber unicameral Congress was more appropriate when creating the 1787 Articles of Confederation. However without the Executive and Judicial Branches of government, the unicameral Legislative Branch became ineffective. Our bicameral Congress was unfortunately modeled after the British Parliament, which has a "House of Commons" having its representatives elected, and a "House of Lords" having its members appointed by the king. Unlike Great Britain and the United States, Provinces in Canada have operated very successfully with unicameral governments.

I truly believe our country needs to return to our founding fathers original confederate-type of Congress; a design having a single-chamber unicameral Legislature, which incidentally had been proposed by William Paterson on June 15, 1787 contained within the New Jersey Plan for our new U.S. Constitution. Unfortunately this concept, which was included in our country's first Constitution, was never implemented in our second and current Constitution. The Garden State actually foresaw the destructive consequences of this legislative structure.

By Marty Piatt, Architect

The bipartisan politics dividing our Congress and the constant infighting between our nation's Senate and House of Representatives must cease immediately. There exists only one solution remaining for our great country to overcome this obstacle, which is to end the struggle for power within Congress between the Democratic and Republican parties governing our bicameral Legislature.

The answer lies in the elimination of our 100-member Senate, leaving intact a single-chamber unicameral Congress consisting of our current House of Representatives. This is the only salvaging solution left to America. With the elimination of our current Senate, the powers vested in the 100-member chamber could be transferred and redistributed to the several sovereign States as was initially intended by our founding fathers.

A Legislative Branch of government consisting of a non-partisan single-chamber unicameral Congress paired with the Executive and Judicial Branch, that without had crippled the first Confederate Congress, appears to be the only logical solution.

It should be noted that the State of Nebraska is the only State legislature having a unicameral legislature. The check and balance of the unicameral State legislature provides that the State Supreme Court and Governor could rule on, or veto, legislation determined to be improper. The unicameral system has little difference from most city, county, and school district governing bodies. In addition, the people would also serve as a check with the right to vote and petition, should there be potential abuse of power by their elected officials.

In 1937, the state implemented the unicameral legislature after a 1934 amendment to the State Constitution. Legislature members were reduced 70% from 133 to 43. The last bicameral legislative session of 1935 passed 192 bills in 110 days at a cost $202,593. The first unicameral legislative session in 1937 passed 214 bills in 98 days at a cost of only $103,445. In 1962, legislative members were increased to 49 after amendment to the State Constitution. One very unique aspect of Nebraska's state legislature, it is nonpartisan. This change was also included in the 1934 amendment. Having a nonpartisan legislature, the political party of the candidate is not listed on the election ballot. The two candidates receiving the majority of votes in the primary election face each other in the general election.

Replacing the functions of our United States Senate would require formation of "A Committee of the States" similar to that of our first government operating under the Articles of Confederation comprised of fifty elected Congressional members appointed to the committee by the sovereign State legislatures or their executive authority. This would result in a greater balance of power between the several sovereign States and the Unites States government.

In addition, elimination of the Senate would rebalance the current Separation of Powers between our Legislative, Executive, and Judicial Branches of government. Other improvements to our Legislative Branch of government should include:

1. Establish a Constitutional structure to our Legislative Branch of government for the total number of congressional representatives;

2. Congressional power to amend or change the Constitution would be eliminated and transferred to the several sovereign States;

3. Congressional power to borrow foreign monies to finance the United States government would be eliminated;

4. Federal laws enacted by Congress could be repealed with a two-thirds majority vote of the several sovereign State legislatures;

5. Congress shall enact no law that applies to its members that does not apply equally to the citizens of the United States;

6. Congressional members shall not personally benefit from intimate knowledge of government information which they may be privy;

7. Congressional compensation and benefits shall not be determined by its members without two-thirds approval of the sovereign State legislatures;

8. Congressional members shall represent only the greater public interest of their State's constituents, and not of the special interest groups, lobbyists, or campaign donors;

9. Congressional powers cannot usurp the authority of the Judicial Branch in matters of Constitutional rulings with enactment of ex post facto legislation.

"I have come to the conclusion that one useless man is a disgrace, that two become a lawfirm, and that three or more become a congress." ~John Adams

"We must especially beware of that small group of selfish men who would clip the wings of the American Eagle in order to feather their own nests." ~Franklin D. Roosevelt

To rephrase an old saying:

"If you are part of the problem, you are not part of the solution."
~Marty Piatt, Architect

"If I was President…"

By Marty Piatt, Architect

EXECUTIVE BRANCH

The Executive Branch of our government was formally established by Article II, Sections 1 through 4 of our U.S. Constitution and created to enforce law, not to enact or interpret law. Also within this Article is described the manner in which our President, and Vice President were to be indirectly elected. As originally envisioned by our founding fathers, the President was to be elected having the greatest number of elector votes, with the Vice President being elected having the second greatest number of elector votes. There was no combined Presidential and Vice Presidential ticket as it exists today in our national election. I believe the rational for this method of election was to give the two greatest Presidential vote winners a power-sharing involvement in administering the Executive Branch of our government.

The Framers of our second Constitution had based their design of the Electoral College on assumptions that the Presidential candidates would not pair together on the same ticket with assumed placements toward each office of President and Vice President. Unfortunately Congress later dismissed the valid assumptions of our forefathers in our modern Presidential politics. The Electoral College consists of the electors appointed by each state who formally elect the President and Vice President of the United States.

The Electoral College is an example of an indirect election, as opposed to a true Democratic election by its citizens. The Constitution specifies the number of electors each State is entitled to have. Each of the State's legislatures decides how its electors are to be chosen. U.S. territories are not represented in the Electoral College. Based upon the total Congressional seats in the House of Representatives, which currently has 435, the Senate, which has 100, and including 3 votes from the District of Columbia, the Electoral College currently consists of 538 elector votes; a total number of electors that has remained unchanged since 1964.

In theory, voters had cast ballots for their favored Presidential and Vice-presidential candidates voting for the correspondingly pledged electors. However, electors were free to vote for anyone eligible to be President and Vice President. But in practice, electors pledge to vote for the constituency-chosen specific candidates.

25

On September 6, 1787, the First Constitutional Convention approved the Committee's Electoral College proposal with minor modifications having concern that the larger States would otherwise control presidential elections. Keep in mind that the United States consisted of only thirteen States. The delegates from the smaller States generally favored the Electoral College method of electing our President. Founding delegates James Wilson and James Madison believed a Democratic popular vote for the Presidency was better suited in establishing our Executive Branch. Given the prevalence of slavery in the South during that period, it would however be difficult to get consensus on that proposal.

James Madison stated that "There was one difficulty however of a serious nature attending an immediate choice by the people. The right of suffrage was much more diffusive in the Northern than the Southern States; and the latter could have no influence in the election on the score of Negroes. The substitution of electors obviated this difficulty and seemed on the whole to be liable to the fewest objections."

Unfortunately, during the elections of 1876, 1888, and 2000, an Electoral College winner did not receive the nationwide popular vote for President and the Republican Party won those respective elections. Outcomes such as these do not properly represent the intended results that a truly Democratic society and election process should express. The dysfunctional aspects of the existing Electoral College voting method results in a national vote bearing no significant Democratic resemblance in determining the final outcome of our Presidential election.

The Electoral College also gives a much larger and disproportionate role to swing states in selecting the President and Vice President. A state with low voter turnout gets exactly the same number of electoral votes as if it had a higher voter turnout. The Electoral College system also appears to unfortunately favor the Republican Party by disproportionately boosting the electoral significance of the lesser-populated states, which have for the most part historically tended to vote for Republican Party Presidential candidates. In direct contrast, if the presidential election were decided by a national popular vote, Presidential candidates would have a much stronger incentive to increase voter turnout. Voters would also have a stronger incentive to persuade their neighbors, friends, and family members to vote in the Presidential elections.

Legal scholars Akhil and Vikram Amar addressing the Electoral College have stated that "The founders' system also encouraged the continued disfranchisement of women. In a direct national election system, any state that gave women the vote would automatically have doubled its national clout. Under the Electoral College, however, a state had no such incentive to increase the franchise; as with slaves, what mattered was how many women lived in a state, not how many were empowered".

The obvious difference in voter turnout between swing states and non-swing states would greatly suggest that replacing the Electoral College with a direct election by popular vote would significantly increase voter participation in our Presidential elections. The Electoral College institution that exists today has become an outdated and archaic method of electing our nation's President. It is an inherently undemocratic method of indirect election needing to be abandoned and replaced with an election having a truly Democratic popular vote. The election of our President and Vice President should be non-partisan in both the primary and general elections, which no single sovereign State should have a distinct advantage in determining the decisive course of any Presidential election by having their own primary elections before any other State.

The Constitutional responsibilities of the Executive Branch must also be more clearly defined with respect to the President's power and authority to issue Executive Orders, Directives, Memorandums, and Presidential Proclamations that are used to clarify, enforce, or act to further law put forth by Congress and our Constitution. In addition, the Constitutional responsibilities of the President should include the "Line-item veto" of Congressional budget legislation giving the President the power and authority to remove all the waste and pork barrel funding proposed by corrupt Congressional members. As Commander and Chief of the Armed Forces, the President shall in the event of a national emergency issue Executive Orders to repel attacks against the United States, its territories or possessions, or its armed forces independent of Congressional approval.

In addition, the actions and responsibilities of the President's spouse or partner should also remain entirely outside the Executive Branch of government. Being an unelected person, they should receive absolutely no compensation or assistance whatsoever from the U.S. Treasury in support of their personal activities on behalf of the President.

The improvements to our current Executive Branch of government should include:

1. Return to our founding fathers original election process of selecting a President and second place Vice-President;

2. Replace the Electoral College with a truly democratic non-partisan popular vote for Presidential elections;

3. Establish uniformly occurring non-partisan Presidential primary and general elections;

4. Defining more clearly the Presidential powers and authority of executive actions including the provision of the line-item veto of Congressional budget legislation;

5. Establishing Executive authority, as Commander in Chief of the Armed Forces, to respond to an attack against the United States;

6. Remove the influence and expense of the Presidents' spouse or partner from Executive politics;

7. Share with the sovereign States the Executive Branch's constitutional responsibility and requirement to enforce all unlawful immigration.

By Marty Piatt, Architect

JUDICIAL BRANCH

The Judicial Branch of our government was formally established by Article III, Sections 1 through 3 of our U.S. Constitution. The judicial power of the United States is vested solely in the Supreme Court; together with any lower courts Congress may establish. The Federal District Courts and Appellate Circuit Courts were created as a matter of law; the Supreme Court having the final appellate authority. Established by the Constitution to interpret law, not to enact or enforce law. The Judicial Branch of government is the system of courts that interprets and applies the law and also provides the mechanism for the resolution of legal disputes. The Judges, of all Courts, hold their offices during good behavior and receive compensation for their services. The Judicial Branch is governed by law enacted by Congress, the Legislative Branch of government.

The current Supreme Court of the United States consists of nine Judge Jurists. The Chief Justice is appointed by the President upon vacancy with the concurrence and approval of Congress. Article II of our Constitution gives the President authority to appoint all other Judicial Branch Judges as well. Our Supreme Court, which is technically not a separate Constitutional Court, does however deal primarily with Constitutional law. The Supreme Court's main authority and objective is to rule on whether or not State or Federal laws that are challenged are in fact constitutional; or laws that conflict with our constitutionally established rights and freedoms, therefore being unconstitutional.

Our Supreme Court, the world's oldest constitutional court, was the world's first court to invalidate a law ruling it unconstitutional in the 1803 case of Marbury versus Madison. This case formed the basis for the exercise of "judicial review" under Article III of the Constitution. Often tasked with ensuring equal justice under law, the Judicial Branch of our government has the power to change laws through the process of judicial review. Courts with judicial review power may annul the laws and rules of the sovereign States when finding the laws incompatible with a higher norm, such as primary legislation, the provisions of the Constitution, or in some cases International law. Critics of judicial review contend that the argument for judicial review must rely on a significant interpretation and over-view on the Constitution's terms failing to address authorizing the Federal courts nullifying the acts of the three branches of our government.

The concept of judicial review was discussed in the Federalist Papers that under the Constitution, the Federal courts would not just have the power, but the duty, to examine the constitutionality of statutes. Alexander Hamilton asserted in Federalist No. 78 that:

"The courts were designed to be an intermediate body between the people and the legislature, in order, among other things, to keep the latter within the limits assigned to their authority. The interpretation of the laws is the proper and peculiar province of the courts. A constitution is, in fact, and must be regarded by the judges as, a fundamental law. It, therefore, belongs to them to ascertain its meaning, as well as the meaning of any particular act proceeding from the legislative body. If there should happen to be an irreconcilable variance between the two, that which has the superior obligation and validity ought, of course, to be preferred; or, in other words, the Constitution ought to be preferred to the statute, the intention of the people to the intention of their agents".

Yet "judicial review" is not clearly defined in our current Constitution. The landmark decision of Marbury versus Madison ultimately assisted in defining the resulting current Checks and Balances of our present Constitutional form of government. There is actually no Constitutional requirement defining that Federal District and Appellate Courts exist at all. Congress could actually abolish our court system at any time. Upon ratification of the Constitution, opponents of a strong Federal Judiciary suggested the U.S. Federal court system should be limited to the Supreme Court; only hearing appeals from the State courts. This view did not prevail, and the first Congress created the U.S. District Court system we now utilize today.

Also established by the first Congress with the Judiciary Act of 1789, the U.S. Circuit Courts were the original intermediate level courts of the U.S. Federal Court system. Having had trial court jurisdiction over civil suits of Diversity Jurisdiction including major Federal crimes, they also had appellate jurisdiction over the U.S. District Courts. The Judiciary Act of 1891 then transferred the Circuit Court appellate jurisdiction to the newly created U.S. Circuit Courts of Appeals. In 1911, the U.S. Circuit Court system was abolished and the remaining trial court jurisdiction was ultimately transferred to the U.S. District Court system.

By Marty Piatt, Architect

Under the presumed doctrine of the Separation of Powers, the Judicial Branch does not create law or enforce law, but rather interprets the laws and applies them to the facts of each individual disputed case. The Legislative Branch enacts laws and the Executive Branch enforces the laws. The current Supreme Court structure is based upon law established by Congress, not by our Constitution.

Under the Judiciary Act of 1789, Congress also organized the Supreme Court, which specified the Court's original and appellate jurisdiction, created thirteen judicial districts, and fixed the number of justices at six, including one Chief Justice and five Associate Justices. Since the passage of the Judiciary Act, Congress has occasionally altered the size of the Supreme Court; historically as a result of the growth of the nation in size. The Supreme Court was decreased to five in 1801; increased in 1807 to seven members; increased to nine in 1837; increased to ten in 1863; then reduced in 1866 to seven. Congress set the Court's size to nine Justices in 1869, and remains in its membership as it presently exists today.

It is my believe the Legislative Branch of our government, while maintaining a Separation of Powers, should not be empowered to enact law defining the organization and establishment of our Judicial Branch of our government. The precise details of the establishment of our Judicial Branch of government should be solely based upon a Constitutional establishment, not Congressional legislation. With the number of current Supreme Court Justices totaling nine, which is an odd number, no single Jurist should determine the decisive course of any Supreme Court ruling. The establishment of the number of Supreme Court Justices should also be based upon a Constitutional establishment, not Congressional legislation.

As any other 12-member judicial trial jury, the Supreme Court should consist of twelve Jurists as well, made up equally of six men and six women Supreme Court Justices; becoming our national "apostles of justice" defending our Constitution. The decisive course of any Supreme Court ruling should be based on major consensus without one single Jurist determining the final outcome. Not unlike the Twelve Apostles of the Church, our Supreme Court should be the messenger of justice conveying the true intentions and interpretation of our U.S. Constitution. And in the unlikely and unfortunate event a ruling consensus cannot be obtained by the Supreme Court, the lower court ruling should therefore stand.

With the recent Supreme Court ruling of Burwell v. Hobby Lobby, it is clear this nation cannot have a male-dominated Supreme Court ruling on matters impacting fifty percent of the population; that being women. As President, I would consider adding three additional women Justices to the existing Supreme Court having a final equal membership of six women and six men Justices. As a result, I would consider nominating Federal Judges Virginia A. Phillips, Susan Bolton, Leah Ward Sears, Sharon L. Blackburn, and Diane Pamela Wood, legal scholar Martha Louise Minow, and former National Security Advisor Condoleezza Rice as potential Supreme Court nominees.

Another relatively recent Supreme Court ruling in the case of Citizens United v. FEC declaring, with respect to political campaign contributions and financing, that corporations are "People", this ruling in my opinion is clearly contrary to what our founding fathers had anticipated in defining our current First Amendment right to free speech. Under the rationale of this ruling, a major American corporation thirty-five years of age should be able to campaign for the office of President, which is undoubtedly and realistically absurd. Corporations are not people. So who shall judge the judges?

It is time to correct a long overdue inequity of our Constitution; the removal or un-appointment of our Federal or Supreme Court judges by the President having a two-thirds concurrence of Congress for those individual judges failing to uphold the Articles of our Constitution. Improvements to our current Judicial Branch of government should include:

1. Reconstruct our Supreme Court with twelve Jurists; consisting equally of six men and six women member Jurists;

2. Remove the power of the organization of our Judicial Branch from the Legislative Branch of government;

3. Establish a Constitutional structure to our Judicial Branch of government for the Supreme Court, District Courts, and Appellate Circuit Courts;

4. Establish Constitution clarification for Judicial Review of actions resulting from the Legislative and Executive Branches of government.

5. Provide a mechanism within the Constitution for the immediate removal and un-appointment of Federal and Supreme Court Judges.

By Marty Piatt, Architect

UNEMPLOYMENT AND THE ECONOMY

Our economy has always performed within a historically occurring cyclical fluctuation and with it unemployment that subsequently follows, which is very unfortunate but naturally occurring. The current unemployment situation began early in the previous administration with the election of former President George W. Bush. Bush's Economic Growth and Tax Relief Reconciliation Act of 2001 cost American's $3.9 trillion of additional national debt over the next 10 years that ultimately failed to stimulate growth in the economy or fuel real job creation.

When Bush took office in 2000 our National debt was about $5.7 trillion and soared 33% to $7.6 trillion in January 2005 as he began his second term, and nearly doubled to $10.6 trillion the day President Obama was inaugurated. It now stands at $18 trillion, nearly doubling since President Obama assumed office. During that time the rich however got much richer. The number "one trillion" actually has twelve (12) zeros. One trillion dollars equals one million, million dollars. Couple the housing crisis with the failure of Wall Street and the Banking industry that resulted from the repeal of the Glass-Steagall Banking Act of 1933, and we end up with a toxic combination leading to financial catastrophe we have now realized. Some would place blame on the Clinton administration and Democrats for this crisis. An unemployment rate unmatched since the Great Depression then followed.

There is a very fine line between the Great Depression and the Great Recession. If you're one of the lucky ones employed, it's a recession. If you're one of the unlucky ones unemployed, it's a depression. Now add this sobering unemployment statistic; the vast number of unemployed and under-employed American citizens roughly equals the same number of illegal foreign nationals unlawfully residing in our country. Like the corny over-used phase says: "you do the math". Excluding Federal jobs, our government does not create jobs. It does however create an environment for job creation and growth. But in any Capitalist economy and society, job creation is solely dependent upon American businesses to provide investment capitol and create jobs. So why were the job-creating American companies hoarding one trillion dollars? Why were American banks hoarding one trillion dollars and not lending to job-creating American companies? The answers to both questions may possibly be "greed".

Federal spending is supposed to create jobs, providing the money that is spent enables people to go to work. Using billions of our taxpayer dollars to bail out the greedy banking industry and Wall Street did nothing to stimulate our economy. No one will ever really know if the Wall Street bailout made the economy better or worse. The rich however got much richer, and the poor got much poorer.

I believe the government would have been better off giving the approximately 310 million American citizens each $20,000 to stimulate the ailing economy at a cost of approximately $6.2 trillion dollars. Most people would have purchased homes or saved for a down-payment, bought cars, took vacations, bought airline tickets, remodeled their kitchens and baths, bought electronic gadgets, paid bills, created college funds, or just saved a portion for a rainy day. Others would have bought drugs, entertained hookers, foolishly spent money on unnecessary illicit stuff, including all other sorts of illegal activities and purchases.

However, all these different avenues and methods would have resulted in spending money that would have most certainly done more for stimulating our economy and job creation then lining the pockets of the banks and Wall Street executives. All this spending would have kept the banking industry and Wall Street very busy.

Instead, Uncle Sam sold-out Main Street, and bailed-out Wall Street.

And here we are now…

Congress and the President wanted to pass legislation creating a "Jobs Bill" spending taxpayer money we don't have to create jobs that the entire previous stimulus spending couldn't accomplish. Again, Congressional racketeers were selling solutions for problems they had created.

Conventional economic wisdom would suggest that unemployment would be low during wartime. War creates an economic environment that would normally remove our men and women warfighters from domestic employment opportunities. This situation decreases the workforce supply while increasing the employment demand for military industrial production. This has conversely been proven wrong in the post-World War II era.

By Marty Piatt, Architect

Within the 21st century Military Industrial Complex, the cost per capita of defense-related employment has skyrocketed with the increased cost of technology and hardware. During the production of the United States Air Force B-2 bomber, it was generally acknowledged that the futuristic aircraft cost more than its entire weight in gold.

The unfortunate result is as the cost of military hardware increases, so does the per capita cost of defense-related employment, which creates fewer overall jobs than any non-defense related employment opportunity. I would hesitantly venture to speculate that the defense-related per capita cost of employment is probably one thousand times greater than non-defense employment costs.

As stated earlier, excluding Federal employment, the government does not create jobs; it creates an environment for job creation. There are many other ways to create jobs rather than relying on wasteful stimulus government spending. Spending taxpayers' money for the sake of spending and stimulus is outright foolish.

The following examples are a few of my proposals to stimulate job growth and creation:

1.   Eliminate the Federal minimum wage standard. The Federal government has no business in a free-market Capitalist economy to dictate employment wage rates. Minimum employment wage rates should be established by the several sovereign States, not the Federal Government. Establishing minimum wage equal to both the western-coastal and the southeastern regions is inherently disproportionate in value compared to their local economies.

2.   For the very same rationale eliminating minimum wage rates, the Federal government should abandon the Davis-Bacon Act wage requirements for prevailing wages. Prevailing wage rates should be established by the several sovereign States, not the Federal government. Paying greater trade wages does not necessarily guaranty the Federal government a higher quality of workmanship. The various trade Unions working within the United States should negotiate with the several States, not the Federal government, to be more competitive in the new world economy.

3.   Replace a portion of our defense-related military spending with much lower per capita employment costs related to American infrastructure construction that is badly needed in all of our sovereign States. All of our interstate transportation systems, roads, railways, bridges, water and sewer systems, electrical energy distribution facilities, telecommunication networks, and natural gas and oil refinement complexes are in dire and immediate need of updating for the 21st century and beyond. Spending a minimum of 15% of our total national budget on American infrastructure would not be excessive.

4.   The Federal Acquisition Regulations (FAR) and all its various military and governmental sub-regulations and sub-sections should be immediately overhauled and simplified for all Federal acquisition of goods and services. Government regulation for acquisition using the FAR has made Federal investment less efficient and less productive, and obviously more costly.

5.   Eliminate all 8(a) "set aside" sole-sourced negotiated Government SBA contracts; all Federal acquisitions should be competitively bid, excluding very limited mission critical and national security situations.

6.   Deportation of nearly twelve million illegal immigrants residing unlawfully within the borders of the United States of American would be the single-greatest Jobs Creation Program ever experienced in American history without any Congressional legislation whatsoever.

7.   The Federal government should mandate that all employers within the United States should utilize the "eVerify" system of employment verification for all its citizens and legal residents. Twelve million illegal immigrants should not be taking valuable jobs away from Black Americans, Veterans, and our teenage U.S. citizens.

8.   Immediately suspend all foreign immigration and naturalization to the United States indefinitely, including those from Mexico until which time the national, or largest State unemployment percent rate falls below the unlawful immigrant population percentage rate.

9.   I would require all banks and lenders to provide FHA Streamline-type Mortgage Refinancing for all mortgage holders in good standing at no cost to millions of homeowners currently having under-water home loans. The Banking industry has sole responsibility for the loss of billions of dollars of all our home equity. No reduction in the loan principle would be required; however, lenders would be required to modify all residential mortgages in good standing with the current low interest rates.

10. I would propose negotiations with Apple Inc. to provide to the Executive branch of government a technologically generic UNIX™-based computer operating system (OS) similar to that first developed by ATT Bell Laboratories. It would utilize an integral Graphic User Interface (GUI) similar to that first developed by XEROX® including all compatible computer hardware in a transition away from the current DOS-based Windows operating system. This would be in exchange for the design and manufacture of Apple™ products within the United States borders employing a minimum of 51% of Apple's total design and manufacturing capabilities in accordance with the "Buy American Act of 1933".

"If I was President..."

By Marty Piatt, Architect

ENERGY POLICY

Energy is our enemy. The lack of energy threatens our nation's security. The use of energy also threatens our planet's security. Global warming is real, or as it is now referred to as: "climate change". Just as our Earth has natural cycles of seasons, it also has cycles of warming and cooling. Our Planet has transformed many times since its creation and throughout its evolution. Historical geological data has shown multiple ice ages have been experienced by our planet, followed by an eventual periods of warming.

Some will dispute that the current warming of our environment is just the natural cycle of our planet. However we may actually be exacerbating an already naturally occurring warming period that our earth quite possibly, if not kept in check, may not be able to recover.

In the evolution creation of our planet and its atmosphere, there came to be a natural balance and equilibrium of gaseous earth element components comprising our atmosphere. The proper amounts of nitrogen, oxygen, carbon dioxide and other gaseous elements that comprise our atmosphere make the symbiotic and synergistic life processes of our planet's plants and animals possible. Having attained a natural gaseous-component equilibrium in our atmosphere, the excess carbon and carbon dioxide ultimately became sequestered beneath the Earth's surface, most notably in the forms of coal, crude oil, and other natural gases all referred to as "fossil fuels".

Using the oxygen in our atmosphere as an oxidizer during combustion, the varied components of hydrocarbons bind with the oxygen atoms to create water vapor, carbon dioxide, and carbon monoxide resulting in the release of energy in the forms of thermal and kinetic energies. This process dramatically depletes the oxygen from our atmosphere, increases the carbon content of our atmosphere, and warms our planet's temperature. In basic terms, and I am no chemist, it really is that simple.

During the years from 1750 to 1850, the Industrial Revolution introduced tremendous advancements in agriculture, manufacturing, mining, transportation, and technology also having a truly profound impact on the financial, economic, social, and cultural environments of the era.

Fueled primarily by coal, the introduction of steam power resulted in a dramatic increase in manufacturing and production capacities. The use of natural gas for lighting also increased, as did the use of gas for other industrial purposes. A great influx of population traveled from the countryside and into the small towns, which swelled in population in turn creating large cities with the transition away from an agricultural-based economy and into machine-based manufacturing and production industry. Unfortunately over the past 260 years our dependence on fossil fuels and other earth-borne hydrocarbons has dramatically increased as quickly as our industrial and scientific technology has increased.

For those that dismiss the theories concerning global warming and climate change, this will be the first unnaturally occurring global warming event with 7,000,000,000 people now inhabiting this planet. The United States Census Bureau (USCB) estimated that on March 12, 2012 the world population would exceed 7 billion inhabitants. We are now seeing the impacts of our global warming and climate change. Fierce hurricanes and typhoons, destructive tornados, drought, flooding, intense heat, and frigid cold represent the resulting climatic changes. Global warming and climate change has affected our oceans and their currents that dissipate both cold and warm temperatures throughout the earth's surface. It seems that the State of Florida has the greatest negative impact from rising ocean levels resulting from global warming and the melting ice at our Earth's North Pole and northern latitudes. Florida needs to begin long-term contingency planning for the future devastation of Florida coastal properties, wetlands, marshes, and everglades. The southern states adjacent to the Gulf of Mexico are also threatened, as was seen in 2005 during Hurricane Katrina.

Can we stop using fossil fuel hydrocarbons to sustain our nation's energy needs and growth? The answers would be yes in the long term; no in the short term. Regardless of what the United States does to change our reliance on fossil fuels, we are only one neighbor in the neighborhood of our planet earth. Developing nations whose economic livelihood depends on cheap energy will inevitably continue to burn cheaper fossil fuels. It is my understanding that if 10% of the area of State of Nevada had photovoltaic generation facilities, 100% of our nation's electrical energy requirements could be met by using solar energy alone. This fact truly supports a solar energy future. 19th century French inventor Augustin Mouchot was the first to convert concentrated solar energy to mechanical steam power during the Paris World Exhibition in 1878.

By Marty Piatt, Architect

Setting aside the critical impacts of global warming and climate change, our nation needs an energy policy to secure our nation's independence from foreign energy sources, most notably oil, imported from the Middle East.

Our country's short-term energy goals should include the following:

1. Rely more heavily on domestic natural gas for our domestic trucking industry;

2. Reduce our need for domestic coal and imported crude oil;

3. Mandatory reclamation and utilization of all petroleum products and oils recycled, refined, and used for bio-diesel fuel production;

4. Mandatory reclamation and utilization of all vegetable, animal, and fish fatty oils recycled from the food industry, refined, and used for bio-diesel fuel production;

5. Burning of our wastewater treatment solids to generate electricity;

6. Burning of our nation's garbage to generate electricity;

7. Mining and extraction of methane gas from our nation's landfills;

8. Increase production of ethanol and methanol to supplement and extend the production volume of gasoline;

Our country's long-term energy goals should include the following:

1. Eliminate both import and export of crude and refined petroleum products;

2. Eliminate the export of domestic natural gas;

3. Focus energy production on sustainable natural energy-generating sources such as solar, wind, water currents, ocean waves, and tidal forces;

4. Production of bio-fuel petroleum replacements for gasoline and diesel;

5. Require all gasoline to be blended with bio-fuel components ranging from E15 minimum to E85 potentially doubling our nations gasoline volume production;

6. Require all diesel fuel to be blended with bio-fuel components ranging from B15 minimum to B85 potentially doubling our nations diesel fuel volume production;

7. Implement mandatory recycling programs in every American community across our nation;

8. Production of hydrogen and oxygen from cleanly generated electricity and ocean water;

9. Promote future fusion and plasma physics technology for energy production.

The price of gasoline, diesel, and commercial jet fuel is dramatically hampers our nation's economic recovery and prosperity. There is no meaningful reason for the volatile price increases of gasoline based upon the barrel-price of crude oil other than speculative greed. The price of gasoline, which has been around $4 per gallon in some areas, is not the result of supply and demand. There currently is no lack of supply of gasoline; we are not waiting in line to fuel our vehicle gas tanks. There is absolutely no reason why the cost of gasoline cannot be well below $3 per gallon.

To fully reduce and minimize the cost of our petroleum fuels, I would require regulation increasing our nation's fuel supply, which appears to be the most appropriate action. When supply increases, cost decreases. It is my understanding that no new petroleum oil refinery has been constructed in the United States in over thirty years. That would immediately change under my Presidential administration. As President I would propose construction of our nation's first hybrid oil-ethanol refinery in 30 years serving the Midway-Sunset oil field, which is our nation's third largest, and California's single largest oil field also central to the production of agricultural resources used for ethanol production.

As President I would propose the following:

1. Initiate government regulation of all forms of energy with respect to price and production, including crude oil, by the Federal Energy Regulatory Commission (FERC);

2. Propose constructing a hybrid petroleum and ethanol refinery serving the Midway-Sunset oil field located in Kern Country, California;

3. Remove financial speculation of all our nation's energy resources;

4. Remove domestically-produced petroleum oil and refined products from the Wall Street futures market;

5. Prohibit all exportation of crude and refined petroleum products from the United States;

I personally believe the production of hydrogen and oxygen from ocean water using solar-generated electrical energy is the ultimate future to meet our nation's clean energy requirements. Hydrogen production will also replenish the oxygen content of our planet's atmosphere helping to reverse the accumulation of carbon dioxide from burning fossil fuels. In addition to mandating cleaner and more sustainably-produced biofuels, a coupling of this policy would include an easing of all EPA standards to increase the fuel efficiency of our nations fleet of trucks and automobiles. Equally maximizing both fuel efficiency and emission control standards would provide an economic posture greatly benefiting our domestic auto industry. A healthy and prosperous automotive industry will help contribute to an overall healthy and prosperous U.S. economy. Most importantly, within the next 100 years, our nation's commercial aviation industry will also be required to transition away from petroleum-based fuels implementing the use of biofuels, natural gas, and hydrogen gas.

Until that transition is achieved, the FAA air traffic control will require a technological update to a GPS-based system controlling the fight paths of our airlines. This would dramatically decrease airliner fuel consumption and increase their profit margin. A healthy and prosperous commercial airline industry will also help contribute to an overall healthy and prosperous U.S. economy.

As President, I would also support the construction of a new Transcontinental Electric High Speed Railroad (EHSR) as part of my transportation and energy policies to reduce automobile traffic and pollution nationwide. I believe the expanded use of our nation's railroads for passenger transportation will be an integral part of our nation's future infrastructure improvements into the next century.

Many American's link our nation's foreign and military policy to our current energy policy. Our politicians have spent more American tax dollars and shed more American blood in the Middle East that our nation will ever recover in the value of oil.

The combined cost to the American taxpayers of both the wars in Afghanistan and Iraq currently approach nearly $1.3 trillion dollars or more, or approximately 9% of our national debt, which does not include the future interest cost of loans used to fund the wars.

Our nation needs to cut our losses and leave the Middle Eastern region to its own destiny and destruction.

Just imagine how $1.3 trillion dollars could have been invested in American alterative energy production instead of overseas crude oil politics and war.

By Marty Piatt, Architect

GOVERNMENT CONSOLIDATION

Before tackling our enormous national debt and annual budget, the entire government of the United States of America needs to be readdressed. There's an old saying in architecture:

"Less is more."
~Ludwig Mies van der Rohe, Architect

This philosophy is so relevant and appropriate when it comes to our government today, especially one with our out-of-control spending. At a time when our government has historically borrowed anywhere between 30 and 40 cents of every dollar it spends annually, American fiscal policy needs to change immediately.

Total expenditures for the fiscal year 2012 was estimated at $3.73 trillion. The estimated total of all government tax revenues for FY12 were estimated to be approximately $2.63 trillion. This would result in a $1.1 trillion dollar budget deficient, leaving about 30% of our budget Congress would have had to borrow to fund. What this means to me is simple arithmetic. We need to slash government spending by 30 to 40%; it is that simple.

So how do we determine what portions of our government to eliminate and what portions to keep and fund? We should reference our Constitution where all-important information pertinent to our Federal government is referenced.

"We the People of the United States, in Order to form a more perfect. Union...

1. "establish justice",
2. "insure domestic tranquility",
3. "provide for the common defense",
4. "promote the general welfare", and,
5. "secure the Blessings of Liberty to ourselves and our Posterity;

...do ordain and establish this Constitution for the United States of America."

Therefore according to our Constitution, we have only five (5) topics to address. All other categories should be left to the several sovereign States.

1. We have established constitutional Justice with the establishment of our three branches of government that enact law, enforce law, and interpret law.

2. One of many concerns our founding fathers was ensuring the Federal government had powers to squash rebellion and end tensions between the several States thus insuring domestic tranquility; either first by persuasion, or by force as a last resort. The Federal government is required to ensure domestic tranquility within all of the sovereign States.

3. Providing for the common defense means adequately funding our military. That is a very subjective goal. Determining to what extent we fund our national defense depends on the overall budget amount and what percentage we want to allocate to the Department of Defense and our national security.

4. Promoting the general welfare would include providing Federal funding for such items as Social Security, Medicare, Medicaid and the State Children's Health Insurance Program (SCHIP), in additional to unemployment benefits.

5. Securing the blessings of Liberty to ourselves and our Posterity was accomplished with the ratification of our Bill of Rights, the first ten amendments to our Constitution, which guarantee our various personal freedoms as lawful citizens of the United States of America.

The next step would be to determine what budget expenditures do not meet the descriptive requirements of the five Constitutional categories that can be either eliminated or consolidated into other budget line items.

The following one hundred (100) listings are only a few of the incredibly numerous departments, boards, administrations, committees, foundations, etc. of our Federal government requiring substantial reduction or possible elimination:

1.   Administrative Conference of the United States
2.   Advisory Council on Historic Preservation
3.   African Development Foundation
4.   American Battle Monuments Commission
5.   Appalachian Regional Commission
6.   Architectural and Transportation Barriers Compliance Board
7.   Arctic Research Commission
8.   Armed Forces Retirement Home
9.   Broadcasting Board of Governors
10. Centennial of Flight Commission
11. Chemical Safety and Hazard Investigation Board
12. Christopher Columbus Fellowship Foundation
13. Commission for the Preservation of America's Heritage Abroad
14. Commission of Fine Arts
15. Commission on Civil Rights
16. Commission on Executive, Legislative, and Judicial Salaries
17. Commission on the Prevention of Weapons of Mass Destruction Proliferation and Terrorism
18. Committee for Purchase from People Who Are Blind or Severely Disabled
19. Commodity Futures Trading Commission
20. Consumer Financial Protection Bureau
21. Consumer Product Safety Commission
22. Corporation for National and Community Service
23. Council of the Inspectors General on Integrity and Efficiency
24. Defense Nuclear Facilities Safety Board
25. Delta Regional Authority
26. Denali Commission
27. Election Assistance Commission
28. Environmental Protection Agency
29. Export-Import Bank of the United States
30. Farm Credit Administration
31. Farm Credit System Insurance Corporation
32. Federal Communications Commission

33. Federal Deposit Insurance Corporation
34. Federal Election Commission
35. Federal Financial Institutions Examination Council
36. Federal Housing Finance Agency
37. Federal Labor Relations Authority
38. Federal Maritime Commission
39. Federal Mediation and Conciliation Service
40. Federal Mine Safety and Health Review Commission
41. Federal Reserve System Board Of Governors
42. Federal Retirement Thrift Investment Board
43. Federal Trade Commission
44. Harry S. Truman Scholarship Foundation
45. Illinois and Michigan Canal National Heritage Corridor Commission
46. Inter-American Foundation
47. International Boundary and Water Commission: United States and Mexico
48. International Boundary Commission: United States and Canada
49. International Joint Commission: United States and Canada
50. James Madison Memorial Fellowship Foundation
51. Japan-United States Friendship Commission
52. John F. Kennedy Center for the Performing Arts
53. Marine Mammal Commission
54. Merit Systems Protection Board
55. Millennium Challenge Corporation
56. Morris K. Udall Scholarship and Excellence in National Environmental Policy Foundation
57. National Archives and Records Administration
58. National Capital Planning Commission
59. National Commission on Libraries and Information Science
60. National Council on Disability
61. National Credit Union Administration
62. National Gallery of Art
63. National Labor Relations Board

64. National Mediation Board
65. National Science Foundation
66. National Transportation Safety Board
67. Nuclear Regulatory Commission
68. Nuclear Waste Technical Review Commission
69. Occupational Safety and Health Review Commission
70. Office of Government Ethics
71. Office of Navajo and Hopi Indian Relocation
72. Office of Personnel Management
73. Office of Special Counsel
74. Office of the Director of National Intelligence
75. Office of the Federal Coordinator for Alaska Natural Gas Transportation Projects
76. Office of the Inspector General for the Federal Housing Finance Agency
77. Overseas Private Investment Corporation
78. Peace Corps
79. Pension Benefit Guaranty Corporation
80. Postal Rate Commission
81. Public Interest Declassification Board
82. Railroad Retirement Board
83. Recovery Act Accountability and Transparency Board
84. Securities and Exchange Commission
85. Selective Service System
86. Small Business Administration
87. Smithsonian Institution
88. Social Security Administration
89. Tennessee Valley Authority
90. Trade and Development Agency
91. U.S. Agency for International Development
92. U.S. Holocaust Memorial Museum
93. U.S. Institute Of Peace
94. U.S. Interagency Council on Homelessness
95. U.S. International Trade Commission

96.   Utah Reclamation Mitigation and Conservation Commission
97.   Valles Caldera Trust
98.   Vietnam Education Foundation
99.   White House Commission on the National Moment of
        Remembrance
100.   Woodrow Wilson International Center for Scholars

The United States government currently has fifteen (15) Executive Departments within the operations of the existing Federal government. My first possible choices targeted for total government elimination include but are not limited to the following departments:

1. Department of Homeland Security

2. Department of Commerce

3. Department of Agriculture

4. Department of Education

5. Department of Housing

6. Department of Labor

The following is a partial list of agencies I would immediately target for elimination:

1. Federal Emergency Management Agency (FEMA)

2. Internal Revenue Service (IRS)

3. Small Business Administration (SBA)

4. Alcohol Tobacco and Firearms (ATF)

5. Drug Enforcement Administration (DEA)

We have the greatest military in the world, the United States Department of Defense. Why would this nation need the Department of Homeland Security (DHS) to defend our country? All activities of the DHS should be integrated into the Department of Defense, and all DHS funding removed from our national budget.

By Marty Piatt, Architect

The Federal Emergency Management Agency (FEMA) has shown in recent history to be entirely ineffective and totally mismanaged and needs absolutely to be eliminated and abandoned all entirely. The Federal disaster emergency-funding portion of the discretionary spending within our national budget can be administrated through various emergency management agencies of the several States eliminating the need for FEMA.

In a purely Capitalist economy, the Small Business Administration (SBA) is truly an unnecessary luxury, particularly with our current budgetary deficit. The SBA should be eliminated and all funding removed from our national budget, and to rely solely of Venture Capitol. The Federal government should encourage small business growth, but not at the expense of the American taxpayer.

Many of the greatest causes of death in our society are the direct result of alcohol, tobacco, and firearms. Other than enforcing of the excise-generating tax collection, the existence of the ATF has not ever in its history made a significant reduction in these death statistics. After the unfortunate disaster in Waco, Texas, the ATF should be eliminated. All ATF responsibilities and tasks can be delegated to the several States and the FBI. All ATF field personnel, activities, and funding could be transferred to the U.S. Customs and Border Protection.

The War on Drugs by the Drug Enforcement Administration (DEA) is a total lost cause, a futile campaign unable to be won, which ultimately is total waste of taxpayer dollars. The DEA should be eliminated, all funding removed from our national budget, and its field personnel, activities, and funding integrated into the U.S. Customs and Border Protection

The Departments of Commerce, Agriculture, Education, Housing, and Labor are a total waste of government assets, should be eliminated, and all funding removed from our national budget. These are activities are better left to be administered by the several sovereign States.

The reconsolidation of the former Department of Health, Education, and Welfare with the consolidation of the Department of Interior, Labor, and Commerce could be an alternative solution.

Having addressed the elimination of many potential government departments and agencies, an examination and analysis of government consolidation is necessary. During challenging economic times such as the period we have experienced, various business industries and corporations, in an effort to become more efficient and cost effective, have undergone considerable consolidation over the past years.

The Federal government also needs to accomplish the very same business goals resulting in increased efficiency and productivity. Many of the major consolidations should involve integrating several existing Federal activities and their related funding into the Department of Defense.

As a Civilian-controlled department, the Department of Defense can better secure our homeland's borders, shorelines, and airspace. In doing so I would proposes the following departments:

1. Integrate all activities and responsibilities of the former Department of Homeland Security permanently into the Department of Defense.

2. Integrate the Department of Veterans Affairs into the Department of Defense to more effectively maintain the health and welfare of our Veterans that have proudly served our country and the Department of Defense.

3. Integrate the United States Coast Guard permanently into the Department of the Navy to protect our sovereign national shorelines and ports of entry;

4. Integrate the U.S. Customs and Border Protection permanently into the Department of the Army to better protect our sovereign national borders;

5. Integrate the National Aeronautical and Space Administration (NASA), the National Reconnaissance Office (NRO), and all other national space-based agencies permanently into the Department of the Air Force to better defend our sovereign national airspace.

By Marty Piatt, Architect

Another major consolidation of our Federal government is our various intelligence agencies. Not unlike the attack on Naval Base Pearl Harbor on December 7, 1941, the attack on the World Trade Center on September 11, 2001 was a direct result of the apparent failures of our national intelligence communities.

Having the undoubtedly most sophisticated and technologically advanced capabilities in the world, our national intelligence-gathering complex has unfortunately failed our nation dramatically in their essential and fundamental responsibility to alert our country of a potential or eminent foreign or domestic terrorist attack against United States territories or its military.

As an unfortunate but necessary result, our intelligence agencies should be consolidated into three, and only three, very distinctive intelligence-gathering agencies consisting of:

1. A "national" intelligence agency consisting of the existing Federal Bureau of Investigation (FBI) that provides all the intelligence gathering responsibilities required within the continental borders of the United States;

2. An "international" intelligence agency (IIA) consisting of the existing Central Intelligence Agency (CIA), National Geospatial-Intelligence Agency (NGA), and National Security Agency (NSA) consolidated into one distinctive intelligence agency that provides all the intelligence gathering responsibilities required outside the continental borders of the United States;

3. A "military" intelligence agency consisting of the existing Defense Intelligence Agency (DIA) consolidating the duties of the National Reconnaissance Office (NRO) that provides all the military related intelligence gathering responsibilities required outside the continental borders of the United States, including its territories, for all military activities and missions worldwide.

All three intelligence agencies would directly communicate and interact with each other, the President, and Congress to better and more efficiently protect our country from domestic and foreign invaders threatening the United States of America and its sovereign territories.

Another major government consolidation would be that of our current healthcare entitlement programs consisting of Medicare, Medicaid, and the State Children's Health Insurance Program (SCHIP).

As President I would initiate the creation of one distinctive all-inclusive healthcare program that I have officially coined and titled the United States "AMERICARE" program. This would be a national medical and dental healthcare program that will provide essential healthcare and prescriptions exclusively to American citizens under the age of 18 and over the age of 64 totally independent of national insurance plans or institutions thus requiring no middleman. Absolutely no benefits would be paid to foreign nationals or illegal aliens through this program. I believe healthy children ultimately grow to become healthy adults, and all American citizen children deserve proper healthcare. All American senior citizens also deserve proper healthcare as part of their social security benefits during their golden retirement years.

Like the old saying: "an ounce of prevention is worth a pound of cure."

American citizens of ages in between 18 and 65 would be left to provide their own healthcare coverage as a matter of choice and freedom, having the ability to voluntarily join the AMERICARE program as an option requiring both co-pays and program premiums.

I believe the recent health care initiative passed by Congress, the "Patient Protection and Affordable Care Act of 2010", unofficially called "Obamacare" is without a doubt unconstitutional in my opinion. The Federal government can no sooner require one to buy healthcare insurance than it can compel one to buy a new car or home. The whole idea and concept of Obamacare is utterly ridiculous, irrespective of the goal it had hoped to achieve. In his decision invoking the Boston Tea Party, a forerunner to the American Revolutionary War, U.S. District Judge Roger Vinson asserted that:

"It is difficult to imagine that a nation which began, at least in part, as the result of opposition to a British mandate giving the East India Company a monopoly and imposing a nominal tax on all tea sold in America would have set out to create a government with the power to force people to buy tea in the first place."

However, let us not confuse healthcare reform with healthcare insurance reform; the latter description referring to Obamacare in my opinion. Taxing Americans to pay for healthcare is one thing, requiring Americans to purchase healthcare insurance is another. If the government can mandate its citizens to purchase healthcare insurance, what will Congress require Americans to buy next?

The only winner regarding "Obamacare" was the national health insurance industry. I believe our nation insurance industry is actually legalized gambling; you're betting you will get sick, the insurance industry is betting you won't get sick; and the gambling odds dictate that the house will always win.

In reality, our national healthcare industry was not reformed. We cannot have healthcare reform until which time we have concurrent "legal" and "tort" reform for medical malpractice; in which the racketeering attorneys and lawyers of our legal system have become the only winners and beneficiaries.

"If I was President..."

By Marty Piatt, Architect

PROHIBITION IN AMERICA

President George Washington signed the Tariff Act of July 4, 1789 authorizing the collection of duties on all imported goods into the United States, including the import of "alcohol". United States customs duties as established by the tariff rates through the year 1860 indicate that approximately 80% to 95% of all Federal revenue received by the U.S. Treasury was tariff-based.

With the passage of the Revenue Act of 1861 on August 5th authorizing the nation's first flat 3% Gross Income Tax (GIT), alcohol excise taxes would cease to be one of the greatest sources of income for the United States Federal government. Having the United States Congress in need of a very reliable and easily collectable source of income, Alexander Hamilton, the first U.S. Treasury Secretary, had recommended implementing and imposing tariffs and excise taxes that were legally authorized by the United States Constitution.

Taxing foreign imports and establish excise taxes would supply the Federal government with sufficient financial resources to pay all of its operating expenses, and to reconcile all U.S. Federal debts at their full value, including all debts incurred by the several States as a result of the American Revolutionary War. Secretary Hamilton believed it was paramount to begin the U.S. Federal government on a sound financial foundation with excellent credit.

The first United States Federal budget was approximately $4.6 million dollars and the population in the 1790 United States Census was approximately four million people. Therefore the average per capita federal tax assessment at that time was approximately $1 per person per year.

As one of the many excise-taxed commodities, alcoholic beverages played a significant and historical role in the beginning development of Colonial America. Some believe the Separatist Pilgrims brought a greater amount of beer than potable water on the Mayflower as they departed on their historic journey and voyage to America. While this fact may seem out of historical context viewing Pilgrims from our modern viewpoint, consuming beer and wine was much safer than drinking water at that time.

The typically polluted water in Europe was usually drawn from sources used for sewer and garbage disposal. Alcohol was believed to provide energy boosts necessary for hard work, proved to be an effective analgesic and painkiller, and without abuse generally improved the quality of American colonial life and health. Our English forefathers had previously consumed beer, wine, and ale for centuries. People of all ages and both sexes typically always drank some sort of alcohol with their meals in both colonial America and in England. The early colonial settlers decided to brew their own beer because the import cost providing a continuous supply of beer regrettably proved much too expensive.

Unfortunately wild American yeasts had also caused the settlers difficulties in the fermentation and brew process that resulted in an unappetizing bitter beverage. This made it difficult to brew the type and quality of beer the colonist settlers were accustomed to drinking. Hop seeds were imported from England and utilized to cultivate a sufficient brew supply for their traditional beer, even though wild hops had actually grown natively in Colonial America. Colonist brew masters improvised a distinctive beer-like beverage brewed from black and red spruce twigs boiled in water, including what may have been an innovative ginger beer. According to its alcohol content beer, not liquor, was categorized with one of either an X, XX, or XXX product rating.

American colonists also learned to make from their native and imported fruits a wide variety of differing fermented wines. They also experimented in fermenting wine using ingredients that would include herbs, flowers, and even oak leaves. Vine-growers were eventually brought from France to America to teach colonial settlers how to cultivate their vineyard grapes. Distilled spirits were considered "aqua vitae", or "water of life" by the Colonist's traditional beliefs they had adhered to. Rum that was distilled and imported from the Caribbean was not commonly available in colonial America until well after 1650.

The colonists began importing molasses and cane sugar directly distilling their own rum resulted in the cost of imported Caribbean rum to plummet. One rum distillery operating in Boston became highly successful and within nearly one generation by 1657 the production of rum had become colonial America's largest and most profitable industry.

By Marty Piatt, Architect

Due to the dramatic increase in American rum consumption, nearly every major city and town from Massachusetts to the Carolinas then had a rum distillery satisfying the local alcohol demand. Within a few years customs duties generated sufficient Federal income to again abolish nearly every Federal excise tax.

When the United States public debt was finally paid off in 1834, then-President Andrew Jackson kept the excise tax zeroed out and reduced the remaining customs duties and tariffs by approximately 50 percent. Until the beginning of U.S. Civil War brought a greater need for more government revenue, Federal excise taxes remained essentially zero. Excise taxes were reintroduced on a wider range of items and income taxes, some declared unconstitutional, were also introduced. Loans taken out during the American Civil War were paid off by around 1916 and thereafter the remaining excise taxes were set very low again.

The foundation was ultimately set by 19th century religious revivalism regarding the relationship between Prohibition and Christianity in the United States. Prohibition also united both the American political progressives against- and the revivalists for- Prohibition.

Author Nancy Koester expressed her belief that Prohibition was a "victory for progressives and social gospel activists battling poverty" stating: "The greater prevalence of revival religion within a population, the greater support for the Republican and Prohibition parties within that population". Prohibition and the Prohibition Party were championed by various Protestant religious denominations in the United States in the early to mid-twentieth century seeking to curtail drunkenness, gluttony, and the overindulgence of alcoholic beverages. Congress passed the 18th Amendment to our Constitution on December 18, 1917. Thereafter all alcohol production, sale, and transport were essentially prohibited. The Amendment would later be officially ratified on January 16, 1919, having been approved by 36 of the then 48 United States. Valuable Alcohol excise taxes would remain essentially non-existent for the following ten years until its repeal. Alcohol excise taxes would have produced virtually no Federal income or revenue. Prior to the official ratification in 1919, Prohibition was also supplemented by the November 18th passage of the Wartime Prohibition Act of 1918 by Congress during the interim period between Congressional approval and official ratification of Prohibition by the several States.

With the loss of nearly all Federal alcohol revenue and the devastating impact on the alcohol production industry and its employment, the final era of Prohibition and its terrible economic impacts, lasting well into the late 1920's, ushered in the beginning of the worst financial depressionary period this county has ever experienced in our history.

I firmly believe that the Constitutional amendment of Prohibition enacted by Congress with the support of American organized religion was the last straw that broke the camel's back in terms of the resulting depressionary American economy that followed. The 1930 Prohibition Commissioner estimated that the average drinking American spent approximately $17 annually on alcoholic beverages in the year before passage of the "National Prohibition Act of 1919". The "Volstead Act", as it was also known, became law on October 28, 1919.

Because enforcement greatly diminished the supply of alcohol, this yearly consumption amount had increased to approximately $35 annually per drinking American by 1930, resulting in an illegal black-market alcohol beverage industry that made approximately $3 billion per year in illegal untaxed income. This amount would be equivalent to approximately $41 billion in 2015 dollars of illegal Federally untaxed income. Organized crime would receive a major boost from the enactment of Prohibition. The Mafia, only until 1920, had limited their activities to prostitution, gambling, and theft. Organizing bootlegging resulted in a more crime-organized response to Prohibition. The Prohibition black market for alcohol beverages flourished and was often both profitable and violent as a result. Federal, State and Local Law enforcement agencies were corrupted by powerful criminals and bootlegging gangs that led to organized racketeering.

As described earlier, Racketeering is a business or syndicate that is based on a belief that it is engaged in the sale of a solution to a problem that the institution itself creates, and perpetuates, with the specific intent to engender continual patronage by the customer.

As a result, Prohibition had actually provided a fertile financial foundation for organized crime to flourish. It was apparent that prohibition had actually transformed various cities into battlegrounds between opposing bootlegging gangs rather than reducing crime as was hoped to accomplish.

By Marty Piatt, Architect

The fact of the matter was that the Volstead Act, despite the persuasive beliefs of the prohibitionist movement that outlawing alcohol crime would be reduced, led to even worse social situations than was anticipated or experienced prior to Prohibition. The establishment of a Prohibition black-market dominated by criminal organizations also demonstrated the increase in crime rates that coincided with the introduction more lethal forms of alcohol.

During the years of Prohibition between 1920 and 1921, a study of over 30 major U.S cities concluded that the overall incidents of crime increased by approximately 24%, theft and burglaries increased by nearly 10%, homicide over 12%, and assaults and battery rose by approximately 13%. Local police department enforcement costs then increased more than 11%. Unfortunately drug addiction coincidentally increased dramatically over 44% as a result of Prohibition. It has been speculated that these increase in crime rates were largely the result of "black-market violence". The demand for stronger liquor surged in popularity because of its greater potency, which in turn made alcohol much more profitable to bootleg and smuggle.

The Federal government ordered the poisoning of industrial alcohols hoping to prevent the bootleggers from utilizing industrial ethyl alcohol to produce illegal beverages. Bootleggers then in response to the poisoned industrial alcohols hired chemists who successfully re-natured the industrial alcohol to supposedly make it safe for public consumption. The Treasury Department then required manufacturers to add more deadly poisons with the addition of the particularly lethal methyl alcohol mixture. Medical examiners in New York City prominently opposed the inherent danger to human life these policies would have as a result. Before the end of Prohibition, more than 10,000 people would die from drinking denatured alcohol. "Canned heat", another lethal substance often substituted for alcohol, was most commonly known as "sterno". After the end of Prohibition, many of those individuals who were poisoned as a result, banded together to sue the Federal government for reparations.

Even though stores and markets sold grape juice concentrate having warning labels listing the steps necessary that should be avoided to prevent the juice from fermenting into wine, the making alcohol at home was very common during Prohibition.

Many drug stores sold a "medical wine" having about 22% alcohol content that was given a medical taste justifying the medical sale. For many, it was easier to home-distill hard liquor rather than the home brewing of beer. The law pursued manufacturers relentlessly because the selling of privately distilled alcohol, which bypassed taxation by the Federal government, was illegal. Home-distilled hard liquor was referred to as "moonshine" in the more rural areas of both North and South Carolina, Georgia, and Tennessee. The term "bathtub gin" was also used in the more northern cities.

The southern-state bootleggers started building their own high-performance, stock-manufactured appearing cars by greatly enhancing their cars' engines, power trains, and suspension systems creating a much faster and more agile performing vehicle. Having a super-fast car during Prohibition would improve all the Runner's chances of outrunning and escaping the agents of the Bureau of Prohibition. These super-cars became known as "moonshine runners" or "shine runners" and were to become the forerunner vehicles of the future NASCAR racing competition.

The Bureau of Prohibition agents were commonly referred to as "revenue agents" or "revenuers". Runners having "ships" also collaborated with the black-market liquor market by loading their vessels with liquor and liquor-making ingredients. The enactment of prohibition resulted in additional enforcement and the resources required also increased, along with other negatively impacting economic effects.

The annual budget of the Bureau of Prohibition increased approximately $9 million during the 1920's from approximately $4.4 million to approximately $13.4 million. The U.S. Coast Guard also spent approximately $13 million yearly enforcing prohibition. These Federal enforcement costs did not include cost incurred by State and local governments. Several of the States had maintained their legal right to enforce their own laws relating to alcohol and its consumption. With the passage of our 21st Amendment to our United States Constitution on December 5, 1933, the repeal of Prohibition was finally accomplished. The repeal of Prohibition was a major blow to the Protestant and other righteous religious-led support of the Prohibition Party. This was yet another example that organized religion has absolutely no business interfering in the secular matters and business of the United States government.

By Marty Piatt, Architect

After Prohibition ended, the several sovereign States were permitted to establish their own laws for the control and consumption of alcohol. During the era of Prohibition from 1919 to 1933, four economic downturns occurred in 1920, 1923, 1926, including the Great Depression of 1929. Occurring during the midst of the depression, the repeal of Prohibition in 1933 came much too late to prevent or reduce the subsequent collapse of Wall Street and the American economy, which I personally blame as a direct result of the enactment of Prohibition by our racketeering Congress.

With the repeal of Prohibition, organized crime lost nearly all of its black market alcohol-generated profits due to the resulting competition with lower priced alcohol sales at legal liquor stores. Prohibition also had a devastating effect on the various alcohol brewing industries in the United States. Only about half of the breweries that existed prior to Prohibition reopened when Prohibition was repealed.

According to wine historians, a fledgling wine industry in the United States was destroyed by Prohibition. Lower quality vines growing thicker skinned grapes that could be more easily transported replaced the productive wine quality grape vines. As winemakers either immigrated to other wine producing nations, or left finally the business, valuable winemaking knowledge was ultimately lost. At the end of Prohibition, some supporters openly admitted its failure. A letter written in 1932 by John D. Rockefeller, Jr. states:

"When Prohibition was introduced, I hoped that it would be widely supported by public opinion and the day would soon come when the evil effects of alcohol would be recognized. I have slowly and reluctantly come to believe that this has not been the result. Instead, drinking has generally increased; the speakeasy has replaced the saloon; a vast army of lawbreakers has appeared; many of our best citizens have openly ignored Prohibition; respect for the law has been greatly lessened; and crime has increased to a level never seen before."

Now we should exchange the word "Marijuana" for the word "Alcohol", and the word "Cartel" for the word "Gang" and we will discover the very same relationship between crime and the Prohibition of marijuana in the present day.

Many economists, law enforcement authorities, reformists, and the pro-marijuana lobby have all established a wide variety of demand- and supply-based marijuana market value estimates utilizing numerous accounting factors resulting in a range of approximately $10 billion to well over $120 billion per year. However, such a wide market range involving the exact marijuana market value is hardly a reliable economic answer or accurate basis for making an educated logical comparison.

A recent National Survey on Drug Use and Health was conducted by the U.S. Department of Health & Human Services' Substance Abuse & Mental Health Administration. This survey stated that approximately 10% of the population over the age of 12 had used marijuana in the past year, while only 6% had used marijuana in any particular month. Of all monthly users, 15% would use marijuana on a daily basis.

Various reports and studies involving marijuana price and volume conclude that a typical marijuana cigarette, or "joint", contains approximately 0.5 to 1.0 gram of marijuana. "High Times", among many other magazines publishing to the interests and needs of the marijuana industry, has conducted surveys of its readers on a monthly basis to approximate marijuana prices from around the nation. The price of marijuana in the United States can vary from as little as $5 to as much as $20 per gram or more depending on the marijuana's potency and area of cultivation.

Based on this and other marijuana-related documented data, most "demand-based" economic studies estimate the overall market for marijuana at approximately $10 to $40 billion annually, possibly even up to $120 billion per year by some estimates. An alternative approach is to analyze the "supply side" rather than the "demand side" of the marijuana market equation. Unlike the steady levels of demand and consumption, the levels of supply, seizures and eradications keep increasing.

Approximately 7 million marijuana plants were eradicated in 2007, an increase of 120% from 2004; the Drug Enforcement Agency (DEA) seized approximately 1.5 million pounds of marijuana in 2008, an increase of 149% from 2005; all according to the DEA's National Drug Intelligence Center (NDIC).

By Marty Piatt, Architect

Dr. John Gettman, a marijuana reform activist and professor at George Mason University, using data from the DEA and other sources in his 2006 study "Marijuana Production in the United States", estimated an annual domestic marijuana harvest of approximately 65 million plants having a gross weight of approximately 22 million pounds. He also estimated another 50% could be harvested in bordering Canada and Mexico.

Based upon the average yields of marijuana plants weighing about 7 ounces per outdoor plant and 3.5 ounces per indoor plant, the total harvest size assumptions, the per ounce price ranges, and consumption rates, estimated the "supply-based" market value for marijuana would approach $120 billion annually, which was nearly identical to the "demand-based" estimate.

Based upon the potential excise (100%) and gross income (10%) taxes generated from the marijuana industry, it could be estimated that the Federal government and the U.S. Treasury could generate nearly $144 billion of tax revenue. Couple these tax amounts with the potential Federal cost savings of eliminating just the ATF and DEA enforcement of existing marijuana laws, the resulting combination of Federal revenue and related cost-savings could easily approach $100 billion or more annually solely from the Federal de-criminalization of the U.S. marijuana industry.

With the combination of marijuana excise tax and Federal tax-savings from enforcement, the Federal government could realize approximately $244 billion per year, or nearly $2.5 trillion dollars over a 10-year period. I believe the immediate repeal all Federal anti-marijuana laws would similarly result in the corresponding incidents of crimes would be decreased by approximately 24%, theft and burglaries by nearly 10%, homicides over 12%, and assaults and battery by 13%. Local police department marijuana-related enforcement expenditures would be reduced by more than 11%. Another important aspect for the Federal decriminalization of marijuana would be the obvious decreased level of crime, specifically in Mexico; creating an environment that the Mexican people would feel safe in their own society. This would also encourage Mexican repatriation and reduce the illegal immigration rate into the United States. If the Mexican government reduced the corruptive elements within their our ranks, their economy could improve, and illegal residents of the United States could return voluntarily repatriated with their homeland and begin to nurture a new era of prosperity at home.

Just as Prohibition helped send our country spiraling into depression, just imaging how ending our marijuana prohibition could rocket our economy forward out of recession into prosperity.

As President I would propose the following recommendations and immediate actions:

1. Repeal the Controlled Substance Act (CSA), Title II of the Comprehensive Drug Abuse Prevention and Control Act of 1970;

2. Repeal all Prohibition era legislation including the Prohibition Act of 1919, Volstead Act, Cullen-Harrison of 1933, and the Wartime Prohibition Act of 1918 that yet may remain unrepealed;

3. Eliminate the Drug Enforcement Administration (DEA) immediately and suspension of all enforcement activities targeted at the various International Drug Cartels (IDC) outside our U.S. borders. Drug regulated enforcement would be the sole responsibility of the several sovereign States;

4. Eliminate the Alcohol Tobacco Firearms (ATF) Agency immediately and suspend all ATF-related enforcement activities. Alcohol regulated enforcement would be the sole responsibility of the several sovereign States;

5. Propose a 100% minimum Federal excise tax on the several sovereign States regulation and sale of marijuana products, including the levy of Federal income taxes on the sale of all marijuana products;

6. Broker a national truce and cease-fire between the Mexican government and the Mexican-based Drug Cartels to stop the killing of innocent Mexican nationals;

7. Assist the Mexican government in their responsibility for the regulation, legitimization, and legalization of marijuana products cultivated and distributed within their country;

8. Command the Mexican government in their request for the repatriation and return of their government's native residents unlawfully residing within the borders of United States of America.

By Marty Piatt, Architect

NATIONAL BUDGET

Our United States nation budget for the fiscal year 2012 (FY12) beginning October 2011 extending through the end of September 2012, proposed in February 2011 by President Obama and submitted to Congress was approximately $3.73 trillion dollars. This was a per capita Budget cost of approximately $12,000 per U.S. resident, substantially greater than the $1 per resident during colonial times.

The total of all government tax revenues for FY12 were estimated to be approximately $2.63 trillion, accounting for a $1.1 trillion dollar budget deficit. Our budget deficit is requiring the United States government to borrow approximately thirty percent (30%) of our national budget. Throughout recent history, the United States has consistently borrowed between 30 and 40 cents of every dollar it spends of your hard-earned tax dollars.

Revenues for Personal Income tax, Social Security, and payroll taxes were estimated at approximately $2.07 trillion; representing approximately 78% of the total tax revenues; or approximately 56% of our national budget. Revenues for Corporate Income tax were estimated at approximately $330 billion; representing approximately 12% of the total tax revenues; or approximately 9% of our national budget. Corporate income taxes paid are significantly less than our personal income taxes.

The income tax revenue statistical differences between Personal and Corporate tax better defines the enormous difference between the rich and the poor, between Wall Street and Main Street. Based upon national income tax revenues for Personal and Corporate income, Main Street pays more than six times the amount of total income taxes than Wall Street.

The FY12 revenues generated from the Federal Reserve were estimated at approximately $66 billion dollars. This is income created by our government lending the United States banking system your money from the U.S. Treasury at a profit. Federal Reserve revenue is essentially a tax generated and levied against the American taxpayers. This is generated from lending the banking industry your hard-earned tax dollars and charging the Banks an interest amount that is absorbed by the American taxpayers that borrow their own money and tax dollars.

The remaining miscellaneous tax revenues of approximately $167 billion dollars represent revenues generated from excise, customs, estate, gift, and others taxes. This amount represents approximately 6% of the total tax revenues; or approximately 5% of our national budget.

Our annual Gross Domestic Product (GDP) is estimated somewhere in the range of approximately $18 trillion dollars. Nearly equal to our GDP, our current national debt is also estimated at approximately $18 trillion dollars. Our National Debt must be defined in two methods to better understand the nature of our financial debt, which can be categorized in "Marketable Securities" and Non-marketable Securities.

Marketable Securities are securities that can be converted quickly into cash at a reasonable price and are liquid because they exhibit high trading volumes that tend to have short-term maturities of less than one year. The rate at which these securities can be bought or sold has little effect on their prices. Examples of Marketable Securities are commercial paper, Treasury bills, banker's acceptances, common ordinary stocks traded on the stock exchanges, and any other money market instruments. Non-marketable securities are stock shares that are held in privately held companies for which there is no readily available market. One would need to find a buyer and negotiate their own price if they wanted to sell non-marketable stock shares.

Our National Debt can be categorized as either "Public Debt" or "Intra-government Debt", which is non-public debt. Public Debt is debt owed to American citizens and foreign governments. Intra-government Debt is debt the Federal government owes itself. In economics, these debts are Government Account Series (GAS) securities held by government trust funds, revolving funds, and special government funds. Intra-government debt is incurred when the U.S. government borrows from Federal trust funds to help fund the current budget deficit of our Federal government operations. Intra-governmental debt holdings are primarily composed of Medicare Trust Funds, Social Security Trust Funds, and Federal Financing Bank securities. Small portions of the Marketable Securities are held by government accounts.

Breaking down our $18 trillion dollar national debt, approximately $12 trillion dollars is in Marketable Securities and approximately $6 trillion is in Non-marketable Securities. Keep in mind I am not an economist.

In other terms, approximately $12 trillion dollars is in Public Debt, and approximately $6 trillion dollars is owed to foreign countries and investors, of which approximately $1.2 trillion dollars is owed to China and $1.21 trillion is owed to Japan. Japan has surpassed China in American debt.

Of the approximately $12 trillion of Public Debt, about $7 trillion dollars is owed to American citizens in the form of Treasury notes and government bonds. The remaining approximately $5 trillion dollars is the amount the Federal government actually owes itself. Now, how can the Federal government owe itself money? Well we would need to ask our racketeering members of Congress. They are the ones that raided the surplus accounts of both the Social Security Administration and the United States Postal Service for starters.

The Social Security Administration (SSA) and the United States Postal Service (USPS) are two of our nation's only "off-budget" Federal organizations that are totally separated and outside of our Federal unified budget as a result of Legislative actions by Congress.

Social Security refers to the Old Age, Survivors, and Disability Insurance (OASDI) Federal social insurance program that was signed into law on August 14, 1935 as part of President Franklin D. Roosevelt's "New Deal". The core part of the program is sometimes abbreviated to OASDI, or RSDI (Retirement, Survivors, and Disability Insurance). The term Social Security also covered unemployment insurance as well. The original Social Security Act of 1935 and its current "off-budget" version as amended in 1983, encompasses several Federal social welfare and social insurance programs. Social Security is funded primarily through a payroll tax referred to as the FICA (Federal Insurance Contributions Act) tax whose dedicated deposits are formally entrusted to the following:

1. Federal OASDI Trust Fund

2. Federal Disability Insurance Trust Fund

3. Federal Hospital Insurance Trust Fund

4. Federal Supplementary Medical Insurance Trust Fund.

The term Social Security was used to refer only to retirement, disability, survivorship, and death benefits that are the four main benefits provided by traditional private-sector pension plans.

The United States Postal Service, also known as the Post Office, U.S. Mail, or USPS, is an independent agency of the United States Federal government. Authorized by the United States Constitution, it is a rare government agency that is explicitly responsible for providing postal service within our nation. The USPS is the 48th-largest employer in the United States employing approximately 574,000 workers. The USPS is also the operator of the largest vehicle fleet in the world utilizing over 218,000 fleet vehicles. The USPS has a legal and constitutional obligation to provide postal service to all American citizens, regardless of geography, at a uniform price and quality. Since the early 1980s, with the minor exception of subsidies for costs associated with the disabled and overseas voters, the USPS has never directly received any taxpayer-funded Federal revenue. The USPS traces its beginnings to 1775 when Benjamin Franklin was appointed the first postmaster general during the Second Continental Congress. The cabinet-level Post Office Department was created in 1792 from Franklin's postal operation. The USPS was transformed into its current form in 1971 under the Postal Reorganization Act.

Congress created the quasi-Federal "off-budget" agencies of the Social Security Administration and the United States Postal Service, which required their independence from the Federal Budget having accountability to sustain the agencies financially. But the resulting greed of our Congress, which spends money belonging to these "off-budget" agencies, will ultimately result in their inevitable future collapse.

As President, using common and otherwise creative accounting practices, I would direct the United States Treasury to:

1. Eliminate all "Intra-government Debt" owed to the Federal government;

2. Reintegrate both the Social Security Administration (SSA) and the United States Postal Service (USPS) back into our Federal Budget eliminating their "off-budget" status;

3. Liquidate all Federal Trusts Funds and accounts and reallocate all the United States financial resources into the U.S. Treasury General Fund;

This would guarantee the financial solvency of both the Social Security Administration and U.S. Postal Service well into our distance future.

Senior citizens will be able to count on their tax-free Social Security income and our Postal carriers will be delivering our mail six times a week. This immediate action would result in lowering our National Debt by nearly one-third, or to about $12 trillion dollars total. With $300 billion dollar annual principle payments, I would pay off all of our foreign-owned debt in approximately 16 years. This could reduce the remaining debt service interest by one-third to approximately $144 billion annually that could also supplement Defense Department spending.

Our GDP technically refers to the market value of all goods and services produced by commerce in a given fiscal year. A leading indicator of a country's wealth and comfort is known as the Standard of Living. One method utilized is represented by the per capita GDP, which is equal to the total value in dollars divided by the population of the country. The United States population currently exceeds 321 million residents. Based upon our estimated population and the current GDP of approximately $18 trillion dollars, the average per capita GDP is approximately $54,000.00 per person, or about $22,000.00 above the 2013 family poverty level of $32,000.00 for parents with four children.

However, our GDP does not include revenues from non-profit organizations, which includes all churches and other religious institutions. Nor does it include the tremendous amount of income revenues generated by our political system, which would include all State and Federal political campaigns, ballot referendums, and initiatives, etc. currently protected and excluded from taxation by our corrupt-redden Congress. Based on Federal Election Commission data released on October 27, 2008, the total amount of just the 2008 presidential campaign contributions totaled nearly $1.12 billion dollars. This does not include any other State and Federal politically generated income.

And yet Main Street, representing approximately 99% of the income-earning population, owns approximately 60% of our national financial wealth, while Wall Street, representing approximately 1% of the income-earning population, owns approximately 40% of our national wealth.

This statistical information also explains the necessity and importance of overhauling our current income tax code. The current tax code, including the Internal Revenue Service (IRS), needs to be entirely abandoned and replaced.

The tax code and tax law enacted and created by Congress, the corrupt gang of criminal racketeers, is the main cause of the vast difference between Main Street and Wall Street incomes.

Politicians and political presidential candidates are now referring to modifying, not abandoning, the existing tax code and implementing a hybrid type of "flat tax" for income revenue. But it must be noted, there is a vast difference between a flat-tax and flat-rate tax. In a flat-tax system, everyone pays exactly the same tax amount. In a flat-rate tax system, everyone pays the identical tax rate. It is very important that our politicians know the tremendous difference between the two definitions of a "flat tax" system.

Our nation's first income tax was a result of the Revenue Act of 1861, which authorized Congress to levy a flat 3% Gross Income Tax (GIT) on all domestic income over $800, and 5% for the gross income of those individuals living outside of the United States.

Tax revenues are just one of two aspects relating to our national budget. The other aspect of our budget is expenditures. But before analyzing expenditures, the government must first address its income potential. In my opinion, we need to abandon the current tax code, and adopt a fair and reasonable flat-rate Gross Income Tax (GIT). Utilizing a GIT flat-rate tax of just ten percent (10%) and using our current GNP, a bare minimum of $1.8 trillion dollars could potentially be generated in Gross Income Tax revenue. If all non-governmental income receiving entities, including but not limited to: a person, group, organization, committee, corporation, religious institution, political party, campaign, referendum, initiative, lobby, etc. was included in tax revenue sources, I believe nearly $3 trillion dollars or more could be generated to support our national budget and debt repayment.

I believe my proposed GIT, a non-religious Patriotic National Tithe of 10% imposed on any and all domestic and foreign "gross incomes", could instantly solve our budgetary deficit problems that we as a nation now face. No deductions, exemptions, credits, or loopholes whatsoever would be allowed or permitted in this flat-rate gross income tax system. Everyone pays the same income tax rate, period! When everyone pays, everyone pays less. With a flat-rate Gross Income Tax system, no one can say they pay more or less tax than anyone else.

Nor does it specifically target higher income-generating individuals or entities. Even the poor will pay the same flat-rate income tax. The more you earn, the more tax you pay. The less you earn, the less tax you pay.

The current income tax system unfortunately rewards financial inefficiency. By allowing and permitting tax deductions for personal and business expenses, the resulting effect is that both profits and tax liabilities are greatly reduced. The current tax system is actually a "lose-lose" situation for both the government and taxpayers. The government loses with less tax revenues; and the taxpayers lose with less profit and disposable income.

The government should instead reward taxpayers for financial efficiency with an overall lower gross income tax rate. Businesses and corporations with a current profit margin less than 10%, while also benefiting from a reduction in payroll taxes, may need to raise revenue accordingly. This may result in a short-term self-adjusting non-permanent rise in economic inflation. There might also be a temporary and positive increase in the resulting tax revenue. Within my 10% flat-rate Gross Income Tax (GIT) proposal, all other payroll deductions including social security would be totally eliminated. An average family earning $48,000 would pay no more than $4,800 in gross income taxes.

Deductions for mortgage interest and tax exemptions for children would however also be eliminated. Without the benefit of the mortgage interest deduction, interest rates would remain at historically low levels as a result. Also, if as parents you choose to have twenty children, be prepared to raise them without help from the Federal government. Single adults and senior citizens without children should not be required to subsidize families in America by paying higher taxes. I believe this childless-taxation is an unlawful situation of "taxation without representation".

A prime encouraging case of the success of a flat tax is the Russian Federation of the former Soviet Union. A 13% flat-rate tax on personal income was implemented and took effect on January 1, 2001. The resulting tax revenues from its personal income tax rose by 25.2% in the first year, followed by a 24.6% increase in the second year, and a 15.2% increase in the third year.

The primary reason for the greater revenue to higher levels of economic growth stemming from the introduction of the flat tax was attributed the theoretical ideals based upon the Laffer curve that predicts such an outcome. An American economist who first gained prominence during the Reagan administration as a member of Reagan's Economic Policy Advisory Board between the years of 1981 and 1989, Arthur Laffer is best known for the Laffer curve. In economics, the Laffer curve is a theoretical representation of the relationship between government revenue raised by taxation and all possible rates of taxation. In the 1970's, Jude Wanniski coined the term after the theoretical economic work of Arthur Laffer who later pointed out his conceptual economic theory was not entirely original. It was described as an illustration of the theory that there exists some tax rate between 0% and 100% that will result in maximum tax revenue.

Economist John Maynard Keynes actually had similar theoretical ideals based upon this theory. The curve is generally represented as a graph, which begins at 0% tax, and zero revenue; then rises to a maximum rate of revenue raised at an intermediate rate of taxation; and then falls again to zero when the revenue is at a 100% tax rate. A potential result of the Laffer curve is that increasing tax rates beyond a certain point would become counterproductive for raising income tax revenue further. The Laffer curve is also associated with supply-side economics and rates of taxation, where its use in debates has been controversial. Some would argue that non-profits should be excluded from this gross income tax system. Some would also argue that religious organizations should be excluded as well. And the politicians will most certainly argue that their politically generated income be excluded too. I would however disagree in all three cases.

First, I will address the taxing of churches and other religious organizations. The term: "Separation of Church and State" is nowhere to be found or referenced within our Unites States Constitution. According to the first amendment, our Constitution states: "Congress shall make no law respecting an establishment of religion, or prohibiting the free exercise thereof"; thus having both an establishment clause, and the free exercise clause. What this amendment means and specifically infers is that the Federal government cannot establish a national religion; nor prohibit, or compel, the free exercise of religious belief by any individual. It is that plain and simple, period.

By Marty Piatt, Architect

The concept of the "Separation of Church and State" refers to the doctrine separating the relationship between religion as an organized institution and the government. The term "wall of separation between church and state," was written in a letter to the Danbury Baptist Association in 1802 by Thomas Jefferson stating: "...I contemplate with sovereign reverence that act of the whole American people which declared that their legislature should 'make no law respecting an establishment of religion, or prohibiting the free exercise thereof,' thus building a wall of separation between Church & State."

James Madison, another early user of the term and the principal drafter of the United States Bill of Rights, wrote in a letter to Edward Livingston Madison stating: "We are teaching the world the great truth that [Governments] do better without Kings & Nobles than with them. The merit will be doubled by the other lesson that Religion flourishes in greater purity, without than with the aid of [Government]."

James Madison also wrote: "Practical distinction between Religion and Civil Government is essential to the purity of both, and as guaranteed by the Constitution of the United States." He also believed that "because if religion be exempt from the authority of the society at large, still less can it be subject to that of the legislative body."

The "Virginia Statute for Religious Freedom", drafted by Thomas Jefferson in 1777, and praised by James Madison states: "...no man shall be compelled to frequent or support any religious worship, place, or ministry whatsoever, nor shall be enforced, restrained, molested, or burthened in his body or goods, nor shall otherwise suffer on account of his religious opinions or belief; but that all men shall be free to profess, and by argument to maintain, their opinion in matters of religion, and that the same shall in no wise diminish enlarge, or affect their civil capacities".

The United States Supreme Court has quoted the phrase first in 1878, and again in a series of cases beginning in 1947. The Court has more than 25 times referenced the "Separation of Church and State" metaphor, though not always fully embracing the principle.

In 1947, Supreme Court Justice Hugo Black used the phrase in Everson versus Board of Education.

The matter involved a tax-funded school district that provided reimbursement to parents of both public- and privately-schooled children taking the public transportation system to school. The plaintiff Everson contended that the reimbursement given for children attending private religious schools violated the constitutional prohibition against State support of religion. The Justices were split over the question whether the New Jersey policy constituted support of religion, with the majority concluding these reimbursements were "separate and so indisputably marked off from the religious function" not violating the Constitution.

Justice Hugo Black's sweeping language in the majority opinion stated: "The 'establishment of religion' clause of the First Amendment means at least this: Neither a state nor the Federal Government can set up a church. Neither can pass laws which aid one religion, aid all religions or prefer one religion over another. Neither can force nor influence a person to go to or to remain away from church against his will or force him to profess a belief or disbelief in any religion. No person can be punished for entertaining or professing religious beliefs or disbeliefs, for church attendance or non-attendance. No tax in any amount, large or small, can be levied to support any religious activities or institutions, whatever they may be called, or whatever form they may adopt to teach or practice religion. Neither a state nor the Federal Government can, openly or secretly, participate in the affairs of any religious organizations or groups and vice versa. In the words of Jefferson, the clause against establishment of religion by law was intended to erect 'a wall of separation between Church and State'."

Even in the minority opinion, Justice Wiley Rutledge also insisted that the Constitution forbid "every form of public aid or support for religion". This Supreme Court decisive precedent clearly suggests the Federal government cannot levy tax to support any church or religious institution; nor could the church or religious institution openly or secretly participate in the affairs of the government, basically establishing a presumed non-interference doctrine separating both the Church and the State. However, and most importantly, the Court's decision does not specifically forbid or infer that the Federal government cannot levy a tax on the income of any church or religious institution in support of the government itself. More recently, in a minority opinion in the matter of Wallace versus Jaffree, Justice William Rehnquist also presented the view that the establishment clause of the first amendment was actually intended to protect local establishments of religion from Federal interference.

Taxing the income of churches or other religious institutions does not specifically "interfere" in the internal affairs and "religious" activities of the Church.

In any case, whether non-profit or not, the Church is forbidden to enter into politics, and the government is forbidden to enter into religion. Taxation is however an entirely a separate matter. I must also mention, in the era of mega-church businesses, it cannot be denied that religion and the Church have not actively entered into the realm of governmental politics. In its obvious involvement in the particularly sensitive moral and political issues such as abortion and same-sex marriage, the church has consistently instilled its religious moral values and doctrine onto their voter congregations, and has made sizable political contributions opposing such issues. The current tax code specifically prohibits non-profit religious organizations and institutions from any involvement whatsoever in governmental political activities. The Church has however more recently also made major political contributions and donations from the religious tithes of its congregations to the opponents of same-sex marriage, which I believe is an absolute and defiant interference into the affairs of State and Federal government and politics. Since religion and the Church is obviously an institution most benefiting from our first amendment rights, I believe the Church should willfully assist in the operation and finance of our government in defending their right to free speech and the free exercise of their religious beliefs.

Second, relating to the taxation of other non-profit organizations, I believe there is no such thing as a non-profit institution in existence that is entirely financed by donations or income without some sort of marginal profit. My point is simply, if everyone pays income tax, everyone pays less income tax. And if everyone pays less, everyone has much more disposable income to make much more donations to the former non-profit organizations. The point of giving, as I believe, should not be for the tax-exemption status of that donation's income, but rather for the selfless, honest, and sincere generosity of giving to those less fortunate in need of financial assistance.

And third, and most importantly, all politically-generated income should be absolutely and entirely taxable. Since the fox is guarding the henhouse, of course Congress would exclude this portion of non-commerce generated income from taxation.

I strongly believe that the gross income tax revenue generated from all of the deep-pocket political actions committees, lobbyist groups, campaign donors, and political parties could be a tremendous windfall for the government, the U.S. Treasury Department, and the American taxpayers.

Having addressed the revenue portion of government, we need now to address and reflect upon our national expenditures. The President's budget for 2012 totaled $3.73 trillion dollars. Approximately $2.35 trillion dollars was for Mandatory Spending; which would include: Social Security (32%), Medicare (20%), Medicaid and State Children's Health Insurance Program (12%), Unemployment and Welfare (26%), and the Interest Only on our National Debt of approximately $15 trillion dollars (10%); items representing 63% of our national budget.

Of the total budget for FY12 expenditures, approximately $1.38 trillion dollars was allocated for Discretionary Spending; which would encompass the Department of Defense including the Overseas Contingency Operations, i.e. War (50%), and all other Federal Departments and Agencies (50%); discretionary spending items representing 37% of our national budget. Democrats and Republicans alike can tell us the United States of America is a Democratic Capitalist society. However, based on our national budget that spends nearly two-thirds of our mandatory budget expenditures on social welfare and entitlement programs, we are Socialists.

I believe this great country has actually become a Socialist state, or more appropriately similar to a Communist Capitalist state, not unlike the Peoples Republic of China; which also has a "Republican" type of Single Political Party-run government.

The Department of Defense and the Overseas Contingency Operations (war) FY12 budget of $679 Billion dollars, was the single-greatest budget line item; representing over 18% of our total national budget. Excluding the current costs of our two wars, this amount would be equal to approximately 15% of our national budget, or approximately 40% of all discretionary budget expenditures.

Our Congressional politicians and national economists try to put these figures into a better perspective by describing the budget amounts in terms of the percentage of the Gross Domestic Product (GDP). Based upon that perspective, our national debt is approximately 100% of our GDP.

By Marty Piatt, Architect

Our annual mandatory expenditures for social welfare, entitlement programs, and interest only payments paid towards our national debt, represent nearly 16% of our GDP. And military spending represents nearly 5% of our GDP. The unfortunate aspect of all these budgetary statistics is that there are no principal payments being paid in any feeble attempt to tackle paying off our national debt principle. If Congress were to quit borrowing money today, it would take well over 100 years to pay off our current debt making just $150 billion dollar annual principle payments paid towards our national debt. That amount does not include interest on the debt.

It's taken over two centuries, but our current bi-cameral Congress, the corrupt gang of criminal racketeers, has finally screwed the United States of America. Our legislative Branch of government is responsible for spending our nation's money. The Executive Branch may propose the spending, but ultimately Congress is solely responsible for budget funding legislation.

Based upon my proposed elimination of our current income tax code and utilizing an implementation of my non-religious "Patriotic National Tithe" of 10% flat-rate tax plan for all gross income, my proposed national budget for **FY18** is approximately one-half trillion dollars ($500 billion) less than the **FY12** budget as follows:

Total revenues: $3.22 trillion dollars

$3.0 trillion – 10 % Gross Income Tax (GIT)
$103 billion – Excise tax
$67.0 billion – United States Postal Service
$30.0 billion – Customs duties
$20.0 billion – Other revenues

Total Expenditures: $3.22 trillion dollars

Mandatory spending: $2.112 trillion

$761 billion – Social Security (36%)
$737 billion – Americare (35%)
$374 billion – Unemployment & Welfare (18%)
$240 billion – Interest on National Debt (11%)

Discretionary spending: $1.108 trillion

$554 billion – Dept. of Defense (50%)
$300 billion – Principal on Foreign Debt (27%)

All other Departments and Agencies (23%)

$67.0 billion – Postal Services
$62.0 billion – Health, Education, and Welfare
$38.8 billion – State
$23.0 billion – Energy
$21.8 billion – Justice
$14.5 billion – Interior, Labor, and Commerce
$10.8 billion – Treasury
$10.4 billion – Transportation
$5.70 billion – Executive Contingency

I am no economist, but I think we all know how to balance and reconcile our checkbooks based on our income. Our National Budget is essentially no different.

To vastly improve Federal acquisition efficiency within the United States government as a whole, as President I would have established the "Federal Acquisition Workforce Improvement Act" of 2017, to be modeled after the military's "Defense Acquisition Workforce Improvement Act" of 1990. This new acquisition program would greatly improve all Federal acquisition assisting in the reduction of waste, fraud, and abuse within the Federal government of the United States.

To assist in reducing the overall size of the Federal government, I would implement a total hiring freeze excluding veteran new hires. With attrition and retirements, the Federal government could slowly reduce its overall size over time.

As President I would also immediately eliminate any and all foreign aid and domestic subsidizes from our Federal budget and spending. After which time 100% of our total foreign debt is paid and entirely reconciled, I would provide 10% of all Federal budget surpluses to be allocated for foreign monetary assistance and aid; our international tithe and charity to the world.

"The divorce between Church and State ought to be absolute. It ought to be so absolute that no Church property anywhere, in any state or in the nation, should be exempt from equal taxation; for if you exempt the property of any church organization, to that extent you impose a tax upon the whole community." ~James A. Garfield

"I don't know how you feel, but I'm pretty sick of church people. You know what they ought to do with churches? Tax them. If holy people are so interested in politics, government, and public policy, let them pay the price of admission like everybody else. The Catholic Church alone could wipe out the national debt if all you did was tax their real estate."
~George Carlin, comedian

"If I was President…"

By Marty Piatt, Architect

FEDERAL RESERVE

"...few people know that the Federal Reserve is not federal,
has no reserves, and is not even a bank."
~Josh M. Black

In 1690, the Massachusetts Bay Colony became the first of the thirteen colonies to issue paper money. But soon thereafter the other Colonies also began printing their own money. Due to the scarcity of coins, which had been the primary means of trade, demand for currency in the colonies had increased. The Colonies' paper currencies were used to pay for their expenses, and lend money to the citizens of the colonies'. Paper money quickly became the primary method used in commerce within each colony, as well as in financial transactions with the other colonies. Not redeemable in gold or silver, some of the currencies were caused to depreciate.

During the American Revolutionary War the first attempt at a national currency was implemented. The Continental Congress began issuing its own paper currency in 1775, calling its bills "Continentals". Used to help finance the American Revolutionary War, the Continentals were backed only by future tax revenue. The value of a Continental quickly diminished as a result. The experience led the United States to be skeptical of unbacked currencies, which were not issued again until the American Civil War.

In 1791, after ratification of the second U.S. Constitution, the government granted the First Bank of the United States a charter to operate as the U.S. central bank until 1811. The First Bank of the United States, chartered by Congress and signed into law by President George Washington on February 25, 1791 at the urging of Alexander Hamilton, was the first Federal institution with central banking responsibilities.

The nation's first Secretary of Treasury, Alexander Hamilton, had advocated the creation of a central bank. The Bank Bill, which he created, was a proposal to establish a National Bank to improve the economic stability of the nation after its independence from Britain. Used as a tool for the government, it was to be privately owned. As a result, the First Bank of the United States was headquartered in Philadelphia, also having branches in other major cities.

Not unlike any other bank, The First Bank of the United States performed the basic banking functions of accepting deposits, issuing bank notes, making loans and purchasing securities. Despite strong opposition from Thomas Jefferson, James Madison, and numerous others, the charter period was for twenty years. Because Congress had refused to renew the charter, it expired in 1811 under President Madison leaving the United States without a central bank for nearly five years, during which time the nation's economy suffered unusually high inflation.

In 1816, President Madison again revived the charter forming the Second Bank of the United States. Early renewal of the bank's charter years later became the primary issue in the re-election of President Andrew Jackson, who was opposed to the central bank, pulled the government's funds out of the bank after he was re-elected. The president of the Second Bank of the United States, Nicholas Biddle, responded by contracting the money supply to pressure President Jackson to renew the bank's charter, thus forcing the country into a recession, for which Biddle blamed the policies of President Jackson.

It must be noted, President Andrew Jackson is the only President in the history of United States to have accomplished completely paying off the entire Federal government's national debt. When the Second Bank of the United States charter ultimately expired in 1836, the United States again went without a central bank for forty years.

Then, in 1873, Congress nationalized money for the first time, imposing what was effectively a gold standard, replacing the bimetallic standard established by our founding fathers. The Coinage Act of 1873 set off cyclical fluctuation of growth and depression that came to be known as the "business cycle". In the pursuing years from 1837 to 1862, known as the Free Banking Era, there was no formal central bank.

Thereafter, from 1862 to 1913, the National Banking Act of 1863 instituted a system of national banks. A series of similarly devastating bank panics and economic downturns occurring in 1869, 1873, 1893, and 1907 again provided strong incentive and necessity for the formation of a centralized banking system. The Black Friday Panic of 1869 on September 24, 1869, was a financial panic in the United States caused by two speculators' efforts to corner the gold market on the New York Gold Exchange.

By Marty Piatt, Architect

Also known as the Fisk/Gould scandal, it was one of several scandals that rocked the presidency of Ulysses S. Grant. After the American Civil War ended and during the reconstruction era, the United States government issued a large amount of money backed by nothing but credit, not unlike the "Continentals" issued in 1775. People universally believed the government would buy back their "greenbacks" with gold at the end of the civil war.

In 1869, speculators sought to profit by cornering the gold market. A group headed by James Fisk and Jay Gould recruited President Grant's brother-in-law, a financier named Abel Corbin. Using Corbin to befriend Grant in social situations, they would argue against the government sale of gold. Corbin supporting their arguments convinced Grant to appoint General Daniel Butterfield as assistant Treasurer of the United States. When the government intended to sell gold, Butterfield agreed to give the men the inside information, possibly becoming one of the first cases of insider trading in American history. Gould began buying large amounts of gold late in the summer of 1869. Stock prices then plummeted causing gold prices to rise. The Federal government then sold $4 million in gold, after Grant finally realized what had transpired. Gould and Fisk started hoarding gold on September 20, 1869, driving the price even higher.

On September 24, 1869 the premium on a gold "Double Eagle" was 30 percent higher than when Grant took office. However, when the government gold hit the market, the premium plummeted within minutes. Investors scrambled to sell their holdings, and many of them, including Corbin, were ruined. Fisk and Gould escaped significant financial harm.

In The Panic of 1873, triggered by the fall in demand for silver internationally, resulted from Germany's decision to abandon the silver standard in the wake of the Franco-Prussian war. A severe international economic depression in both Europe and the United States resulted lasting until 1879. Known as the first Great Depression until the 1930s, it is now known as the Long Depression. Starting on September 20, the New York Stock Exchange closed for ten days. Of the country's 364 railroads, nearly 89 went bankrupt. The railroad industry had been the nation's largest employer outside of agriculture. During that period, great infusions of cash from speculators caused abnormally high growth in the railroad industry, which included uncertain risks associated with the investment.

85

An estimated total of 18,000 businesses failed between the years 1873 and 1875. By 1876 unemployment had reached nearly 14%, construction work was halted, wages were cut, real estate values fell, and corporate profits vanished.

The Panic of 1893, an economic depression occurred in the United States that was not unlike the Panic of 1873, the collapse of railroad overbuilding and risky railroad financing resulting in a series of bank failures. The Northern Pacific Railway, Union Pacific Railroad, and the Atchison Topeka & Santa Fe Railroad failed.

Followed by the bankruptcy, over 15,000 companies and 500 banks failed. At the panic's peak, up to 19% of the workforce was unemployed according to high estimates. With the loss of life savings kept in failed the banks combined with huge spikes in unemployment, a once-secure middle-class could not make mortgage payments and as a result, many walked away from recently built homes, not unlike today.

During the Panic of 1907, also known as the 1907 Bankers' Panic, a financial crisis occurred when the New York Stock Exchange fell nearly 50% from its high of the previous year. As panic ensued at a time of economic recession, many runs on the banks and trust companies occurred. Panic then extended across the nation as vast numbers of people withdrew deposits from their regional banks, resulting in several banks and businesses filing for bankruptcy protection. The primary cause of the run was a retraction of market liquidity by many of New York City banks resulting in a loss of confidence among depositors, worsened by unregulated side bets.

In October 1907, the United Copper Company failed in an attempt to corner the market on stock of the crisis, actually triggering the crisis. The banks that had lent money to the cornering scheme suffered runs that later spread to affiliated banks and trusts, leading just days later to the downfall of New York City's third-largest trust, the Knickerbocker Trust Company. This collapse spread fear throughout New York's trusts as regional banks withdrew reserves from New York City banks. If not for the intervention of financier J. P. Morgan, the panic may have deepened. Pledging large sums of his own money and convincing other New York bankers to do the same, Morgan shored up and stabilizing the banking system.

By Marty Piatt, Architect

During that crisis, the United States did not have a central bank to inject liquidity back into the market. By the following November, the financial crisis had ended.

However, a following crisis arose when a major stock brokerage firm borrowed heavily using the stock of Tennessee Coal, Iron and Railroad Company (TC&I) as collateral. The collapse of TC&I's stock price was averted by an emergency takeover by Morgan's U.S. Steel Corporation, an action hesitantly approved by President Theodore Roosevelt, an anti-monopolist. The following year, Senator Nelson W. Aldrich established and chaired a commission to investigate the crisis and propose future solutions, unfortunately leading to the creation of the Federal Reserve System.

On December 23, 1913, with what would essentially become the Third Bank of the United States, Congress created the Federal Reserve System with the enactment of the Federal Reserve Act. Becoming the central banking system of the United States of America, the Federal Reserve Banks opened for business in November 1914.

Then the recession of 1918 occurred, only four years after the Federal Reserve began operation. It was a brief, but a very sharp recession caused by the end of World War I wartime industrial production. High unemployment was also a result of troops returning home from combat.

Then came another recession in 1920, which was the single most deflationary year in American economic history. Wholesale prices declined by 36.8%. However, production did not fall as much as might have been expected from the deflation, and the GNP may have declined from about 3% to 7%.

Then came yet another recession in 1923, lasting about two years. It was a mild incident compared to others.

Then in 1926, three years prior to the Great Depression, another mild yet unusual economic recession struck, lasting little more than two years as well. The recession was thought to be caused largely in part by the six month halt in production at Henry Ford's automotive factories while in transition from the Model T production to the next generation Model A production.

87

Then came the Great Depression of 1929, only fifteen years after the introduction of the Federal Reserve. The previous panics of 1869, 1873, 1893, and 1907 were great, all unbelieving the next could be even greater until 1929. The Great Depression, a severe worldwide economic depression that varied across most nations, started in 1929 and lasted until the late 1930s or early 1940s. It became the longest, most widespread, and deepest depression of the 20th century. Beginning from the initial fall in stock prices in September 1929, the depression resulted in the subsequent October crash of the stock market.

On October 28, 1929, the stock market dropped 12.82%, losing 38.33 points down to 260.94, which become the second largest single-day percentage loss in American history. The very next day, the stock market fell again. This time dropping 11.73%, losing another 30.57 points down to 230.07. It became the third largest single-day percentage loss in American history. Known as Black Tuesday, the stock market had a two-day loss of 68.9 points, dropping a total of 23.12%.

During the Crash of 1929, stock brokerage firms would lend $9 for every $1 the investor had deposited, basically creating margin requirements that were only 10%. The brokers called these loans in as the market fell, but the loans could not be repaid. As depositors attempted to withdraw their deposits and debtors defaulted on their loans, banks began to fail, triggering multiple bank runs. Federal Reserve banking regulations to prevent such panics including government guarantees were ineffective or not utilized, leading to the loss of billions of dollars in bank assets.

The Great Depression had devastating effects in every country. Personal income, tax revenues, profits, and overall prices plummeted. International trade plunged by more than 50%. U.S. unemployment rose to 25%, and in some countries 33% worldwide. Cities dependent on heavy industry were hit hard and construction was virtually at a halt. Rural farming areas suffered as crop prices fell by nearly 60%. Areas dependent on primary sector industries such as cash cropping, mining and logging suffered the greatest.

There were multiple causes for the first downturn in 1929. Historians emphasized structural factors like major bank failures and the stock market crash, in contrast to economists that pointed to monetary factors such as actions by the Federal Reserve that contracted the money supply.

By Marty Piatt, Architect

In a world of inexact balances between supply and demand, recessions and business cycles are thought to be a normal part of economic cyclical fluctuation. A subject of much debate and concern is what turns a normal recession or business cycle into a depression. The search for causes is closely connected to the issue of avoiding future depressions. Many financial scholars and economists still have not agreed on the exact causes, and their relative importance. Was The Great Depression primarily a failure of free markets or a failure of government efforts to regulate interest rates, curtail widespread bank failures, and control of the money supply? This rhetorical question remains unanswered. Those who believe in a lesser role for the state believe that it was primarily a failure of government, while those who believe in a greater economic role for the state believe it was primarily a failure of free markets that compounded the problem. I believe both possibilities were to blame.

On June 16, 1933, the "Glass-Steagall Act" was enacted as a result of The Great Depression. It established the Federal Deposit Insurance Corporation (FDIC) in the United States that also imposed many banking reforms, several of which were intended to control speculation. Named after its Congressional sponsors, Senator Carter Glass (D) of Virginia, and Representative Henry B. Steagall (D) of Alabama. It is often referred to as the "Banking Act of 1933".

Then came the recession of 1937. Except for unemployment, which remained high, all the main economic indicators had regained the levels of the late 1920s after the Great Depression. The economy in America unexpectedly fell, lasting through most of 1938. Production, profits, and employment declined sharply. Unemployment jumped from 14.3% in 1937 to 19.0% in 1938. While considered only minor in comparison to the Great Depression, the 1937 recession lasted more than four years. It was by far one of the worst recessions of the twentieth century. A tightening of monetary policy by the Federal Reserve was a contributing factor to this recession. Between August 1936 and May 1937, the Federal Reserve doubled the banking reserve requirements leading to a contraction in the money supply. The Roosevelt Administration reacted by launching a rhetorical campaign against monopoly power, which was cast as the main cause of the depression. President Roosevelt appointed Thurman Arnold to break up large trusts, which ending up being ineffective. The campaign ended once World War II began and corporate energies had to be directed to winning the war.

By 1939, the effects of the 1937 recession had disappeared. Employment in the private sector recovered to a 1936 level and continued to increase until the beginning of World War II. Manufacturing employment leaped from 11 million in 1940 to 18 million in 1943. Ignoring the cautious pleas of the Treasury Department, Roosevelt embarked on an antidote to the depression, reluctantly abandoning his efforts to balance the budget while launching a $5 billion spending program in the spring of 1938. This program was an effort to increase mass purchasing power.

Then the recession of 1945 occurred, which lasted only eight months. Not unlike the decline in government spending at the end of World War I, the end of WWII also led to an enormous drop in gross domestic product, technically making this a recession a result of demobilization and the shift from wartime to peacetime economies, having a decline in GDP of approximately 12.7%.

Then came the 1948 recession, lasting just eleven months, which was very mild having a reduction of GDP of a mere 1.7%. it was followed by a period of monetary tightening. The recession began shortly after President Truman's "Fair Deal" economic reforms, which peaked with a 7.9% unemployment rate.

In 1952, approximately one year after the Federal Reserve reasserted its independence from the U.S. Treasury, its monetary policy became more restrictive in fears of furthering perceived higher inflation. During this period, unemployment was about 6.1% and the nation's GDP declined approximately 3.7%. The actions of the Federal Reserve resulted in the recession of 1953, also lasting approximately 10 months. Following a post-Korean War inflationary period, additional budgetary allocations were obligated to national security.

In 1956, to bolster the Glass-Steagall Banking Act of 1933, Congress enacted the "Bank Holding Company Act" that was to regulate the actions of bank holding companies. The legislation required that the Federal Reserve Board of Governors must approve the establishment of a bank holding company. It prohibited banks headquartered in one state from acquiring a bank in a different state. It was implemented to regulate and control banks that had formed bank holding companies, which enabled them to own both banking and non-banking businesses.

The law prohibited a bank holding company from engaging in non-banking activities or acquiring voting securities of certain non-banking companies.

Then in 1958, another recession emerged, which lasted eight months. It had an unemployment rate of about 7.5% having a duration trend in between recessions of just over three years for the two prior recessions. Having a change in budget surplus of 0.8% of the GDP in 1957 to a budget deficit of 0.6% of the GDP in 1958. The budget deficit fell again to 2.6% of the GDP in 1959. The net result of the 1958 recession was an overall decline in the total GDP of approximately 3.7%.

Then in 1960 came a very short recession lasting only ten months, which had a decline in the GDP of approximately 1.6%. Occurring after the Federal Reserve began raising interest rates in 1959, the government transitioned from deficit of approximately 2.6% in 1959, to a surplus of approximately 0.1% in 1960. Having a peak unemployment rate of about 7.1%, the economy finally emerged from its short recession and began the second-longest recorded period of economic growth lasting 13 years.

Then the 1973 recession occurred, which among the various causes, was the Vietnam War. The war turned out to be costly, both economically and politically, for the United States of America. Coupled with the 1973 oil crisis and the fall of the Bretton Woods monetary management system, the 1973-1974 stock market crash made the recession much more evident Between January 1973 and December 1974, the DJIA lost over 45% of its value, becoming the seventh-worst percentage loss of the stock market in the history of America. In the two years beginning in 1972 to 1974, the American economy slowed from 7.2% GDP growth to a 2.1% contraction, while inflation jumped from 3.4% in 1972 to 12.3% in 1974. The 1973 recession had an unemployment rate of 9.0% and a reduction in the GDP of approximately 3.2% lasting about sixteen months.

As a result of this 1973 recessionary period, the United States Congress passed the little known "Federal Financing Bank Act of 1973", that created the Federal Financing Bank. This was yet another secretive quasi-Federal government corporation created by Congress under the general supervision of the Secretary of the Treasury. The Act was established to centralize and reduce the cost of Federal borrowing, including federally assisted borrowing from the U.S. public.

It was also established to deal with federal budget management issues that occur when "off-budget" financing had inundated the government securities market with offers of a variety of government-backed securities that competed with U.S. Treasury securities. Having statutory authority to purchase any obligation issued, sold, or guaranteed by any Federal agency, it ensured that the fully guaranteed obligations would be financed more efficiently.

Then came The Severe Recession beginning in July 1981, which technically ending in November 1982. Contractionary monetary policy established by the Federal Reserve System to control high inflation was the primary cause of the recession. Starting as a mild recession in January 1980, unemployment was about 7.8% in July. Beginning in 1979, the Savings and Loans industry began losing money due to spiraling interest rates. The net S&L income that totaled $781 million in 1980, fell to a loss of $4.6 billion in 1981, and again at a loss of $4.1 billion in 1982. The total net worth for the entire S&L industry was then virtually zero. Unemployment continued to grow, reaching 10.8% nationally in November 1982, later peaking at a record of 25% in parts of the northern Midwest. Bank failures rose steadily, reaching a post-depression high of 42 by mid-1982. By year's end, in an effort to keep banks solvent, the Federal Deposit Insurance Corporation (FDIC) had spent $870 million to purchase bad loans. Another 49 banks failed in 1983, which easily beat the Great Depression record of 43 failures set in 1940. The Continental Illinois National Bank and Trust Company, the nation's seventh-largest bank with $45 billion in assets, failed in 1984. Lasting nearly two years, the recession period ended with a decline in GDP of between 2.2% and 2.7%.

Then there was Black Monday, which refers to Monday, October 19, 1987, when the Dow Jones Industrial Average (DJIA) dropped 22.61% losing 508 points down to 1738.74. This now became the largest single-day percentage loss of the stock market in American history.

The crash initially started in Hong Kong, spread to Europe, and finally hit the United States after other markets had already significantly declined. Selling by program traders was the most popular explanation for the 1987 crash. U.S. Congressman Edward J. Markey stated: "Program trading was the principal cause", warning about the possibility of such a crash. In program trading, computers perform rapid stock executions based on external inputs, such as the price of related securities.

By Marty Piatt, Architect

The recession of 1990 occurred in the aftermath of Black Monday. With the start of the first Gulf War and the resulting spike in oil prices, economic stagnation had returned ten years after the last recession. In the next several years, high unemployment, massive government budgetary deficits, and slow growth in our GDP lasted well into 1992. Unemployment peaked at 7.8% in June 1992, resulting in a modest decline in the GDP of approximately 1.4%

In 1994, the "Riegle-Neal Interstate Banking and Branching Efficiency Act" was enacted by Congress to repeal many aspects of the "Bank Holding Company Act of 1956". It amended the laws governing federally chartered banks restoring the laws' competitiveness with the recently relaxed laws governing state-chartered banks. The unfortunate goal of this legislation was to return to a balance between the benefits of federal versus state bank charter.

In September 1998, the Federal Reserve, in unlawful violation of both the "Glass-Steagall Banking Act of 1933" and the "Bank Holding Act of 1956", criminally issued a waiver to merge Citicorp and the Travelers Group to form the mega-conglomerate Citigroup, which combined banking, insurance services, and securities. Citibank was a commercial bank holding company, and the Travelers Group was an insurance company. The Citigroup Corporation included Citibank, Smith Barney, Primerica, and the Travelers Group. I am unaware of any resulting investigation concerning the blatant criminal activity of the Federal Reserve. Under what legal or constitutional authority did the Federal Reserve possess to issue a Glass-Steagall Act waiver usurping the authority of Congress?

On November 12, 1999, Congress enacted the Gramm–Leach–Bliley Act of 1999, also known as the Financial Services Modernization Act, which was later signed into law by President Bill Clinton. This ex post facto law repealed the Glass–Steagall Banking Act of 1933, thus removing any remaining barriers in the market among banking, insurance, and securities companies, which would have prohibited any single institution from acting as any combination of a commercial and investment bank, and an insurance company. This formally legalized these types of mergers on a permanent basis. This legislation also removed any criminal culpability of the Federal Reserve unlawfully issuing Glass-Steagall waivers.

As a result, only commercial and investment banks, insurance companies, and securities firms were permitted to consolidate. The law also repealed the conflict of interest prohibitions "against simultaneous service by any officer, director, or employee of a securities firm as an officer, director, or employee of any member bank" contained within the Glass–Steagall Act of 1933. Less than 10 months after the repeal of Glass-Steagall, in combination with the ongoing global economic situation beginning in December 2007, The Great Recession of 2008, took a particularly sharp spiral down.

On September 29, 2008 the DJIA dropped 6.98%, losing 777.68 points down to 10,365.45, which became the reigning single-day stock market point loss in American history.

On October 3, 2008, less than one week later, President George W. Bush signed into law what was thought to be the $700 billion Troubled Asset Relief Program (TARP). It provided a financial mechanism for the United States government to purchase toxic assets and equity from failing financial institutions hopefully to strengthen the financial sector from the sub-prime mortgage crisis. It would later be discovered that former President Bush and the Federal Reserve secretly lent approximately $7.7 trillion dollars to the failing financial institutions, which was disguised as the $700 billion TARP initiative. Where did the Unites States get $7.7 trillion dollars?

On October 15, just twelve days after signing TARP, the DJIA dropped 7.87%, losing 733.08 points down to 8,577.91. It became the second largest single-day stock market point loss in American history, which was believed the result of the late-2000s financial crisis.

On December 5, 2008 the financial industry would require an unprecedented combined total of $1.2 trillion dollars in Federal aid, becoming the single greatest day requiring financial bailout funds. The Federal Reserve did not disclose to the public at the time the actual extent and depth that banks were in trouble.

The Great Recession technically ended in mid-2009 according to government statistics and information. There are two schools of thought for meaning of a recession. The first and less exact definition refers more broadly to a "period of reduced economic activity".

The second and more exact economic definition refers to a "contraction phase of a business cycle, with two or more consecutive quarters of negative GDP growth".

Despite official data showing a historically modest recovery, a 2011 poll found that more than half of all Americans believed the nation was still in recession, or even in depression. Those that are not employed call it a depression, while those that are game fully employed call it a recession; the difference between the two being very subjective. With persistent high unemployment, low consumer confidence, declining in home values, increases in foreclosures and personal bankruptcies, escalating federal debt and inflation, and rising prices of both gas and food, it is very hard for most Americans to believe the current recession had ended.

During the time period between the creation of the Federal Reserve in 1913 to the present day, the United States has sustained seventeen (17) different major economic turndowns, some much more devastating than others. These economic turndowns, averaging nearly 16 months each, resulted in an average reduction in our GDP of approximately 9.4%. The average duration in between the recessionary or depressionary periods averaged nearly four years. Since the post-1929 Great Depression era of economic downturns, the average unemployment rate in the United States has been approximately 10.5%.

What exactly has the Federal Reserve accomplished to prevent recessions or depressions? The official responsibilities of the Federal Reserve are to establish the nation's monetary policy, supervise and regulate our banking institutions, maintain the stability of the financial system, and to provide financial services to depository institutions, the United States government, and foreign institutions. In addition, the responsibilities include maintaining employment, stabilizing prices of commerce, and establishing banking interest rates at a predetermined level by regulating monetary policy necessary for a fluctuating economy.

Various components of the Federal Reserve also supervise banks, provide financial services, and conduct research on the economy and the economies in the surrounding region. Providing the government with a ready source of loans, the Federal Reserve System is also the safe depository for Federal monies.

The Federal Reserve, an inexpensive agent for meeting payments on the national debt and government salaries, is a low cost mechanism for transferring these funds. The United States government receives all the annual profits after a statutory dividend is paid. Federal Reserve Banks issue shares of stock to member banks. Federal Reserve Bank stock is quite different from owning stock in a private company, as it does not technically operated at a profit, or so they say. Ownership of a certain amount of the stock is, by law, a condition of membership in the system. The Federal Reserve stock cannot be sold, traded, or pledged as security for a loan, and dividends are limited by law to 6 percent per year.

Considered partial compensation, the Federal Reserve dividends are paid in lieu of interest paid on member banks' required reserves. By law, banks in the United States must maintain fractional reserves, most of which are kept on account at the Federal Reserve. Twelve Federal Reserve Banks form a major part of the Federal Reserve System. Together they divide the nation into twelve Federal Reserve Districts, and are jointly responsible for implementing the monetary policy set by the Federal Open Market Committee (FOMC). Within its own particular district, each Federal Reserve Bank is also responsible for the regulation of the commercial banks within that district.

The Federal Reserve System's structure is composed of the Board of Governors, appointed by the President, the FOMC, the twelve regional Federal Reserve Banks located in major cities throughout the nation, and numerous privately owned U.S. member banks, including various advisory councils. The FOMC is the committee responsible for setting monetary policy, consisting of all seven members of the Board of Governors and the twelve regional bank presidents. However, only five bank presidents vote at any given time.

The Federal Reserve System, having both private and public components, was designed to serve the interests of both the general public and private bankers. The resulting structure is considered very unique among central banks because the Department of the Treasury, which is an entity outside of the central bank, creates the currency used. Established as the operating arms of the nation's central banking system, the twelve regional Federal Reserve Banks are organized much like private corporations, which lead to confusion about its ownership.

By Marty Piatt, Architect

The Federal Reserve Banks have an intermediate legal status, with features of private corporations and features of public federal agencies. As federally created instrumentalities whose profits belong to the federal government, the United States has an interest in the Federal Reserve Banks, however this interest is not proprietary. In Lewis v. United States, the United States Court of Appeals for the Ninth Circuit stated that:

"The Reserve Banks are not federal instrumentalities for purposes of the FTCA [the Federal Tort Claims Act], but are independent, privately owned and locally controlled corporations." Further stating, however, that: "The Reserve Banks have properly been held to be federal instrumentalities for some purposes."

The Federal Reserve is a quasi-independent tax-exempt entity within U.S. government, and "its monetary policy decisions do not have to be approved by the President or anyone else in the Executive or Legislative branches of government" according to its Board of Governors. Deriving its authority from law enacted by the U.S. Congress, the Federal Reserve System is however subject to congressional oversight. Its chairman, vice-chairman, and other members of the Board of Governors are chosen by the President and confirmed by Congress.

The government also exercises some control over the Federal Reserve by appointing and setting the salaries of the system's highest-level employees. Thus the Federal Reserve has both private and public aspects. After a statutory dividend of 6% on member banks' capital investment is paid, the U.S. Government receives all of the annual profits and an account surplus is maintained.

In 2010 the Federal Reserve made a profit of approximately $82 billion dollars, and of that amount transferred approximately $79 billion dollars to the Department of the Treasury. The Federal Reserve made another profit of $76.9 billion dollars in 2011.

The FY12 revenues generated from the Federal Reserve were estimated at approximately $66 billion dollars. I believe the Federal Reserve revenues are essentially a tax generated and levied against the American taxpayers. The Federal Reserve has been taking money from the wallets of all American citizens since its creation, while enabling the greed and corruption of Wall Street, all at the expense of Main Street.

During the period of post-creation of the Federal Reserve in November 1914, a series of eighteen similarly devastating bank panics, economic downturns, or declining Wall Street events subsequently occurring in: 1918, 1920, 1923, 1926, 1929, 1937, 1945, 1948, 1953, 1957, 1960, 1969, 1973, 1980, 1987, 1990, 2001, and throughout 2008 again provide serious questions and profound reflection for the necessity of the formation of a centralized banking system.

Absolutely the most serious was The Great Depression of 1929, and The Great Recession of 2008, which still troubles our present economy. Again I ask; what exactly has the Federal Reserve done to prevent recessions or depressions? What has the Fed really accomplished?

In nearly every case in American economic history from 1869 to 2008, and continuing to the present, the unbridled greed and corruption of the banking industry and Wall Street investment firms, including actions of the Federal Reserve and its various Chairmen, including Congress has resulted in the near collapse of the American economy with devastating results. I believe that the Federal Reserve and its member counterparts are all criminal accomplices to the greed and corruption of our banking system and Wall Street institutions.

It is my opinion that the Federal Reserve Act of 1913 should be immediately repealed and the Federal Reserve System as we know it abandoned. I believe most people would agree knowing the full disclosure of all the so-called quasi-Federal activities of the Federal Reserve. All responsibilities of Federal Reserve could be performed by the Department of the Treasury and Treasury Secretary, if not better, while also being held accountable. The Federal Reserve essentially became the middleman for Wall Street greed and corruption.

I believe with proper oversight, the Department of the Treasury could establish the nation's monetary policy, supervise and regulate our banking institutions, maintain the stability of the financial system, maintain and encourage employment development, stabilize the economy, establish reasonable banking interest rates at a predetermined level by regulating monetary policy necessary for a fluctuating economy, and conduct research on the economy and the economies in the surrounding region.

By Marty Piatt, Architect

The United States government, in the absence of what was the Federal Reserve, could very well establish the first "Federal Reserve Savings Bank of America", becoming the official Federal Depository of our nation's wealth and prosperity. This national savings bank would be tasked to protect the monetary assets of U.S. citizens, and would eliminate the need for any foreign and international investment in our country. This would leave the banking industry and Wall Street institutions to fend for themselves; conducting business independently with their own financial assets and reserves.

In a truly Capitalist economy, the banking system and Wall Street institutions are not too big to fail. Until they are held accountable to a higher standard of conduct and ethics, the past will keep repeating itself. In my opinion, Uncle Sam should not be there to bail them out again. Relying solely on their own assets, the banking system and Wall Street institutions will have to conduct their businesses more professionally, and cautiously. Gone are the million dollar bonuses and CEO salaries. Gone are the speculative and risky transactions. Gone are the greedy gamblers and the usurious moneychangers.

Past protesters in New York calling their protest "Occupy Wall Street", have brought to the attention of America the plight of "We are the 99%". One percent (1%) of our country controls 40% of the wealth while, 99% of our country controls only 60% of the wealth. Some accounts suggest that over 40% of the country's wealth created from 1983 to 2004 went to the upper 1% of our population, leaving the bottom 80% receiving a marginal 6% of the new wealth. Estimates of the wealth of the American population vary, but they all share one commonality.

The top 1% in the United States population starts with household annual incomes approaching $600,000, which may encompass most all the bankers and investors working on Wall Street.

In 1929, just prior to the Great Depression, the wealth of the richest 1% had control of was approximately 44%, which has an extremely strong correlation with the activity of the stock market. A recent Congressional Budget Office report found that income for the top 1% increased 275% since 1979, while increasing only 18% for other Americans. Coincidentally during that period, we had economic financial crisis and turmoil in 1981, 1987, 1990, 2001, throughout 2008, and lingering on to today.

In every instances beginning with the election of former President Ronald Reagan, whose first action was to lower taxes on the richest 1%, we have entered deep and severe recessions.

Studies have concluded the richest 1% of Americans have been getting richer over the last three decades while the middle class and poor have seen their after-tax household income increase marginally in comparison. The top 1% made $165,000 or more in 1979, jumping to $347,000 or more in 2007. The income for the top one-fifth started at $51,289 in 1979 and climbed to $70,578 in 2007.

On the other end of the spectrum, those in the bottom 20% went from $12,823 in 1979 to $14,851 in 2007. The top 20% percent of Americans currently control approximately 84% of U.S. wealth. I attribute all these economic situations and statistics as a result of the policies and actions of the Federal Reserve and the United States government under Republican control. A recent Federal Reserve report stated that as the Great Recession reduced household net worth to a level not seen since the early 1990s, the typical American family lost approximately forty percent (40%) of its wealth between the years 2007 and 2010.

I don't however favor taxing the rich more than taxing the poor. I believe that a flat-rate Gross Income Tax (GIT), or as I prefer to refer to it as a non-religious "Patriotic National Tithe" consisting of 10% tax assessed on all national gross income, is the most reasonable and fair income tax solution to our nation's current revenue and budget challenges. Utilizing my proposed Gross Income Tax (GIT) system, the top 1% may also pay approximately 40% of the government's needed revenue in proportion to their wealth. Congress and the last two administrations alike have sold out Main Street and bailed out Wall Street. The Federal Reserve needs to be permanently dismantled, its assets sold, and its surplus reserves, if any truly exist, recovered and returned to the U.S. Treasury and the American taxpayers. The Federal Reserve has consistently shown throughout its history their actions and subsequent results have enabled the persistent greed and corruption of Wall Street to continue and perpetuate.

As President I would propose the immediate repeal of both the Federal Reserve Act of 1913 and the Federal Financing Bank Act of 1973 abandoning both the Federal Reserve and the Federal Financing Bank.

I would also propose the creation of the first Federal Reserve Savings Bank Act of 2017. Its focus would be to become the Federal Depository of American's wealth and prosperity, and to establish national saving interest rates that indirectly impact the commercial lending interest rates of the American banking system. I want to turn the Federal Reserve upside down, in favor of Americans, rather than greedy banks.

In addition, I would propose the nationalization of our American currency and debt. I would convert all outstanding debt into financial assets to be invested within the Federal Reserve Savings Bank. Congress would then be prohibited from borrowing from foreign countries to satisfy national budgetary expenditures.

I would propose the immediate repeal of both the Riegle-Neal Act of 1994, and the Gramm–Leach–Bliley Act of 1999. All Federal government ties to the banking industry and Wall Street need to be immediately and permanently severed, thus allowing the banking system and Wall Street to either prosper or fail in our capitalist market economy. Our nation needs to implement a separation of bank and state. Economic history has shown us one important thing, Wall Street greed and corruption will continue to prevail until which time they actually do fail.

"The money powers prey upon the nation in times of peace and conspire against it in times of adversity. It is more despotic than a monarchy, more insolent than autocracy, more selfish than bureaucracy. It denounces, as public enemies, all who question its methods or throw light upon its crimes. I have two great enemies, the Southern Army in front of me and the bankers in the rear. Of the two, the one at my rear is my greatest foe." ~Abraham Lincoln

"The eyes of our citizens are not sufficiently open to the true cause of our distress. They ascribe them to everything but their true cause: the banking system... a system which if it could do good in any form is yet so certain of leading to abuse as to be utterly incompatible with the public safety and prosperity." ~Thomas Jefferson

"Government is instituted for the common good; for the protection, safety, prosperity, and happiness of the people; and not for the profit, honor, or private interest of any one man, family, or class of men."
~John Adams

"If I was President..."

By Marty Piatt, Architect

DEPARTMENT OF DEFENSE

On October 13, 1775 the Continental Congress passed a resolution establishing what was then known as the Continental Navy. Under our nation's "first" Constitution, the Articles of Confederation, the Congress reserved for itself greater control over the nation's naval forces than the land forces. This had less to do with a judgment of the importance of sea power than with the fear of standing armies. The national government could be trusted with control of less politically dangerous and more expensive naval forces.

While naval power clearly had played an extremely important role in the Revolution, the years immediately following the War were difficult ones for the Continental Navy. Two years after the end of the Revolutionary War, the nearly bankrupt Continental Congress sold the last ship of the Continental Navy, the frigate Alliance, and the Continental Navy was disbanded. The founding of the Board of Admiralty later succeeded the Continental Navy.

The War Department, founded in 1789 shortly after the establishment of a Constitutional government under President George Washington, was also known as both the United States Department of War and the War Office. The U.S. Constitution gave the government and Congress the power "to raise and support armies" but "to provide and maintain" a Navy. Nevertheless, no consensus had yet existed to support a large national Navy, and until the mid-1790s, the United States continued as it had under the Confederation Congress without any naval force.

Originally a civilian agency responsible for the operation and maintenance of the United States Army, the War Department was established to administer the field army under the President as Commander in Chief and the Secretary of War. Retired senior General Henry Knox, then in civilian life, served as the first Secretary of War.

Eleven years after the disbanding of the Continental Navy, conflicts between American merchant shipping and pirates in the Mediterranean Sea resulted in the United States Congress passage of "The Act to Provide a Naval Armament". Also known as the Naval Act of 1794, it established the country's first naval force on March 27, 1794.

Until the official founding of the United States Navy on April 30, 1798, the War Department also assumed responsibility for both the naval forces and the air forces, until the creation of the Department of the Air Force in 1947. The Secretary of War headed the United States Cabinet war department throughout its entire existence.

Existing from 1789 until September 18, 1947, the War Department split into what is now the Departments of the Army and the Air Force, joining the Department of the Navy as part of the new joint National Military Establishment (NME), and was subsequently renamed the United States Department of Defense in 1949. Created with a single secretary as its head to preside over the former War Department, the Department of Defense was established to reduce the inter-service rivalry between the military armed forces that was believed to have resulted in the reduction of military effectiveness during World War II.

With the beginning of the Cold War, the United States began to maintain a permanent state of readiness for war that permanently increased our Defense Department expenditures. World War II proceeded a new era of a permanency in a greater United States defense budget.

The Department of Defense is the U.S. federal department allocated with the largest level of budgetary resources. The military budget pays the salaries, training, and health care of uniformed and civilian personnel, maintains arms, equipment and facilities, funds operations, and develops and buys new equipment for all the branches of the military: Army, Navy (including the Marine Corp), Air Force, and Coast Guard, which is actually a civilian department of the Department of Homeland Security.

Among the many agencies of the Department of defense are the Missile Defense Agency, the Defense Advanced Research Projects Agency (DARPA), the Pentagon Force Protection Agency (PFPA), the Defense Intelligence Agency (DIA), the National Geospatial-Intelligence Agency (NGA), and the National Security Agency (NSA), and several joint service schools including the National War College. The organization and functions of the Department of Defense are set forth in Title 10 of the United States Code. It was established and charged with coordinating and supervising all agencies and functions of the government relating directly to national security and the United States armed forces.

By Marty Piatt, Architect

Our 34th President and 5-star United States Army General Dwight David Eisenhower wrote at the conclusion of his second term:

"Our military organization today bears little relation to that known by any of my predecessors in peacetime, or indeed by the fighting men of World War II or Korea. Until the latest of our world conflicts, the United States had no armaments industry. American makers of plowshares could, with time and as required, make swords as well. But now we can no longer risk emergency improvisation of national defense; we have been compelled to create a permanent armaments industry of vast proportions. Added to this, three and a half million men and women are directly engaged in the defense establishment. We annually spend on military security more than the net income of all United States corporations. This conjunction of an immense military establishment and a large arms industry is new in the American experience. The total influence - economic, political, even spiritual - is felt in every city, every State house, every office of the Federal government. We recognize the imperative need for this development. Yet we must not fail to comprehend its grave implications. Our toil, resources and livelihood are all involved; so is the very structure of our society. In the councils of government, we must guard against the acquisition of unwarranted influence, whether sought or unsought, by the military industrial complex."

"The potential for the disastrous rise of misplaced power exists and will persist. We must never let the weight of this combination endanger our liberties or democratic processes. We should take nothing for granted. Only an alert and knowledgeable citizenry can compel the proper meshing of the huge industrial and military machinery of defense with our peaceful methods and goals, so that security and liberty may prosper together" wrote President Eisenhower.

But the rhetorical question remains; is the existence of Department of Defense based upon war, or defense?

The December 7, 1941 attack on Pearl Harbor should have changed everything; but it did not.

Then on September 11, 2001, the attack on the World Trade Center finally changed everything.

How could the greatest Military organization in world history coupled with the most extensive international and military intelligence agencies not have foreseen these events, is yet another outstanding rhetorical question remaining unanswered. I believe the time has come for our county and military to profoundly reflect on these issues of "war and defense". Albert Einstein, a genius and great thinker once stated: "You cannot simultaneously prevent and prepare for war." I disagree.

The 1949 transition from the previous War Department to the current Defense Department should have been the defining moment; but it was not. Yet in the six decades since that transition, the United States military doctrine of war rather than national defense unfortunately remains unchanged. We now face a time in history with financial and military budget constraints unprecedented in modern times that will require new approaches to national defense and international warfare.

In the recent past wee have seen in the nations of Egypt, Tunisia, Yemen, Libya, and Syria that other methods are available at a lesser cost than American blood and tax dollars, achieving better short-term results. We as a nation need to remove ourselves from the perceived unwanted influence in the Middle East. Israel will be just fine… they fight wars in terms of days, not years.

Our nation will never recover in oil what it has cost us in terms of priceless American life and debt-increasing hard-earned American tax dollars. We need to cut our losses, leave the Middle East to their own destruction, and develop an appropriate twenty-first century energy policy unreliant on Middle Eastern oil reserves.

Our Department of Defense, not Congress, must decide for itself, how to obligate allocated military funding from our national budget more efficiently in terms of national defense. We can no longer police the world, and must drastically reduce our perceived world imperialistic occupations and presence internationally.

Securing the borders, shorelines, and airspaces of our country and sovereign territories must finally take first and utmost priority. The reduction of our military expenditures may unfortunately include the closure of many of our foreign military bases, which I believe would be a very prudent, necessary, and realistically ambitious goal.

By Marty Piatt, Architect

The focus of the Department of Defense's Base Realignment and Closure (BRAC) should be concentrated on foreign base closures rather the closure of domestic military bases, which provide domestic employment in this economic time of higher unemployment.

The time has also come for the United States to finally withdraw from the North Atlantic Treaty Organization (NATO). I believe the perceived threat to the United States and Europe from the former Soviet Union and the current Russian Federation has been greatly reduced; yet some amount of uncertainty may still remain.

The United States needs immediately to readjust its priorities and spending habits to address the current and changing nature of military threats in the world. In 2009, former United States Secretary of Defense Robert Gates wrote the following:

"What all these potential adversaries- from terrorist cells to rogue nations to rising powers- have in common is that they have learned that it is unwise to confront the United States directly on conventional military terms. The United States cannot take its current dominance for granted and needs to invest in the programs, platforms, and personnel that will ensure that dominance's persistence. But it is also important to keep some perspective. As much as the U.S. Navy has shrunk since the end of the Cold War, for example, in terms of tonnage, its battle fleet is still larger than the next 13 navies combined- and 11 of those 13 navies are U.S. allies or partners."

With potential government consolidations such as permanently integrating the Customs and Border Patrol into the Army, the Coast Guard into the Navy, and NASA and NRO into the Air Force, among others, these civilian departments can better fund and help protect our borders, shorelines, and airspace by assisting the Department of Defense in its responsibility to do so.

I believe the percentage of our National Budget allocated to the Department of Defense should remain the absolute greatest percentage of our nation's budget. The allocation of military appropriations could possibly apportioned amongst the branches of the military possibly based upon the warfighter members serving within each branch of the military as determined by the military, not Congress.

But with a needed balanced budget and uncertain future revenues supporting our budget, the exact amount and allocation for the Department of Defense spending also remains unclear and uncertain in the future. I believe the national budget allocation for discretionary spending should be no less than a minimum of fifty percent (50%) for the total Federal budgetary expenditures in the future.

With the abolition of unnecessary government departments and agencies such as: the Department of Homeland Security (DHS), the Alcohol, Tobacco, Firearms, & Explosives (ATF), the Drug Enforcement Agency (DEA), and the Federal Emergency Management Agency (FEMA) among other possible eliminations, their associated budgets could possibly be reintegrated into our military budget and it's requirements.

The national spending for the Department of Defense can and must be maximized to its greatest and fullest potential possible for a new era in warfare fighting international terrorism and those that may threaten our country, our Constitution, our freedom and democracy, and our way of life.

Never to be used as a "pre-emptive" military strike weapon, as President I want it known perfectly clear that I would never hesitate to utilize tactical nuclear devices in swift and rapid retaliation to horrific foreign or terrorist attacks, such as the December 7th or 9/11, on or against our country, military forces, and sovereign territories.

Make no mistake, as Commander and Chief of the American Armed Forces I will use any and all means available within our vast military arsenal to smite all those who wish harm on the United States of America, its citizens, and its sovereign territories.

By Marty Piatt, Architect

NASA

The National Aeronautical and Space Administration (NASA) became operational on October 1, 1958, "to provide for research into the problems of flight within and outside the Earth's atmosphere and for other purposes". NASA was established by the National Aeronautics and Space Act of July 29, 1958 replacing its predecessor, the National Advisory Committee for Aeronautics (NACA). This occurred one year after the former Soviet Union successfully launched the Sputnik 1 satellite, which ultimately lead to a space race as a result of the "technology gap" that had become both a military and scientific crisis as part of the Cold War rivalry with the Soviets.

NASA's manned missions began with the "Project Mercury" that was initiated in 1958 to discover if man could actually survive in outer space exploration. The ranks of recruits wanting to become astronauts came from all military services of our Armed Forces. Astronaut selections were coordinated and facilitated with defense research, contracting, and military test pilot programs. Project Mercury, operationally lasting from 1959 to 1963, had "manned" missions beginning in 1961.

On May 5, 1961, astronaut Alan Shepard became the first American in space on a 15-minute suborbital space flight while piloting the Mercury-Redstone 3, called Freedom 7. On February 20, 1962, astronaut John Glenn became the first American to orbit the Earth on during the flight of Friendship 7. Since it was apparently clear that the Mercury spacecraft had reached its technological limit of endurance in space, only 3 more Mercury orbital flights were made after Friendship 7, the last in 1963, and 3 additional orbital flights were later cancelled. The next NASA program, "Project Gemini", was to focus on conducting experiments and developing and practicing techniques required for future lunar missions.

On March 23, 1965, Gus Grissom and John Young piloted the first manned flight with astronauts onboard the Gemini 3. Nine Gemini missions followed, proving that long-duration human space flight with rendezvous and docking with other space vehicle was possible, including the gathering of medical data regarding the effects of outer space weightlessness on human beings. In addition, the Gemini missions also introduced the first spacewalks for NASA and American astronauts.

Following Project Gemini, the NASA project titled the "Apollo" program, was one of the United States most expensive and extensive programs ever attempted. The Apollo program used the extremely successful "Saturn" family of rockets as launch vehicles. Based upon derivatives of the U.S. Army's "Redstone" and "Jupiter-C" rocket designs, the Saturn rockets were more powerful than the rockets previously built for the Mercury and Gemini space programs. Consisting of two (2) different rocket variations, the Saturn 1B (C-1) and Saturn V (C-5), the latter becoming the largest and most powerful launch vehicle ever used in the Apollo program. The Saturn V still remains the most powerful rocket in United States manned space flight history using the massively successful F-1 and J-2 rocket engines. The Apollo spacecraft had two main parts: the combined command and service module (CSM) and the lunar landing module (LM). The LM was to remain on the Moon and only the command module (CM) containing the lunar astronauts would return to Earth.

Lasting from 1961 through 1972, the Apollo project originally had 20 separate planned missions; however Apollo's 18 through 20 were cancelled to provide greater resources to be devoted to the future Space Shuttle program. In addition the premature cancellation of the remaining three Apollo program launches enabled one of the remaining Saturn V launch vehicles to be utilized for the launching of the Skylab orbital laboratory program in 1973. The final cost of project Apollo was reported to Congress in 1973 to total $25.4 billion dollars.

I may not be a rocket scientist, but the bottom line to successful launch vehicles is the total "cost per pound" of payload lifted to low-earth orbit (LEO). It really is that simple. The Saturn V maximum LEO payload was about 260,000 pounds. Having a program cost in 2015 dollars of approximately $140.3 billion, having 18 launches (Apollo & SkyLab), and placing roughly 4,680,000 pounds (assuming max. payload) into at least LEO, the bottom line cost per pound for the Apollo Saturn Rocket Program equates to about $29,985.04 per pound, or about ~$30K/lb.

During the active development of the Apollo program, NASA designer's commenced looking at future needs for a post-Apollo era, and it appeared very obvious that the next step should be a manned mission to the planet Mars.

By Marty Piatt, Architect

For the proposed Mars mission tasks, the Saturn V rocket was determined to be insufficiently powerful. The "Nova" project was a series of proposed rocket designs, originally as NASA's first heavy launchers for similar missions utilizing the Saturn V rocket, and later as more powerful subsequent versions of the Saturn V intended for extended missions to the planet Mars.

On January 27, 1959 NASA presented their in-house designs for the first "Nova" rocket series to then-President Dwight D. Eisenhower. Essentially separate, the two series of designs were in most cases a rocket that was substantially more powerful than the Saturn V rocket. The final Saturn V rocket design was actually larger than early Nova proposed concepts. However, the Nova C8 model concept was noted to be nearly identical to the proposed Saturn C-8 model concept. When it soon became clear that the post-Apollo NASA funding would be considerably less, NASA would unfortunately abandon the Nova rocket program in 1964. The name "Nova" was used in over 30 large rocket programs from the late 1950's throughout the 1980's. Unlike the original Nova rocket series designed exclusively by NASA, major aerospace companies that had not been awarded any major Apollo-related NASA contracts performed new Nova-designated rocket designs under contract.

In 1968, using surplus material from the Apollo program, the Apollo Applications Program (**AAP**) was established by NASA to develop future manned space missions, including a manned mission to the planet Mars. AAP was the pinnacle development of many official and unofficial post-Apollo follow-on projects studied by NASA. Initially the AAP was a off-shoot of the Apollo "X" bureau, also known as the Apollo Extension Series (AES) that was developing technology concepts for proposed manned mission based on the Saturn IB and Saturn V family of rockets. Missions potentially included a manned lunar base, an earth-orbiting space station, the "Grand Tour of the Outer Solar System", and the original "Voyager program" of Mars Lander probes.

The Apollo manned lunar base proposal utilized an unmanned Saturn V rocket to land a shelter habitat based on the Apollo Command/Service Module (CSM) on the lunar surface. A second Saturn V rocket would carry a 3-man astronaut crew and a modified CSM and Apollo Lunar Module (LM) to the Moon.

A 2-man astronaut exploration team would have a lunar surface stay time of approximately 200 days while using an advanced lunar rover and a lunar flier in addition to logistics vehicles to construct a larger shelter. Isolation of the CSM astronaut-pilot was a major concern for NASA mission planners. As a result of this concern, it was also proposed to either have a 3-man exploration team, or have the CSM rendezvous with an orbiting module.

Also studied was a hybrid "Saturn-Shuttle" based Space Launch System (SLS). Consisting of a Shuttle-like orbiter strapped to the side of a Saturn V rocket, the Saturn-Shuttle hybrid was a proposed interface of a space shuttle orbiter and external fuel tank with the S-IC stage on a Saturn V rocket. An "interstage" would be fitted directly on top of the S-IC stage to support the external fuel tank, previously occupied by the S-II stage. This design tactic enabled NASA to steer completely away from segmented solid propellant rocket engines similar to those that destroyed the space shuttle Challenger.

In hindsight, this interstage design would have been far superior to the future STS design of the Space Shuttle program. The addition of wings on the S-IC stage would allow the booster to fly back to the Kennedy Space Center (KSC) for technicians to refurbish the booster by replacing the five (5) F-1 rocket engines and reusing the fuel tanks and other hardware for later space flights.

Having need to keep costs down and permit President Nixon to approve the proposed Space Shuttle program in 1972, NASA decided to utilize segmented Solid Rocket Boosters (SRB) similar to those used on the Titan III rocket instead of the Saturn S-IC. This decision unfortunately formally ended the Apollo Saturn rocket program. Along with the rest of the AAP program, "Man-on-Mars" program was canceled and replaced by the Skylab "dry workshop" space station and the Space Transport System (STS). If the AAP Mars mission had not been canceled, the very first manned landing on Mars was scheduled to have occurred back in 1985. The currently planned Orion Mars Mission, when launched, would occur in the 2030's, forty-five years later than planned.

Prior to the Apollo XI lunar moon landing in 1969, NASA began early conceptual studies of space shuttle-type orbiter designs.

By Marty Piatt, Architect

In 1969, then-President Richard Nixon formed the Space Task Group (STG) to evaluate the preliminary shuttle studies completed to date, and ultimately recommend a national space strategy including the construction of a space shuttle fleet. The goal presented by NASA to Congress, was to provide a low and cost-effective means of frequent access to low earth orbit that could be utilized by both NASA and the Department of Defense. This could be later deemed a complete failure.

The Space Shuttle program became the predominant focus of NASA beginning in the late 1970's throughout the 1980's. The "Space Transportation System" (STS), the official shuttle program title, was NASA's only manned launch vehicle program beginning in 1981 and ultimately ending in 2011. The 30-year shuttle program was initially proposed as a frequently launch-able and reusable space vehicle, and by the end of 1985, in initial four space shuttle orbiters had been constructed; the space shuttles named: Columbia, Challenger, Discovery, and Atlantis.

On April 12, 1981, the Columbia became the first space shuttle to launch having a crew complement consisting of only two NASA astronauts. The Space Shuttle programs major components were a reusable rocket-powered winged orbiter plane including an expendable external fuel tank and two reusable side-mounted solid fuel launch rocket boosters. The space shuttle's external fuel tank, which was actually larger than the shuttlecraft itself, was the only launch system component that was neither reutilized nor recycled.

The winged earth orbiter was launched vertically, carrying NASA shuttle crews of between two and eight astronauts, some of which could also be foreign guest astronauts. A crew complement of four was typically used as a minimum.

The space shuttle could orbit at altitudes between 115 to 400 miles above earth sea level and carry a maximum payload to low earth orbit (LEO) of 54,000 lbs. or 27 tons. Shuttle mission durations could usually last anywhere from 5 to 17 days. With the shuttle mission completed, the space shuttle would independently navigate itself out of orbit using the shuttle Maneuvering System. The shuttle would then become its own re-entry vehicle utilizing the shuttle's Orbiting Maneuvering System (OMS) system and actuating flight surfaces to make re-entry flight adjustments during the gliding controlled-descent and landing.

Columbia, designated OV-102, was delivered to Kennedy Space Center (KSC) on March 25, 1979 after being assembled in Palmdale, California becoming the shuttle fleet's first fully functional orbiter vehicle; flying two years later;

Challenger, designated OV-099, was delivered to KSC in July 1982;

Discovery, designated OV-103 was delivered in November 1983; and,

Atlantis, designated OV-104 was delivered in April 1985.

The shuttle Challenger was originally constructed as a Structural Test Article (STA-099) but was later converted to a complete and operational shuttle orbiter. According to NASA, it had been estimated to be far less expensive than converting the very first flight test space shuttle vehicle, Enterprise, designated OV-101, from its Approach and Landing Test (ALT) orbiter configuration to a fully functional space shuttle orbiter.

Never intended for orbital flight and used exclusively for atmospheric test flights only, Enterprise had many of its original internal parts removed and cannibalized for reuse on the other orbiters. After visual and cosmetic restoration, the Enterprise is currently on display at the National Air and Space Museum in Washington, D.C. The first orbiter vehicle which was originally intended to be named "Constitution", later changing the orbiter name to "Enterprise" by the Ford administration in response to a massive and ultimately successful write-in campaign by fans of the television series Star Trek and its legendary "Starship". NASA also used two modified commercial-use Boeing 747 jetliners as Space Shuttle Carrier Aircraft (SCA) to piggyback the space shuttles back to Florida.

On January 28, 1986 Challenger (STS-51-L) was destroyed during ascent due to an "O-Ring" failure on the right solid rocket booster (SRB), with the tragic loss of all 7 astronauts on board.

In August 1987 Congress authorized a replacement for the Space Shuttle orbiter Challenger. The shuttle replacement, named Endeavor, designated OV-105, was to be built and constructed utilizing structural spare parts from the construction of Discovery (OV-103) and Atlantis (OV-104) that were originally manufactured and intended to facilitate the potential repair of any orbiter in the future.

By Marty Piatt, Architect

On May 7, 1991 the orbiter replacement for the Challenger loss, christened Endeavor, arrived at Kennedy Space Center's (KSC) Shuttle Landing Facility piggy-backed on top of one of NASA's two Space Shuttle Carrier Aircraft (SCA). Endeavor was launched one year later.

On February 1, 2003, Columbia (STS-107) disintegrated during earth reentry also tragically killing all 7 astronauts on board the shuttle. Congress never replaced the Columbia orbiter.

In 2005, realizing the ultimate fate of the STS program and the shuttle fleet, Congress passed the "NASA Authorization Act of 2005" that created the next possible successor to the STS Space Shuttle program called the "Constellation" program which included the "Ares" family of rockets, the "Orion" multipurpose crew vehicle (MPCV) space, and the "Altair" lunar surface access module (LSAM).

Since February 2006, NASA's mission statement has been to "pioneer the future in space exploration, scientific discovery and aeronautics research". NASA also provides oversight of launch operations and countdown management for unmanned NASA launches and is responsible for the Launch Services Program (LSP) as well.

On July 8, 2011 the space shuttle program ended with the final orbiter launch of Atlantis. Adjusted for inflation, the final cost of the shuttle program through 2011 was estimated to be approximately $196 billion dollars. The average per-launch cost to fly a space shuttle orbiter through the STS program end in 2011 has now been estimated at approximately $450 million per STS mission, or nearly 60 times its originally estimated mission cost. During early development of the orbiter, NASA had estimated that the shuttle program would cost approximately $7.45 billion in developmental and non-recurring costs, and approximately $9.3 million per mission cost. The cost to deliver payload to low earth orbit was originally estimated as low as $118 per pound of payload assuming a 65,000-pound payload capacity and an aggressive 50 orbiter launches per year, or about $7.7 million dollars per STS mission. Unfortunately this didn't happen. With a program cost in 2015 dollars of approximately $209.9 billion (~$70B more than Apollo), having 133 launches and placing roughly 7,128,800 pounds (assuming max. payload) into at least LEO, the bottom line price per pound for the Space Transport System (STS) equates to about $29,455.17 per pound, or about ~$30K/lb.

I was surprised to discover that STS achieved parity with Apollo relative to the Program cost per pound to LEO. Both the Apollo and STS programs, having entirely different hardware, launch frequencies, and mission capabilities, achieved parity delivering a cost per pound to LEO of nearly $30K/lb. It is amazing that the two (2) entirely different programs, one expendable and the other reusable, basically achieved the same result.

Clearly the winner was the expendable launch system, having achieved parity in a fraction of the amount of launches. Only proving when it comes to rockets, bigger is better! Future American manned space exploration will require a cheaper, larger, greater dependable launch vehicle than the SLS or Saturn V.

STS proved itself far inferior to the Apollo Saturn-Shuttle concept and far more costly in terms of the loss of American astronaut lives. With the asset loss of two orbiters, the tragic disasters also included the unfortunate loss of all 14 precious human lives onboard the shuttles Challenger and Columbia.

Recently declassified information has revealed that NASA's STS shuttle cargo bay is nearly the exact same size the National Reconnaissance Office (NRO) spy satellites known as "Key Hole". The KH models consist of the series KH-1 through KH-13. The Space Shuttle was nothing more than a military delivery vehicle occasionally used for civilian space missions. The predominant mission objectives of STS were military. And the Soviets knew this.

The former Soviet Union had developed its own version of the Space Shuttle in direct response to the military STS. Known as the BURAN program, which translated into English means "Snowstorm or Blizzard", the Soviet version had an uncanny aerodynamic similarity to STS, some would say copied. Looks can be deceiving. Under closer examination, the Soviet Buran space shuttle was actually far superior to STS.

The main and significant difference between the Buran and STS was the lack of main engines. The Buran had only two Orbital Maneuvering System (OMS) engines, including a series of much smaller Vernier attitude thrusters used in the Attitude Control System (ACS).

By Marty Piatt, Architect

With the addition of three (3) R-25 rocket engines, the Space Shuttle Main Engine (SSME) would require an external fuel tank during STS launch leaving the SSME useless in orbit. Unfortunately, the three (3) RS-25 rocket engines alone were incapable of lifting the Shuttle and payload. Two (2) solid rocket boosters (SRB) each having four (4) segments joined by "O-rings" would be required to provide addition launch trust for liftoff. Upon achieving orbit the three (3) RS-25 rocket engines would become useless and present a return mass liability. Weighing nearly 16,000 lbs or about 8 tons, the SSME would also greatly reduce the payload capacity of the STS orbiter.

Without main engines, the Buran would require an expendable heavy-lift launch system. Not unlike the Apollo-Shuttle variant explored by NASA, the Buran program relied upon the Energia heavy-lift expendable liquid-fueled rocket for liftoff. The Energia rocket had a payload to LEO of approximately 190,000 pounds or about 95 tons.

The Buran space shuttle had a launch-payload capacity of approximately 60,000 pounds or about 30 tons, and a return-payload capacity of approximately 40,000 pounds or about 20 tons. The STS launch- and return-payload capacities were about 25 tons and 15 tons, respectively. Without solid rocket boosters, the Buran's launch safety would greatly surpass that of our STS. NASA soon realized this fact after the Challenger disaster. The possibility of O-ring failure still poses a significant and tremendous threat to the SLS program.

Launched in 1988, seven years after the launch of the space shuttle Columbia in 1981, the crew-less Buran performed two (2) orbits, and re-entered the atmosphere in a controlled flight landing autonomously. This had a tremendous advantage in the unlikely event the crew was unable to maintain control of the spacecraft during reentry. Our STS Space Shuttle would never achieve this huge technological milestone. Buran never flew again with the collapse of the Soviet Union. In all, three (3) Buran spacecraft were constructed. One used for atmospheric flight-testing, one flown in its maiden space voyage, and one sister ship that was never flown.

The original planned successor to the STS space shuttle was to be Project Constellation and its Ares I and Ares V rockets. In early 2010 Congress was then asked to endorse a scaled-back Space Launch System (SLS) program relying much heavier on private capitol ventures.

On October 11, 2010 the Constellation program and Ares rocket program was cancelled with the signing of the program ending legislation, leaving the United States with no immediate means for military or scientific manned access to outer space. The "NASA Authorization Act of 2010" authorized creation of the current Space Launch System (SLS). The SLS utilized SRB- and SSME-derived STS components designed specifically for the space shuttle.

NASA envisioned the integral combination of both the ARES rocket designs of the Constellation program and STS into a single launch combination of liquid- and segmented solid-fuel Challenger-type rocket vehicle system to be utilized for both crew and cargo missions. The Orion and Altair program portions of Constellation were exempt from cancellation and continue in their research and development.

On September 14, 2011, declaring that the newly-envisioned Space Launch System would take NASA astronauts farther into space than ever before, NASA announced the potential maiden flight possibly schedule for December 2017. The success of SLS technology utilizing flawed segmented solid-fuel booster technology that destroyed the space shuttle Challenger remains doubtful. Development of SLS technology is entirely based upon leftover STS junk consisting of (15) left-over RS-25 rocket engines and junk engine parts for (1) more, including SRB bombs strapped to the rocket; technology that cost the lives of our 14 brave astronauts. The future of US manned space flight is based upon flawed garbage.

In a nutshell, the first stage of the SLS rocket consists of (4) RS-25 engines, just one (1) more than the three (3) SSME utilized on the space shuttle. Keep in mind, just (1) Saturn F-1 rocket engine provides more thrust than (3) RS-25 rocket engines combined. The Saturn V had (5) F-1 rocket engines. The SLS solid rocket boosters (SRB) now utilize (5) sections, rather than the 4-section SRB components of STS; having (2) additional O-rings posing even greater destructive potential. I presume SLS will most likely follow the same demise as NASA's previous Nova and Ares rocket programs. Without any reliable or consistent access to outer space until most likely after 2017, the United States presently utilizes the space launch services of our former space adversary, the Russian Federation, and their successful Soviet-era Soyuz rocket and spacecraft program at a significant cost to NASA and the American taxpayer.

By Marty Piatt, Architect

Despite its recent past, NASA has achieved extraordinary tasks throughout its history such as:

1. Built extremely successful human spaceflight programs;

2. Launched probes and landers throughout our solar system and beyond into our universe;

3. Constructed and orbited telescopic observatories of both Earth and our galaxy; and,

4. Conducted scientific research into aeronautic and aerospace technologies.

As of 2010 NASA had budgeted approximately $59 billion for the International Space Station (ISS) from 1985 through 2015, or approximately $72 billion previously adjusted in 2010 dollars. The total cost of the ISS is nearly $150 billion dollars including the 36 shuttle flights at nearly $1.5 billion dollars each, and foreign contributions of Russia's $12 billion, Europe's $5 billion, Japan's $5 billion, and Canada's $2 billion. Each person-day on the ISS would have cost $7.5 million assuming 20,000 person-days of use by two to six-person crews from 2000 to 2015, or about 60% less than the nearly $20 million per person-day on the United States Skylab program.

However, having completed extraordinary scientific accomplishments, including the construction of the International Space Station, NASA's space shuttle program would not provide the required heavy-lift capabilities necessary for our future post-shuttle era interplanetary exploration. NASA really dropped the ball with respect to manned spaceflight. NASA has lost sight of what our nation's space exploration goals should be.

With the cancellation of the Nova rocket program in 1964, the Apollo Saturn-Shuttle program in 1972, and the Ares rocket program in 2010, the future of the current Space Launch System (SLS) still remains uncertain.

NASA should fast track the re-design and construction of the former Saturn program faster and better than the current SLS system with the new and improved "**Saturn 2.0**" program. As President, I would engage NASA to refocus their ambitions on the Mars exploration program to be accomplished in four (4) phases of development as follows:

Phase 1: Saturn 2.0 Heavy-Lift Launch System

The current SLS launch vehicles would be cancelled in lieu of a "reboot" of the existing Apollo space vehicle launch system and "Saturn" rocket program.

The **"Saturn 2.0"** reboot would include transforming the existing Jupiter-C class of similar **C1, C3, C5**, and **C8** family of rocket designs used in both the "Nova" and "Saturn" rocket programs having uprated F-1X and J-2X rocket engine technology:

Saturn IC (C-1.1):

1st stage: S-IC1 with (1) F-1X rocket engine;

2nd stage: S-IVB with (1) J-2X or RS-25 rocket engine;

3rd stage: S-IVB with (1) J-2X rocket engine. (optional)

Saturn C3 (C-3.1):

1st stage: S-IC3 with (1) F-1X rocket & (2) S-IC1 F-1X booster engines;

2nd stage: S-IVB with (1) J-2X or RS-25 rocket engine;

3rd stage: S-IVB with (1) J-2X rocket engine. (optional)

Saturn V (C-5.1):

1st stage: S-IC5 with (5) F-1X rocket engines;

2nd stage: S-IIC5 with (5) J-2X rocket engines;

3rd stage: S-IVB with (1) J-2X rocket engine. (optional)

Saturn C8 "Supernova" (C-8.1):

1st stage: S-IC8 with (8) F-1X rocket engines;

2nd stage: S-IIC8 with (8) J-2X or (4) RS-25 rocket engines;

3rd stage: S-IVC/D with (1) RS-25 or RS-68 rocket engine. (optional)

By Marty Piatt, Architect

The **Saturn C8 "Supernova"** would become the world's most powerful rocket ever built utilizing the uprated F-1X rocket engines that will provide nearly 1,800,000 lbf (pounds-force) of thrust each, having a total C8 combined engine thrust approaching 14 million lbf for the first stage alone. The "Supernova" payload amount placed into low Earth orbit (LEO) could potentially exceed approximately 463,000 lbs. or 232 tons; as opposed to the Space Shuttle's maximum payload to LEO of approximately 54,000 lbs. or 27 tons. The Saturn C8 was estimated in 1985 to have a flyway-cost of approximately $58.3 million. Based upon a maximum payload of 463,000 lbs. and a flyaway-cost adjusted for 2015 dollars of $130 million, the Saturn C8 "Supernova" could easily achieve a $280 per pound to LEO launch cost; over 100 times "less" than STS.

Two (2) optional variants, derived for both the Saturn V and Saturn C8 "Supernova" rockets, similar to the **Saturn INT-21** could be developed using the first and second rocket stages, but omitting the S-IVB third stage. This configuration would facilitate the ability for massive mission payloads having maneuvering thrusters to replace the third rocket stage for placement of various mission payloads into LEO to be later towed and repositioned for various assembly or mission location operations. The rocket guidance unit of the **Saturn INT-21** would be relocated from the top of the third stage to the top of the second stage. The proposed **Saturn INT-21** C5/C8 versions have never before flown in these rocket derivative configurations.

On May 13, 1973, a similar **Saturn INT-21** rocket variant was launched only once by NASA which lifted the "Skylab" space station into orbit. Skylab was built from a S-IVB stage that eliminated relocating the rocket guidance unit to the second stage. The **Saturn INT-21** was also intended for other NASA space flights in the AAP, and would be used to launch other massive payloads for military and defense-related projects, in addition to other American space stations and orbital outpost components, the proposed Skylab "B", and the International Space Station (ISS). During the original design and construction of the **Saturn IB**, the F-1 rocket engine that was under development had not sufficiently progressed to the stage of implementation into the rocket. Greater number of small rocket engines is less efficient and more problematic than fewer large rocket engines. The newly configured **Saturn IC** would eliminate the need for the H-1.1 rocket engine type thus simplifying the production of the Saturn 2.0 rocket engines exclusively to the F-1X and J-2X.

NASA could also re-evaluate and re-boot the previous hybrid "Saturn-Shuttle" program utilizing **Saturn 2.0** technology with a winged Transport Orbital Vehicle (TOV) similar in design to the NASA **HL-20** for astronaut crew only transport to low Earth or Earth/moon L1 orbit as the third stage mounted on top of the newly proposed **Saturn IC** rocket. The vertical-takeoff horizontal-landing (VTHL) crewed orbital lifting-body vehicle to replace NASA manned space capsules would be similar to the various space plane designs like the "Dream Chaser" being developed the Sierra Nevada Corporation, the "Kliper" developed by the Russian Federation Space Agency (FSA) to replace the "Soyuz" space capsule, the "Hermes" developed by the European Space Agency (ESA), and the USAF developed "X-20" Dyna-Soar.

It must be noted that the incredibly successful Apollo program using the **Saturn V** rocket had an unprecedented reliability record never losing one single NASA mission payload in all of the entire thirteen (13) Saturn V launches. I believe the **Saturn 2.0** rocket program could quickly fast-track the design and development beyond Post-milestone "B" in the Federal Acquisition Process.

Phase II: Libra Station

After the successful completion and implementation of the upgraded Saturn 2.0 launch system, the next phase for Mars exploration would be the establishment of the Earth/Moon L1 outpost called "Libra Station". Located nearly midway between the Earth and the Moon is an area of outer space where the gravitational forces of the Earth and Moon exerted on an orbiting object are cancelled; a point referred to as a "Libration Point". Also known as a Lagrange Point, named after the 18th century Italian-French mathematician Joseph Louis Lagrange, this L1 point marks a "sweet spot", an exact position where the combined gravitational pull of the Earth and Moon provides exactly the necessary centripetal force for an object to orbit along with them in an configuration where the object can theoretically become fixed and stationary relative to both the Earth and Moon. Libra Station would become a destination axis for all Earth, Moon, and Mars space travel. Unlike the other Libration points of L2, L3, L4, and L5, the L1 location of Libra Station in within the Earth's magnetosphere, and would provide substantial protection from deep-space radiation. It is also outside the boundary of Earth orbital debris.

By Marty Piatt, Architect

Consisting of a stationary rotating permanent and sustainable manned space outpost, Libra Station would be beneficial during the pre-Martian colonization phase. A rotating portion of the Station could potentially provide a simulated earth-equivalent gravitational environment within berthing and habitat modules. Libra Station's construction could begin with the re-utilization of many portions of the ISS, consisting of the United States Orbital Segment (USOS), existing space and ISS modules, and all other NASA spare parts that are available for future integration. The time has come for America and Russia to divide the existing ISS into their respective owners property and possession and go their way. Additional Station construction parts under consideration could be the "Node 4" Docking Hub System (DHS) to provide the main colony connection point. Node 4 would be constructed using the Node Structural Test Article (STA) originally constructed to become Node 1 to facilitate testing of ISS hardware that was later was put into storage at the Kennedy Space Center.

Spare parts from the STS Orbital Maneuvering System (OMS) and an Orbiter External Airlock (OEA) could then be combined to construct a Libra Station utility module for maneuvering, orientation, including a remaining Multi-Purpose Logistics Module (MPLM), and potentially a Nuclear Power Generator (NPG). The Canadian ISS Robotic Arm could also be salvaged to assist with logistical and station keeping. The potential inclusion of other new United States and international components including "Bigelow" inflatable modules used for life support systems, astronaut accommodations, storage, and laboratory research facilities. A reusable lunar lander would also be stationed at Libra Station for lunar landings and refueling purposes as well as a Transport Utility Grunt (TUG) for travel between both Earth orbit and lunar orbit, similar in concept to the proposed Russian "Parom", or "ferry" in Russian. Libra Station would provide: an outpost for scientific research, a graving dock for construction, assembly, and maintenance of space transport vehicles, a fuel depot module for refueling, assist in the pre-Martian lunar outpost construction, and a launch facility for Mars-bound and other interplanetary space ships. The continued growth of Libra Station could become the largest human space Colony greater than both the future Mars and lunar outposts combined. Not that the future mission to colonize Mars is not important, I believe the long term goals of manned space exploration could be focused in future space colonization extending outside our solar system in search of Earth-like planets for human colonization.

123

Phase III: Peary Lunar Outpost

After the establishment of "Libra Station", the next phase for Mars exploration would be the establishment of the manned lunar orbit and moon surface "outpost" location at Peary Crater, a large lunar impact area closest to the lunar North Pole, most likely one of the favorite lunar outpost locations currently planned.

The main purpose of this phase would be accomplished, not for sake of lunar colonization, but rather for trial and test runs verifying program safety and technology reliability for lunar-versions of future Martian habitat and support structure construction including unmanned structure placement.

Future lunar colonization could be accomplished and completed with private venture capital investments. Full colonization of the moon remains questionable when considering the trade-offs evaluating the ultimate costs and rewards. Lunar mining and resource recovery is one of the various possible reasons for lunar colonization.

Phase IV: Martius Colony

The final phase of the Mars Exploration Program would be the initial establishment of a permanent and sustainable manned Martian outpost and colony, called "Martius Colony". Latin for "Field of Mars", the "Martius" colony would begin as a single Martian surface habitat and orbital outpost becoming a complete and full-fledged Station growing in time to a colony with the assistance and cooperation of private venture space exploration programs. The location of the future Martius Colony would most likely be established near the Martian North Pole where the search for iced water has recently been confirmed. The means for achieving Martian colonization could result from four different approaches similar to those considered during the Apollo program for lunar exploration:

1. Direct Martian Ascent (DMA): A Saturn spacecraft would travel directly to Mars as a single mission unit, land, and return leaving the landing stage on Martian surface. This plan would require a more powerful launch vehicle such as the Saturn C8 "Supernova" rocket.

2. Earth Orbit Rendezvous (EOR): Multiple Saturn rockets would be launched, with each rocket carrying various parts of a Direct Martian Ascent spacecraft and propulsion unit, which would enable the Mars spacecraft to escape Earth orbit. After docking and assembly in Earth or Libra Station orbit, the spacecraft would then travel to Mars and land as a space vehicle unit.

3. Mars Surface Rendezvous (MSR): Multiple Saturn spacecraft would be launched in succession. The first spacecraft, an unmanned and automated vehicle carrying propellants and habitat facilities, would land on Mars and would be joined some time later by a manned vehicle. Propellants would be transferred from the automated vehicle to the manned vehicle before the manned vehicle could return to Earth.

4. Mars Orbit Rendezvous (MOR): A Saturn V and/or C8 "Supernova" would launch Martian spacecraft composed of modular parts. The Command Module (CM) would remain in Mars orbit, while an Excursion Module (EM) would descend to the Martian surface and return to dock with the CM still in Martian orbit. In contrast to other the plans, MOR requires only a small part of the spacecraft to land on Mars, thereby minimizing the total mass to be launched from the Martian surface for the return trip back to Earth.

5. Mars Direct (MD): This hybrid approach for a manned mission to Mars is both cost-effective and possible with current rocket technology. This concept was originally described in a research paper by NASA engineers Robert Zubrin and David Baker in 1990, and later expanded upon in the 1996 book: "The Case for Mars".

The plan involves several launches making use of heavy-lift booster rockets similar in size to the Saturn C8 "Supernova" rocket. The Mars Direct proposal includes an Earth Return Vehicle (ERV) and a Mars Habitat Unit (MHU). Similar in nature to the MSR and MOR mission methods, the first MD flight would send an unmanned Earth Return Vehicle (ERV) to Mars, with a supply of hydrogen, a chemical plant, and a small nuclear reactor. After landing on Mars, a series of "Sabatier" chemical reaction processes coupled with electrolysis would combine approximately 8 tons of hydrogen carried by the ERV with the existing carbon dioxide of the Martian atmosphere to manufacture up to approximately 112 tons of methane and oxygen.

Approximately 96 tons of this combination would be required to return the ERV to Earth at the end of the mission. The remaining fuel components would then be available for Mars rovers and other equipment. This chemical manufacturing process is expected to require approximately 10 months to complete. After the Earth Return Vehicle is launched from Earth, about 26 months later a second vehicle, the "Mars Habitat Unit" (MHU), would be launched on an approximate 6-month long low-energy transfer trajectory to Mars. Carrying a required crew of only 4 astronauts so that the team can be split in two preventing any astronaut from being alone, the ERV would not be launched until the automated fuel factory had signaled the successful fuel production of chemicals required for operation on Mars and the return trip home to Earth.

During the Mars mission, connecting the spent upper stage of the Saturn C8 booster rocket to the Mars Habitat Unit, and rotating them both about a common axis could generate artificial gravity. After reaching Mars, the upper rocket stage would be jettisoned, with the MHU aero-braking into Mars orbit prior to a soft-landing in close proximity to the ERV. Precise landing would be assisted by a radar beacon initiated by the first Mars lander. Once on Martian surface, the crew would spend 18 months on the surface, carrying out a range of scientific research, aided by a small rover vehicle carried aboard their MHU, and powered by the methane produced by the ERV. In returning to Earth, the ERV would be used leaving the MHU for the possible use of subsequent explorers and future colonization. On the return trip to Earth, the propulsion stage of the ERV would be used as a rotating counterweight to generate artificial gravity for the trip back.

A modified version called "Mars Semi-Direct" proposal came in response to major criticisms. Consisting of three (3) spacecraft that would include a "Mars Ascent Vehicle" (MAV). The ERV would remain in Mars orbit for the return journey home to Earth. The unmanned MAV would land and manufacture propellant fuel for the ascent back to Mars orbit. This proposal architecture has also been used as the design basis of numerous Mars mission studies, including the NASA "Design Reference Mission" (DRM). The DRM calls for a significant upgrade in rocket hardware with at least 3 launches per mission, rather than two, and launches the ERV to Mars fully fueled, where it is parked in Martian orbit above the planet surface for subsequent rendezvous with the MAV.

By Marty Piatt, Architect

The Mars Society and Stanford Mars exploration studies retain the original 2-vehicle mission profile of Mars Direct, but increase the crew size from four to six astronauts.

Another modified proposal, referred to as the "Mars to Stay" (MTS) proposal, involves not immediately or possibly never returning the first Mars astronaut explorers back home to Earth. It has been suggested that the cost of sending a four or six person crew could be one-fifth to one-tenth the cost of returning that same four or six person crew back home to Earth. Depending on the precise mission approach taken, a complete lab could be launched and landed for less than the cost of sending 110 pounds of Martian rocks back to Earth. Approximately twenty or more future Mars colonists could be sent for the cost of returning one crew complement of four.

Also in consideration is the "Ballistic Capture Trajectory" method for travel to the Martian planet. Different than the "Hohmann Transfer" method, which uses a more direct path for the spacecraft to catch up with Mars and enter its orbit, the "Ballistic Capture Trajectory" uses an indirect path that allows Mars to catch up with the spacecraft permitting entering Martian orbit. The Hohmann transfer is usually quicker, however expends much greater energy and fuel to achieve Martian orbit. The Ballistic Capture Trajectory method requires more time to achieve Martian orbit, but yet at a fraction of the energy and fuel required for the Hohmann Transfer method.

Now not to be confused with the previously cancelled Constellation rocket program, the ultimate goals of these four phases for Martian exploration would be accomplished under the "re-branded" program launched as the "**ARES**" program, brother of **APOLLO**.

Based upon past NASA budgets and the actual adjusted costs for the Saturn, Apollo, and ISS programs using "parametric" and "analogy" cost estimating methods to provide a preliminary Rough Order of Magnitude (ROM) program cost, my personal cost opinion for the 4-phase "Ares" program mission to Mars could cost approximately $400+ billion dollars, or an average of approximately $20 billion dollars per year expenditure for the likely 20-plus year initial Mars mission duration.

127

The "parametric" cost estimating method, or "statistical" method is the cost estimating methodology that uses statistical relationships between historical costs and other program variables such as system physical or performance characteristics, measures of contractor output, or loading of manpower.

The "analogy" cost estimating method, or "top-down" method is an estimate of costs based on historical data of a similar item. The analogy method compares a new or proposed system with one analogous (i.e., similar) system that was acquired in the recent past, for which there is accurate cost and technical data.   There must also be a reasonable correlation between the proposed and "historical" system. The parametric and analogy cost estimating methods are only two of four methods used by the United States government for cost estimating which would include the "engineering" and "actual" as the two other cost estimating methods available.

The **Saturn 2.0** reboot could have the exciting new design revisions completed and flight-testing accomplished prior to the end of one presidential term in 2020 with construction of the Libra Colony substantially completed in its infant operational state shortly thereafter.

Construction of the Peary Lunar Outpost and Mars expedition and Martius Colony could potentially be substantially completed by 2030 with proper program funding and implementation.

The new Saturn 2.0 program could also utilize the Orion, CST-100, Altair, Dream Chaser, Dragon, and possibly the Russian Klipper designs as potential hardware and technology used in conjunction with the new Saturn 2.0 Space Launch System.

It must be noted that the former Apollo program provided approximately 400,000 new NASA and aerospace engineering jobs within the nearly two decades the program was active. The future "Ares" program 4-phase Mars expedition and "Libra Station" program could very well achieve the same employment growth as the Apollo program if not greater employment results possibly approaching 1,000,000 new American jobs located within the continental United States.

By Marty Piatt, Architect

Based upon a bare minimum job creation of 400,000 new jobs and the total Ares program cost of approximately $400 billion dollars, the per capita employment cost would be approximately $1 million per new job over the entire 20-year life of the Ares program.

To put this cost into better perspective, the Department of Defense current wartime cost to deploy just one warfighter overseas nearly exceeds on average one million dollars each year. Since 9/11, the US military has spent on average more than approximately $337 million dollars per day.

The list of all American-made rocket engines and their launch thrust capabilities, excluding all Russian-made RD-170 and RD-180 rocket engines that are now banned, include the following:

1. F-1X (RP-1/LOX)   1,800,000 lbf

2. RS-68 (LH2/LOX)   705,000 lbf

3. RS-25 (LH2/LOX)   512,000 lbf

4. AR-1 (RP-1/LOX)   500,000 lbf

5. J-2X (LH2/LOX)   294,000 lbf

6. RS-27A (RP-1/LOX)   200,000 lbf

7. RL10 (LH2/LOX)   25,000 lbf

NASA should refocus their rocket engine technologies on the F-1X, AR-1, and RS-27A rocket (RP-1/LOX) engines for developing first stage launch systems. Renowned NASA rocket scientist and Apollo rocket designer Wernher von Braun chose RP-1 as the preferred first stage rocket fuel because of its much greater fuel density, irrespective of rocket engine's lower Specific Impulse. That rocket science rationale has not changed.

Specific Impulse is considered the thrust efficiency of a rocket engine. Like rocket miles per gallon, it is the thrust force produced by each pound of fuel per unit of time. Having greater density, RP-1 required less volume to produce the same amount of thrust force as liquid hydrogen.

The overall cost effectiveness and affordability of NASA's rocket engines should also be analyzed in terms of dollars per pounds-force ($/lbf), rather Specific Impulse efficiency.

NASA could then concentrate their efforts on the remaining RS-68, RS-25, and J-2X rocket (LH2/LOX) engines for developing upper stage launch systems. It should be noted that the RS-25, or SSME, is the most expensive rocket engine ever designed, built, and maintained in the entire history of NASA's space programs. The RL10 could also potentially be used in future Orbital Maneuvering Systems (OMS) designs. With the potential to manufacture liquid methane (LM) and oxygen (LOX) on Mars, interplanetary travel back to Earth would require the use of rocket (LM/LOX) engines.

The United States has more than sufficient American-made rocket engine technology available, which eliminates the need for a Russian-made RD-170 or RD-180 rocket replacement program. Mars exploration and exploration outside of our solar system will also require the creation and implementation of new and updated rocket technologies including the proposed new "NJ-2" class of rocket motors.

Used as a potential replacement for the Saturn S-IVB, the new NJ-2 rocket would utilize current and forthcoming nuclear and plasma technologies consisting of the following potential Saturn third stage S-IVN nuclear rocket types such as:

1. VASIMR – Variable Specific Impulse Magneto Plasma Rocket

2. NTR – Nuclear Thermal Rocket

3. NERVA – Nuclear Energy for Rocket Vehicle Applications

4. NSWR – Nuclear Salt-Water Rocket

5. EM DRIVE – Electro Magnetic Drive

A nuclear thermal rocket uses fluid, usually liquid hydrogen, which is heated to an extremely high temperature in a nuclear reactor vessel, which then expands through a rocket nozzle to create rocket thrust. The nuclear reactor's energy replaces the chemical energy of the rocket propellant's reactive chemical oxidation occurring in a typical chemical rocket.

Due to the higher energy density of the nuclear fuel as compared to chemical fuels, which is over 100 times, the resulting fuel efficiency or effective exhaust velocity of the engine is at least double the performance of chemical fuel rocket engines.

By Marty Piatt, Architect

The overall gross lift-off mass of a nuclear rocket is nearly half that of a typical chemical rocket, and when used in an upper rocket stages, it nearly doubles or triples the payload capacity carried into orbit, and beyond.

The Electro Magnetic Drive, or "RF resonant cavity thruster" as it is technically known, is still theoretical and experimental. The EM Drive promises extraordinary capabilities to reduce space travel to a fraction of the time if proven feasible.

As President, I would propose to NASA to separate crew launches from mission payload launches. Astronauts would launch separately when possible and then rendezvous with their mission payloads. This would provide greater astronaut safety when launching huge mission payloads. Private commercial crew launches could also supplement NASA launches.

In addition to aerospace research and design, NASA should also concentrate on future aeronautical research and design for civilian commercial aircraft. A radical and revolutionary design concept for a passenger aircraft utilizing a partially double-decked winged lifting-body design maximizing both lift and fuel efficiency would be an exciting future American aeronautical goal.

I would also propose studying a future Ares program secondary launch site to be located at the existing Vandenberg Air Force Base nestled on the central California coast.

To moderate future NASA budget costs to better afford the "Ares" program, as President I would have NASA suspend indefinitely or cancel all non-essential "unmanned" space exploration programs and projects and reallocate those resources and personnel to the renewed mission of exploring Mars. As an added economic windfall, NASA research and space center locations in Florida, Texas, Louisiana, Mississippi, Alabama, Virginia, Maryland, Ohio, and California will all benefit from this renewed mission to the red planet Mars and the new "NASA economy".

"If I was President…"

By Marty Piatt, Architect

AFGHANISTAN AND IRAQ

"Of course the people don't want war. But the people can be brought to the bidding of their leader. All you have to do is tell them they're being attacked and denounce the pacifists for somehow a lack of patriotism and exposing the country to danger. It works the same in any country."
~Hermann W. Goering, Adolph Hitler's Reich Marshal

The first Persian Gulf War against Iraq in response to Iraq's invasion and annexation of Kuwait lasted from August 1990 to February 1991, also codenamed "Operation Desert Storm". More commonly referred to simply as the Gulf War, it was a war waged under a United Nations authorized coalition force from the 34 participating international countries all led by the United States.

On August 2, 1990 the invasion of Kuwait by Iraqi troops was met with international condemnation, and brought immediate economic sanctions against Iraq by members of the United Nations Security Council. United States President George H. W. Bush deployed American military forces into Saudi Arabia, and urged other international countries to deploy their own military forces in coalition. The great majority of the military forces in the coalition were from the United States, with Saudi Arabia, the United Kingdom and Egypt as leading contributors, in that order.

On January 17, 1991 the initial conflict to remove Iraqi troops from Kuwait began with an aerial bombardment.

On February 23, 1991 a ground assault consisting of aerial and ground combat confined to Iraq, Kuwait, and border areas of Saudi Arabia followed. For the coalition forces that liberated Kuwait and advanced beyond the Iraqi border this was a decisive victory. The coalition declared a cease-fire 100 hours after the ground campaign began and ceased their military advance into Iraq.

Iraqi military forces including the Republican Guard loyal to Saddam Hussein desperately launched Scud missile attacks against U.S. and coalition military targets in Saudi Arabia in addition to random targets within the country of Israel.

On February 28, 1991 the Persian Gulf War formally ended. Saddam Hussein unfortunately remained in power in Iraq against better judgment and logical rationale. The total cost relating to the Persian Gulf War through has been estimated to be approximately $61 billion dollars, including approximately 225 American warfighter deaths, approximately 776 American warfighters wounded and maimed. The total amount of both Iraqi and Kuwaiti civilian deaths has been estimated to be approximately 4,700 non-combatants. Some estimates of enemy deaths range greatly anywhere from 20,000 to 200,000 combatants.

Then on September 11, 2001, ten years after the end of the Persian Gulf War, everything changed. This date will live on in infamy until the next unknown terrorist attack, not "if" but "when". Not since December 7, 1941 has our nation experienced the terrible and tragic loss of precious life with the attacks on the World Trade Center, Pentagon, and failed White House target resulting in a commercial airliner crash in Pennsylvania. These were not acts of war; these were acts of cowardice by perpetrators taking the lives of thousands of American innocents. An act of terrorism by Islamic extremists, justified in their demented minds with God's approval, they believed they would enter into the gates of heaven with their martyrdom. I truly believe God has other eternal accommodations awaiting the 9/11 terrorists. The Islamic extremists known as "al-Qaeda" (translated as "the cell") were based and trained in Afghanistan supported by the Taliban-controlled government and headed by Osama bin Laden, the mastermind of the 9/11 attacks on New York's World Trade Center in America.

After the August 1998 U.S. Embassy bombings in Tanzania and Kenya were linked to Osama bin Laden, then-President Clinton ordered missile strikes on militant training camps in Afghanistan that were later cancelled due the belief that the death of a Saudi Prince at the strike site would have been included in the collateral damage.

During a March 2001 visit to Belgium and Europe, Ahmad Shah Massoud warned the European Parliament in Brussels that his intelligence sources had gathered information regarding an imminent and large-scale attack to occur on United States soil. He stated that the Taliban and al-Qaeda had introduced "a very wrong perception of Islam".

By Marty Piatt, Architect

Without the military support of Pakistan and financial support of Saudi Arabia, Bin Laden and Taliban would not be able to sustain their military campaign against the Afghan Northern Alliance. During that time the United States and the European Union would decide to provide no support to Massoud for the fight against the Taliban.

Massoud, an engineering student at Kabul University who became a military leader having a commanding role in driving the Soviet Union out of Afghanistan, had strongly rejected the literal interpretations of Islam and the Quran followed by the Taliban al Qaeda, and the Saudi government. A Sunni Muslim and anti-communist, Massoud was known as the "Lion of Panjshir" by his followers. Not only seeing him as their military commander, his devout followers also saw him as their spiritual leader.

On September 9, 2001, just two days prior to 9/11, Massoud, then 48, became the successful assassination target of a suicide attack by two Arabs posing as journalists that detonated a bomb hidden in their video camera during an interview in Khoja Bahauddin, in the Takhar Province of Afghanistan.

Having had survived numerous assassination attempts over a 26-year period, the death of Massoud was considered to have had a strong connection to 9/11 and appeared to be the actual terrorist attack that Massoud had warned against in his speech to the European Parliament several months earlier. Following his assassination, Massoud would later be nominated for the Nobel Peace Prize in 2002.

John P. O'Neill, a counter-terrorism expert and the Assistant Director of the FBI until late 2001, retired from the FBI and was offered the position of Director of Security at the World Trade Center (WTC). He accepted the position at the WTC two weeks before September 11, 2001.

On September 10, 2001, one day before the attack on the World Trade Center, O'Neill told two of his friends: "We're due. And we're due for something big... Some things have happened in Afghanistan [referring to the assassination of Massoud]. I don't like the way things are lining up in Afghanistan... I sense a shift, and I think things are going to happen... soon." John O'Neill died on September 11, 2001, during the collapse of the South Tower of the World Trade Center.

On October 5, 2001, providing that the United States submitted what it called "solid evidence" of his guilt the Taliban, offered to try Bin Laden in an Afghan court, but the U.S. would not hand over its evidence to the Taliban.

On October 7, 2001, the armed forces of the United States, with the international coalition assistance of the United Kingdom, Australia, and the Northern Alliance (Afghan United Front) launched the war in the Islamic Emirate of Afghanistan, known as "Operation Enduring Freedom". The primary goal of the invasion was to find Osama bin Laden and other high-ranking al-Qaeda members to be put on trial, to completely dismantle the al-Qaeda terrorist organization, and to remove the Taliban government with the ultimate task of introducing and supporting a democratic government within Afghanistan.

Second only to the Vietnam War which lasted from 1959 to 1975, the war in Afghanistan has now become the second longest running military conflict in American history. The United States continues to battle a defiant and widespread Taliban and al-Qaeda insurgency worldwide, throughout Afghanistan, Pakistan, and its neighboring countries, including many tribal areas within those same countries. The United Nations Security Council (UNSC) did not authorize the U.S.-led military mission Operation Enduring Freedom in Afghanistan.

Pursuant to the United Nations Charter, which the Coalition Forces countries are all signatories, provides that all UN member states, except in self-defense, must settle their international disputes peacefully and no member nation can authorize military force. Our United States Constitution states that international treaties, such as the United Nations Charter, that are ratified by the United States congress remain part of the law of the land.

Critics of Operation Enduring Freedom maintain that the invasion and bombing of Afghanistan were not legitimate self-defense measures authorized under Article 51 of the United Nations Charter because the 9/11 attacks were not "armed attacks" by another member nation.

Rather the 9/11 terrorist attacks were perpetrated by groups of individuals, and the attackers supposedly had no proven connection to the Afghanistan nation or government.

Further, it is their opinion that even if a member nation had perpetrated the 9/11 attacks, no bombing campaign would constitute self-defense since the necessity for self-defense must be "instant, overwhelming, leaving no choice of means, and no moment for deliberation."

Proponents of the legitimacy of the United States led invasion argue that United Nations Security Council authorization was not required because the invasion was an act of collective self-defense by Coalition Forces authorized under Article 51 of the UN Charter, and therefore was not a war of aggression.

I personally believe the invasion of Afghanistan was entirely justified. However, I would have used an alternative resolve to end the conflict.

The total cost relating to the war in Afghanistan through the fiscal year 2011 is expected to be approximately $470 billion dollars with the annual cost of deploying one U.S. warfighter in Afghanistan estimated at over $1 million dollars per year.

Eleven years of continuous war in Afghanistan have resulted in approximately 1,900 American warfighter deaths, approximately 15,000 American warfighters wounded and maimed, the Taliban being removed from power, and a democratic Middle Eastern government was installed with American-style corruption and racketeering.

The total amount of both Afghanistan civilian deaths has been estimated to range from between 14,000 to 34,000 non-combatants. Some estimates of enemy deaths range greatly anywhere from 37,000 to 41,000 combatants.

The United States has yet to really end the war in Afghanistan.

Less than seven months after the United States invasion of Afghanistan in April 2002, President George Bush held meetings with British Prime Minister Tony Blair at Bush's Crawford, Texas ranch to discuss the future invasion and war in Iraq.

During a secret July 23, 2002 meeting involving British government, Ministry of Defense, and British intelligence discussed the build-up to the Iraq war including direct references to classified U.S. policy of the time.

The memo known as the "Downing Street memo" stated:

"[President] Bush wanted to remove Saddam [Hussein], through military action, justified by the conjunction of terrorism and WMD. But the intelligence and facts were being fixed around the policy".

The memo also stated: "It seemed clear that [President] Bush had made up his mind to take military action, even if the timing was not yet decided. But the case was thin. Saddam was not threatening his neighbours, and his WMD capability was less than that of Libya, North Korea or Iran".

The "Downing Street memo" was later published in the UK in The Sunday Times on May 1, 2005, in the Los Angeles Times on May 12, 2005, in the Washington Post on May 13, 2005, and nearly one year later in The New York Times on March 27, 2006. In a Memorial Day editorial, The Star Tribune revisited the Downing Street Minutes as part of the evidence stating explicitly:

"President Bush and those around him lied, and the rest of us let them. Harsh? Yes. True? Also yes. Perhaps it happened because Americans, understandably, don't expect untruths from those in power. But that works better as an explanation than as an excuse... It turns out that former counterterrorism chief Richard Clarke and former Treasury Secretary Paul O'Neill were right. Both have been pilloried for writing that by summer 2002 Bush had already decided to invade [Iraq]."

Criticism of the initial intelligence leading up to the Iraq war included a former CIA officer who described the Office of Special Plans (OSP) as a group of ideologues who lied and manipulated intelligence to further its agenda of removing Saddam Hussein, were dangerous to our national security, and a credible threat to world peace.

Between 2001 and 2003, according to the nonpartisan Center for Public Integrity, President George W. Bush and six other top members of his administration allegedly made a total of approximately **"935"** false statements regarding Iraq's threat to the United States.

In what was phrased as a "carefully launched campaign of misinformation" during the 2-year period following September 11th attacks on the World Trade Center to rally international support for the invasion of Iraq.

"Thou shalt not bear false witness [lie]…"

~The Bible, [Exodus 20:16, Deuteronomy 5:20]

In July 2002, before the 2003 invasion, CIA Special Activities Division (SAD) Paramilitary teams entered Iraq and later joined by members of the U.S. military's elite Joint Special Operations Command (JSOC). SAD teams then combined with United States Army Special Forces to organize the Kurdish Peshmerga forces. In a battle in the northeast corner of Iraq the combined joint team defeated Ansar al-Islam, who was an alleged ally of al Qaeda. The US forces consisted of the Army's 10th Special Forces Group and Paramilitary Officers from SAD.

On February 15, 2003, one month before the invasion of Iraq, there was Iraq war protests that attracted between six and ten million people in more than 800 cities worldwide, becoming the largest such protest in human history according to the Guinness Book of World Records. This includes a three million-person rally in Rome, Italy, which is also listed in the Guinness Book of World Records as the largest ever anti-war rally.

On March 20, 2003 at 05:34 Baghdad time or approximately 02:30 UTC nearly 90 minutes after the lapse of the 2-day, 48-hour deadline explosions in Baghdad were heard. The military invasion of Iraq had just begun. The CIA's Special Activities Division consisting of special operations commandos from the Northern Iraq Liaison Element infiltrated throughout Iraq and called in the early air strikes.

Led by United States Army General Tommy Franks, the 2003 invasion of Iraq began under the codename "Operation Iraqi Liberation" and later would be renamed "Operation Iraqi Freedom". The coalition's mission according to President George W. Bush and British Prime Minister Tony Blair, was "to disarm Iraq of weapons of mass destruction, to end Saddam Hussein's support for terrorism, and to free the Iraqi people."

At 03:15 UTC, or 10:15 p.m. EST, President George W. Bush announced that he had ordered the 'attack of opportunity' against Iraqi targets. The objectives of the United States invasion of Iraq were to:

1. End the Saddam Hussein regime;

2. Eliminate whatever weapons of mass destruction could be found;

3. Eliminate whatever Islamist militants could be found;

4. Obtain intelligence on militant networks;

5. Distribute humanitarian aid;

6. Secure Iraq's petroleum infrastructure;

7. Assist in creating a representative and compliant government as a model for other Middle Eastern nations.

On April 9, 2003 Baghdad fell to U.S. and coalition forces, ending Saddam Hussein's 24-year dictatorial rule.   U.S. forces then seized the deserted Ba'ath Party ministries and stage-managed the tearing down of a huge iron statue of Saddam Hussein.   A widespread outpouring of gratitude toward the coalition invaders with the quick fall of Baghdad was accompanied by massive civil disorder, including drastically increased crime and the looting of public and government buildings.

On May 1, 2003, in a Lockheed S-3 Viking, President George Bush landed on the CVN-72 aircraft carrier USS Abraham Lincoln, where he spoke announcing the end of major combat operations in the war in Iraq. The President's carrier landing was criticized and characterized by opponents as an unnecessarily theatrical and expensive stunt. Criticized as premature, a banner stating "Mission Accomplished" that was clearly visible in the background was made by White House staff and supplied by the request of the United States Navy.

On September 16, 2004, Kofi Annan, the United Nations Secretary General, said of the invasion by President George Bush: "I have indicated it was not in conformity with the UN Charter. From our point of view, from the Charter point of view, it was illegal."

By Marty Piatt, Architect

An April 2004 USA Today/CNN/Gallup Poll reported 66% of the Iraqi people believed that the American-led occupation of their country did more harm than good, and supported an immediate military withdraw even though they feared they could be put in a far greater danger after the withdraw of American forces.

In 2004, London's conservative International Institute for Strategic Studies (IISS) had concluded that the invasion and U.S.-led occupation of Iraq became "a potent global recruitment pretext" for the Mujahedeen that "galvanized" al-Qaeda and "perversely inspired insurgent violence" in Iraq.

In a January 2005 report, The U.S. National Intelligence Council concluded that the war in Iraq had become a breeding ground for a new generation of terrorists. David Low, the national intelligence officer for transnational threats, indicated that the report concluded that the war in Iraq provided terrorists with: "...a training ground, a recruitment ground, the opportunity for enhancing technical skills... there is even, under the best scenario, over time, the likelihood that some of the jihadists who are not killed there will, in a sense, go home, wherever home is, and will therefore disperse to various other countries."

Robert Hutchings, the Council's chairman, stated: "At the moment, Iraq is a magnet for international terrorist activity." Also in 2005 in a released report, the Central Intelligence Agency (CIA) stated and confirmed that absolutely no weapons of mass destruction (WMD) had been found in Iraq.

In 2006, The Pew Global Attitudes Project reported that majorities in the Netherlands, Germany, Jordan, France, Lebanon, China, Spain, Indonesia, Turkey, Pakistan, and Morocco believed the world was safer prior to the invasion of Iraq and removal of Saddam Hussein from power.

The newly declassified 93-page document titled "2006 National Intelligence Estimate" (NIE), which was used to justify the Iraqi invasion, also claimed that Iraq possessed no weapons of mass destruction and did not contribute aid to the Afghanis. The 2006 National Intelligence Estimate outlining the conclusion of all 16 U.S. intelligence agencies, held that: "The Iraq conflict has become the 'cause celebre' for jihadists, breeding a deep resentment of U.S. involvement in the Muslim world and cultivating supporters for the global jihadist movement."

141

In 2006 it was found that majority of people in the United Kingdom (UK) and Canada believed that the Iraqi war was "unjustified". Most people in the UK were very critical of their government's support of United States military policies in Iraq.

On December 30, 2006 Saddam Hussein was hanged until death, after a yearlong trial having been found guilty of crimes against humanity by an Iraqi court.

In January 2007, a British Broadcasting Corporation (BBC) World Service poll in 25 countries consisting of more than 26,000 people, found that 73% of the global population disapproved of United States handling of the Iraq War. Another poll conducted in September 2007 by the BBC found that 66% of the world's population believed the United States should withdraw its military forces from Iraq.

Four years after the 2003 invasion of Iraq, polls conducted in 2007 by the Arab American Institute (AAI) concluded that 83% of Egyptians, 68% of Saudi Arabians, 96% of Jordanians, 70% of the population of the United Arab Emirates, and 76% of the Lebanese had a negative view of the United States role in Iraq.

On May 10, 2007, 144 Iraqi Parliamentary lawmakers, calling on the United States to set a timetable for withdrawal, signed onto a legislative petition for such.

In November 2008, Iraqi protesters staged a massive demonstration stomping on and burning of an effigy of President George W. Bush.

On December 4, 2008, the U.S.-Iraq Status of Forces Agreement was approved establishing that United States combat and military forces would withdraw from Iraqi cities by June 30, 2009. The agreement also established that all United States military forces would be out of Iraq completely by December 31, 2011.

On February 17, 2010, United States Secretary of Defense Robert Gates announced "Operation New Dawn", the name for the new military mission that would replace "Operation Iraqi Freedom" on September 1, 2010.

By Marty Piatt, Architect

On October 21, 2011, our President announced that all U.S. warfighters and trainers would leave Iraq by the year's end, finalizing the United States mission and war in Iraq.

On December 15, 2011, at a flag lowering ceremony in Baghdad, Defense Secretary Leon Panetta officially declared the war in Iraq ended.

On December 18, 2011 at 4:27 UTC the last U.S. warfighters left Iraqi territory in accordance with the U.S.-Iraq status of Forces Agreement.

After nine years of Iraqi war, approximately 4,500 American warfighter deaths, approximately 32,000 American warfighters wounded and maimed, and $800 billion dollars of American tax dollars spent, Saddam Hussein was finally and permanently removed from power, executed by hanging, and a democratic Middle Eastern government was installed with seemingly American-style corruption and racketeering.

For a better perspective of the unnecessary Iraqi War, its cost would be equal to twice the proposed $400 billion dollars cost of the 20-year duration of a future Libra Station and Martius Colony and their related NASA "Ares" rocket program components.

With the unnecessary war in Iraq resulting in the American loss of life, spouses will never experience love and intimacy with their lost loved ones, children will grow up without mothers and fathers, siblings will mourn the loss of brothers and sisters, and parents will suffer the premature loss of their children.

The Iraqi War was a "premeditated" George W. Bush war based upon blatant lies and deception launched to complete the unfinished war of George H. W. Bush, his father, which failed to meet our future objectives.

Had I been President at the launching of the first Persian Gulf War, the military conflict would not have ended without the complete removal of Saddam Hussein from power of the country of Iraq eliminating the future U.S. military operations. Using the very same rational used for the second invasion of Iraq, Saddam Hussein must not have remained in power during the first Persian Gulf War.

On February 5, 2003, Colin Powell, United States Secretary of State, stated the following to the United Nations Security Council:

"We know that Saddam Hussein is determined to keep his weapons of mass destruction; he's determined to make more. Given Saddam Hussein's history of aggression... given what we know of his terrorist associations and given his determination to exact revenge on those who oppose him, should we take the risk that he will not someday use these weapons at a time and the place and in the manner of his choosing at a time when the world is in a much weaker position to respond? The United States will not and cannot run that risk to the American people. Leaving Saddam Hussein in possession of weapons of mass destruction for a few more months or years is not an option, not in a post–September 11 world."

This would have resulted in preventing approximately 4,500 American warfighter deaths, approximately 32,000 American warfighters wounded and maimed, and saving $800 billion dollars of American hard-earned tax dollars. Without the second invasion of Iraq, approximately 132,000 to 150,000 future Iraqi military and civilian deaths would have been prevented.

The combined cost to the American taxpayers of both wars in Afghanistan and Iraq approaches nearly $1.3 trillion dollars, or approximately 9% of our national debt, which does not include the future interest cost of loans used to fund the wars. After eleven years of war, approximately 6,400 American warfighter deaths, nearly 47,000 American warfighters wounded and maimed, the Middle East is actually much less stable than it was prior to the invasion of Afghanistan.

Of the thousands of wounded and maimed warfighters, the most devastating are the IED blast wounds that have left hundreds of American warfighters severely and horribly maimed with genital injuries.

In addition to the horrible amputations and severe burns, thousands of young American warfighters have suffered genital injuries, tragically leaving these young men unable to father children, while also struggling to engage and perform in something resembling the intimate relations and sexual intercourse they have previously had with their loving spouses, often without the benefit and aid of what some would consider of the primary symbol of male manhood.

By Marty Piatt, Architect

More than 1,500 American warfighters have been carried off the battlefield with devastating genital wounds since 2005.

Since 2009, when the President ordered the "surge" of 30,000 combat troops into Afghanistan approving a new tactic of increased foot patrols, the pace of very severe genital injuries had dramatically accelerated. About 170 combat troops had suffered genital wounds, from Improvised Explosive Devise (IED) blasts in the year prior to the surge.

In 2010, according to Pentagon data, the number of genital injuries of American warfighters increased to approximately 259. In 2011, the Department of Defense cited approximately 299 cases of genital wounds that were characterized as "devastating" according to urologist Dr. James Jezior, who performs genital repair surgery for our veterans at Walter Reed Medical Center.

IED blasts have become the primary cause of U.S. battlefield death during the past decade, killing or wounding 34,360 American warfighters in Afghanistan and Iraq, according to recent Department of Defense data. One reason for the increasing incidence is that modern body armor leaves the lower torso exposed to the upward blast of buried bombs yet protecting the upper torso and chest area; a vulnerability unfortunately exploited by the terrorist insurgents.

The combined American and enemy military and civilian deaths resulting from three Middle Eastern wars waged by the United States number somewhere between approximately 214,000 and 433,000 precious lives lost. Had I been Commander in Chief during the 9/11 attacks on the United States, I would have authorized immediate military response no less than those utilized by our military to bring an end to World War II. Using tactical nuclear devices, as President I would have unleashed the entire wrath of our massive and awesome military arsenal. This would have ultimately saved thousands of lives as it did ending World War II.

Having confirmed the identities of terrorist perpetrators, I would have approved a nuclear resolve to end the Taliban control of Afghanistan including all training bases and facilities for their assault on the United States of American.

Using a similar second ultimatum, I would have unconditionally requested the immediate surrender, arrest, and extradition to the United States of Osama bin Laden, the mastermind of the September 11, 2001 attacks. Failure to satisfy this request would have resulted in a second military mission against the Afghanistan government again using nuclear resolve. Make no mistake, the radical Islamic terrorists having "awakened the sleeping giant" would have reaped my firm and absolute resolve responding to the situation. The United States would have not repeated the unsuccessful military campaign waged against the Taliban in Afghanistan that the former Soviet Union armed forces had unfortunately failed to accomplish. Saddam Hussein would most certainly have then complied with future American mandates for weapons of mass destruction (WMD) inspections, and Iraq would have continued to contain Iran, which was the existing American military doctrine implemented for decades. The government of Iraq and Saddam Hussein might possibly have fallen during the same "Arab Spring" period of political turmoil that resulted in the recent revolutions in Egypt, Tunisia, Yemen, and later in both and Libya and Syria spreading to other Middle Eastern nations.

I find it both interesting and ironic that the United States waged war under Republican administrations against two previous perceived allies that were both "enemies of our enemies"; unfortunately arming and training both the Taliban fighting the Soviets, and the Iraqi fighting Iran. Based upon this military track record, is the Taliban in Pakistan next on our nation's potential war agenda? Or is Iran in our military crosshairs? Nevertheless, by international and world standards, it is actually George W. Bush that is the ultimate terrorist, the great Satan.

As President I would prepare executive orders providing "Conditional" Pardons to all American warfighters convicted of any and all war crimes not committed against fellow United States warfighters while serving in Afghanistan and Iraq. Not one American warfighter shall remain incarcerated for war crimes, which are ultimately the responsibility having been committed by George W. Bush, while the former President remains a free man. There remains no statute of limitations for war crimes.

Resulting from the invasion of Iraq, as President I would propose the establishment of a War Crimes Tribunal in cooperation with the International Criminal Court, the International Court of Justice, and the sovereign country of Iraq, to be administered in The Hague, Netherlands.

This tribunal would formally investigate and become judicator of war crimes allegedly committed by members of the George W. Bush Presidential administration including but limited to the former President involving the seemingly unlawful invasion of Iraq. The indictments, not unlike the war crimes of WWII, would consist of the following allegations:

1. Participation in a common plan or conspiracy for the accomplishment of a crime against peace;

2. Planning, initiating and waging wars of aggression and other crimes against peace;

3. War crimes; and Crimes against humanity.

The resulting Tribunal verdict would help in the healing our nation and the healing of our world. This will show the international community that no American president is above reproach in matters relating to domestic or international law.

As of March 13, 2012, the United States Central Command has confirmed at a minimum of 6,364 American warfighter casualties during the missions: Enduring Freedom, Operation Iraqi Freedom, and Operation New Dawn.

Added to the massive cost of the Iraqi war, the new Embassy of the United States in Baghdad would become the largest and most expensive embassy in world history. Costing a purported $750 million to initially build having approximately 4.7 million square feet, it is nearly as large as the Vatican. One week after submitting his FY2006 budget to Congress, President Bush sent Congress an emergency FY2005 supplemental funding request that included more than $1.3 billion for the embassy. In addition, an emergency supplemental appropriation that included $592 million more for embassy construction was signed into law on May 11, 2005. A grand total of nearly $2.642 billion dollars in funding was needed for construction of the U.S. Embassy in Baghdad, according to the Department of State.

Under my Presidency, the current defense-related industrial military complex will easily transition away from war-related military production into a peaceful military production industry for outer space exploration, the colonization of Mars, and lunar resource recovery on the our moon.

"Iraq is an unjust war. I thought then, and I think now, that the invasion if Iraq was unnecessary and unjust. And I think the premises on which it was launched were false." ~Jimmy Carter, former U.S. President

"There is no greater guilt than the unnecessary war."
~John Adams

"War is horrible. War is sickening. Wars started for supremely righteous causes are just as horrible [and] sickening in their consequences as wars started for less than righteous causes. Politicians who sit in office chairs and start wars and wave flags as young men and women go off to kill and die and be psychologically and emotionally damaged for life are the most sickening of all. Politicians start wars and are rewarded with an appearance on weekend talk shows and Very Respectable Discussions with Very Respectable media figures and jokes at the White House Correspondent's Dinner and appearances on Leno and ghostwritten self-glorifying memoirs and lavishly catered fundraising parties with corporate executives. They should be rewarded with outrage. They should be rewarded with scorn. Starting a war is a monstrous, monstrous crime against humanity, as we know when it begins that no matter how cleanly it is conducted it will result in thousands upon thousands of bullets smashing men's skulls and arms and legs blown off by shrapnel and mothers and children incinerated by high explosives. And every extra day that a war is perpetuated unnecessarily is a crime anew. And we as a nation could not be more bored by the unceasing industrial strength violence being carried out in our names in nations where none of us will travel, or vacation, or think about much at all as long as sports and American Idol and Downtown Abbey are on TV. We skim past those stories of the latest bombing or drone strike or gunfight or civilian massacre. We joke about the personal foibles or funny accents or minor gaffes of the politicians who hold it in their power to stop war, but won't. We're bored and petulant and self-absorbed until that video of some soldier pissing on dead bodies comes along, at which point we can have an outrage contest and feel good about ourselves for being more outraged than the next completely uninvolved person, for a day or two, until the big game comes on."

~ LtCol Julian Myers, USMC, retired

IMMIGRATION

On June 25, 1978, a drunk driving illegal alien from Mexico murdered Kevin Francis Piatt. Kevin was only 22 years old. He was my brother. The illegal Mexican national was charged with driving under the influence of alcohol, hit-and-run, leaving the scene of an accident, and vehicular manslaughter. He served less than one (1) year in the Sutter County Jail.

Presently, over 12 million unlawful foreign nationals illegally occupy the United States of America, and more than half of them are from Mexico. Some would argue the total is greater. Because the Federal government refuses to properly enforce all immigration laws protecting American citizens from foreign invasion, the several States have decided to take action to stem the invasion of illegal immigrants into their States.

The Federal government has filed court petitions to halt the States enforcement of their illegal immigration laws in every case. Twenty-four percent of the States, 12 in all, have passed anti-immigration laws to date. And more State-enacted anti-immigration laws are pending. These States are obviously willing to absorb the cost to enforce the illegal immigration in many cases. Many opponents of these anti-immigration laws feel we need Immigration Reform legislation, again.

The Democrats tend to agree with the idea of more amnesty and reform, not because it is the right thing to do, but because they are courting the Hispanic vote for their re-election. The Republicans obviously tend to prefer enforcement, but until the current Democratic administration takes real and prudent action, substantial enforcement is not forthcoming. Failing to admit it, the Republicans privately prefer the status quo because with the decrease in wages from illegal immigration, profits increase for those unlawfully utilizing illegal Mexican nationalists for labor.

The 2016 Democratic Presidential candidates will also be courting and pandering to the Hispanic Mexican-American vote; so don't anticipate a change in policy any time soon. To be fair to the current administration, the deportation rate under the current administration is greater than the previous administration. I would however rescind all executive orders issued by the current administration that support illegal immigration and repatriate those brought here unlawfully.

149

The Immigration Reform and Control Act of 1986 that was approved by Congress under President Ronald Reagan included amnesty provisions that failed to resolve the same illegal immigration issues that we are facing today that are undermining our country's security. The United States of America really needs to enforce our current Immigration Laws that are in effect now. All illegal undocumented foreign nationals currently residing unlawfully within the borders of the United States of America need to be repatriated with their country of origin as required by our current immigration law.

The illegal immigration issues our country is facing today are also related to the corruption within the Mexican government, as well as the situation with the Mexican Drug cartels. Our nation may have no control of our southern neighbor's government, but our actions can impact the drug trade and crime on both sides of our southern border, which is another topic of discussion.

I can sympathize with the Mexican people wanting to come to our country and their wanting a better life, but it must be done legally. Their problems must not become our problems. Mexican people fleeing the corruption and illegal entitlements received by their politicians, only to arrive in the United States expecting unearned entitlements at the expense of American taxpayers. They are no different than their corrupt politicians and government they are intending to flee. The apparent lack of the their people's patriotism for their own country symbolizes their failure to spur a "revolucion" against the drug cartels and seemingly corrupt government. Now not all illegal aliens are of Mexican origin, however, the vast majority of them are, this cannot be disputed. This is an absolute fact. Approximately one of every two illegal aliens is from Mexico.

This is definitely NOT a racial issue. I prefer the use of the term: "Statistical Profiling". There is no "Racial Profiling" argument whatsoever that can diffuse this fact; it is a reality. Technically speaking, the term "Hispanic" is not a racial term, but rather an ethnic category, and many people treat it as a racial category, which leads to unnecessary confusion.

"A racist is not only one who hates another of a different race, but is also one that supports another of their own race for no other reason than they share the same race, irrespective of any rational reasoning against it."
~Marty Piatt, Architect

By Marty Piatt, Architect

Those aliens that are here illegally must have some sort of false documentation justifying their residency, forged identifications, or stolen identities all in violation of Federal law. This would make them criminals. If common American citizens were caught possessing unlawful identification documentation not unlike those possessed by illegals, we would realize the full wrath of the law upon us. This is not the case for undocumented foreign nationals. We cannot reward them with amnesty for their criminal actions. They too must realize the full brunt of America's laws.

Then there is the issue of birthright. Ratified on July 9, 1868, our 14th amendment to our Constitution intended only to give birthright and citizenship to the newly freed black slaves and native Indians. It was never ever intended by our forefathers to be applied to unlawful foreign invaders. And it seems Congress has never enacted legislation to clarify or properly enforce the Constitution, in which the fourteenth amendment contains such a clause "subject to the jurisdiction thereof". The Supreme Court has unfortunately ruled in favor of the illegally acquired residency in past rulings without the legislative action clarifying the situation by Congress. It should be noted that is the case precedent of United States v. Wong Kim Ark, 169 U.S. 649 (1898), the United States Supreme Court ruled that a child born in the United States of Chinese citizens, automatically became a U.S. citizen. This case ruling established the precedent in the interpretation of the Citizenship Clause of the 14th Amendment to the Constitution. However, Wong Kim Ark's parents were actually legal residents of the United States, were permanent domicile having a business here, which was not for the Chinese government.

The term now coined: "anchor babies" refers to the pregnant mothers residing or coming to the United States wanting to give birth to their future American citizen children, thus giving them an anchor to stay. "Birth Tourism" is also another unjust means of obtaining citizenship through lawful visits to the United States. The ongoing illegal immigration originating from our southern Mexican border is disproportionately diluting our American "melting-pot" culture, English language, and North American territorial heritage our nation has realized historically for generations as a result of lawful worldwide international immigration. If you don't speak English, you probably shouldn't be here. If you don't want to speak English, you probably shouldn't be here. The issue of illegal immigration has also impacted our current situation of unemployment.

151

There is a Texas court case in its pretrial stage concerning the issuance of birth certificates and U.S. citizenship, which the State refuses to issue to "anchor babies", without proper identification of the illegal alien Mexican parents. A court document filed by the government of Mexico adds to the national debate of illegal immigration and anchor babies. This legal brief, which includes a sworn affidavit by Mexico's Consul General for Texas, Carlos Gonzalez Gutierrez, admits openly that the official policy of Mexico is to encourage its people to migrate to the United States illegally to have access our country's very generous welfare system. It is very sad that a county cannot take care of its own citizens.

The brief declares that "Mexico is responsible to protect its nationals wherever they may be residing", and a clarifying footnote in the Mexican Constitution states that "Mexican nationality is granted to children born abroad of a Mexican born parent". This clearly implies that anchor babies born in our country retain the nationality of their parents, and the anchor babies' citizenship belongs in Mexico, not the United States.

Many liberals Americans claim our U.S. Constitution guarantees automatic U.S. citizenship to all children born our soil. Our Fourteenth Amendment to our constitution begins with the words "All persons born or naturalized in the United States, subject to the jurisdiction thereof." This means someone born in the United States is "subject to the jurisdiction" of the parents national citizenship. The anchor babies should not receive U.S. citizenship unless laws are enacted by our Congress to provide such. In filing the legal brief and submitting sworn testimony in the Texas case, Mexico is officially declaring children born to Mexican citizens residing illegally in the United States shall remain "subject to the jurisdiction" of Mexico. The sworn testimony of the Mexican Consul General stated:

"My responsibilities in this position include protecting the rights and promoting the interests of my fellow Mexican nationals" and "The main responsibility of consulates is to provide services, assistance, and protection to nationals abroad".

The assertion of Mexico's continuing jurisdiction over its "nationals abroad" remains inconsistent with claims to automatic U.S. citizenship strictly by virtue of their birth on American soil, "subject to the jurisdiction thereof" contained in our United States Constitution.

By Marty Piatt, Architect

In the Texas case, filed on behalf of about 24 mothers, who admittedly are citizens of Mexico living illegally in Texas, complain that without proper identification they cannot receive official birth certificates for their Texas-born children, or "anchor babies". Without Texas birth certificates, they cannot enroll in Medicaid, apply for food stamps, receive Section 8 housing, and other American taxpayer-provided benefits they do not deserve. Not unlike other states, Texas only issues birth certificates to family relatives upon proper submission of valid identification issued by either a United States Federal or State agency. Adopted to combat the growing epidemic of identity theft, these restrictions attempt to prevent the widespread abuse and unlawful use of forged or fake documents by illegal aliens from Mexico.

The Mexican consulates, in order to assist its citizens living illegally outside of Mexico within the United States who are unable to produce the required identification, issue an official-looking document called the "Matricula Consular", which includes a photo laminated to the document. Refusing to accept this foreign identity document, which the State has no way to verify, Texas will not issue birth certificates to anchor babies born to illegal aliens living within the borders of their state. The lawsuit alleges that by refusing to accept the "Matricula Consular" issued by the Mexican government as valid identification to obtain a birth certificate for their anchor baby, Texas is depriving the children of United States citizenship in violation of our 14th Amendment to our Constitution. The reliance of this Mexican identification document clearly proves that the anchor babies born to illegal alien parents are actually "subject to the jurisdiction" of the Country of Mexico, and therefore are not Constitutionally eligible for automatic citizenship of the United States.

"In the first place, we should insist that if the immigrant who comes here in good faith becomes an American and assimilates himself to us, he shall be treated on an exact equality with everyone else, for it is an outrage to discriminate against any such man because of creed, or birthplace, or origin. But this is predicated upon the person's becoming in every facet an American, and nothing but an American... There can be no divided allegiance here. Any man who says he is an American, but something else also, isn't an American at all. We have room for but one flag, the American flag... We have room for but one language here, and that is the English language... And we have room for but one sole loyalty and that is a loyalty to the American people". ~U.S. President Theodore Roosevelt

The staggering statistics as a consequence of unlawful foreign nationals residing in our country illegally resulting in the following very approximate financial figures:

1. $11 to $22 billion is spent each year by our state and local governments on welfare to illegal aliens;

2. $2.5 to 7.5 billion is spent each year on Medicaid for illegal aliens;

3. $12 billion is spent each year on primary and secondary school education for children that are here illegally;

4. $17 to $27 billion dollars are spent each year for education for the American-born children of illegal aliens, known as anchor babies;

5. $90 billion is spent each year on illegal aliens for welfare and other related social services paid by American taxpayers;

6. $3 million is spent each day to incarcerate illegal aliens;

7. $200 billion each year in suppressed American wages are caused as a result of illegal aliens;

8. In 2006, illegal aliens sent home $45 billion in income tax-free remittances to their foreign countries of origin;

9. Currently, second only to oil exports, financial remittance from Mexican nationals living in the United States is the largest source of income for Mexico.

In 2007, the Department of Homeland Security (DHS) estimated the cost of deporting all illegal aliens to be approximately $94 billion, or about $110 billion adjusted for 2015 dollars.

In July 2010, the Federation for American Immigration Reform (FAIR) released the results of the study that examined the costs of illegal immigration at the federal, state, and local levels. The study found both state and local governments spend about $84.2 billion annually in various law enforcement, school, and social services. California taxpayers alone spend in excess of $21 billion each year for illegal alien entitlements and benefits. The same study also found that illegal aliens receive over $29 billion dollars each and every year in Federal assistance. The key findings of the study also discovered that illegal aliens from Mexico cost hard working American taxpayers an average per household of approximately $1,214.57 adjusted for 2015 dollars.

By Marty Piatt, Architect

Educational expenditures for children of illegal aliens are the single largest expense to American taxpayers, having a cost of nearly $52 billion annually, all of which are absorbed by state and local governments. At the federal level, nearly one-third of costs are offset by taxes paid by illegal aliens. At the state and local level, less than 5 percent of the average costs associated with illegal immigration are recovered by taxes paid from illegal aliens. Most illegal aliens do not pay income taxes, and those who do are refunded when they file tax returns. Illegal aliens also receive tax credits resulting in payments paid to them from the U.S. Treasury having paid no income taxes.

On December 10, 2012, Department of Homeland Security Assistant Secretary for Legislative Affairs, Nelson Peacock, responding to several requests from United States Senators, including Sen. John Cornyn (R-TX), wrote: "Our conservative estimate suggests that Immigration and Customs Enforcement (ICE) would require a budget of more than $135 billion to apprehend, detain and remove the nation's entire illegal immigrant population." Having a one-time cost of about $135 billion, or $45 billion per year to deport every single illegal alien in the country, it would be a huge windfall when considering that it already costs American taxpayers $113 billion annually to keep them here. In other words, the mass deportation would pay for itself in less than 3 years using the 1954 deportation rate of 5.2 million illegal aliens per year.

To better put this into perspective, over the period of ten (10) years the Federal government has provided the State of Louisiana about $113 billion in reconstruction assistance to rebuild the city of New Orleans from the devastating effects of Hurricane Katrina in 2005. The United States spends well over the same amount in aid to illegal aliens every single year.

According to various reports published in Los Angeles newspapers:

1. 40% of workers in L.A. County work under the table being paid in cash not paying taxes (L.A. County's population is 10.2 million);

2. 95% of warrants for murder in Los Angeles are for illegal aliens;

3. 75% of those most wanted in Los Angeles are illegal aliens;

4. Over 66% of all births in L.A. County are to illegal alien Mexican nationals on Medi-Cal, whose births were paid for by taxpayers;

155

5. Nearly 35% of all inmates housed by the California Department of corrections (CDC) detention centers are illegal Mexican nationals;

6. 29% of inmates in Federal prisons are illegal aliens;

7. Nearly 60% of all occupants of HUD properties are illegal aliens;

8. Less than 2% of illegal aliens pick crops, while 29% are on welfare;

9. Illegal aliens have a crime rate 2.5x that of non-illegal immigrants.

First, we start with self-deportation. I would permit the States to assist the Federal government in its responsibility to enforce the current Federal immigration laws and give them greater latitude in creating their own laws to assist the enforcement of illegal immigration. The Federal government should not hinder the States using judicial proceeding opposing laws that are wasting hard-earned American taxpayers' dollars that could be better spent on enforcement.

As a result, most illegal alien would voluntarily leave and return home. Let's make their stay in the United States so difficult as to make them return to their homeland voluntarily. If illegal aliens cannot get jobs, get driver's licenses, register vehicles, utilize the American banking system, or find homes to rent or purchase they will be forced to leave and return to their country of origin. When the well runs dry, they'll move back home. Even Cesar Chavez, founder of the United Farm Workers, was very vocal about not hiring illegal aliens for farm work because it undermined the wages of legal immigrants and American Citizens.

Second, the Federal government should accept its responsibility to enforce its own illegal immigration laws and take immediate appropriate action for legal deportation; it is that plain and simple. The Federal government should properly protect and secure our nation's borders to stop the influx of illegal aliens entering our country.

I would immediately appoint Arizona Sheriff Joe Arpaio to lead our border protection efforts in our country's southwestern territories. To better enforce our borders I would immediately transfer all ATF and DEA Federal employees to the U.S. Customs and Border Protection to patrol our nation's borders and assist in the deportation of all illegal immigrants. The residual effect will also reduce the amount of drugs and Mexican gang criminals entering our country.

To achieve this goal, as President I would propose and initiate "OPERATION GET BACK". Beginning back in May of 1954, President Dwight D. Eisenhower deported 1.3 million illegal Mexican aliens using about 750 border agents, 300 vehicles, and 7 airplanes during a 3-month period in what was called "OPERATION WETBACK". Although the Border Patrol operation also occurred in large cities, the main focus concentrated on the border areas of California, New Mexico, Arizona, and Texas. "OPERATION GET BACK" would utilize the same tactics and methods as those used in 1954.

Using the same 1954 deportation rate of 5.2 million per year (1.3M/3-month), about 12 million illegal aliens could be deported in less than three years costing about $45 billion per year. When you include seizing the assets of these foreign national criminals to pay their fines and deportation costs, and eliminating all foreign aid to Mexico, the net cost of OPERATION GET BACK could be zero, if not profitable. In 1954, without 21st century technology, President Eisenhower did far more with much less. The U.S. Customs and Border Protection (CBP) currently have more than 62,400 Federal employees with a FY16 budget of nearly $13.6 billion. According to the Bureau of Justice Statistics, there are well over 460,000 local, county, and State law enforcement officers in the United States. Excluding the CBP, Federal law enforcement personnel alone account for more than 120,000 officers. If you add another 20,000 deputized CBP volunteers who are American citizens, there are more than 662,400 law enforcement personnel and volunteers available to enforce illegal immigration deportation. If all local, county, and State law enforcement officials were given the authority to enforce our existing Federal immigration laws, nearly all of the 12 million illegal aliens could be identified and deported much quicker than three (3) years.

Assuming the unavailable local and State law enforcement officers who are administrative managers, Sheriffs, or local Police Chiefs, the total number of law enforcement personnel available to assist CBP would be about 600,000 officers. If you divide 12 million illegal aliens by 600,000 officers, that would equal a deportation rate per officer of about 20 illegal aliens. If the combined number of local, State, and Federal law enforcement officers apprehend and deport only one (1) illegal alien per week, it could potentially only take twenty (20) weeks to apprehend and deport 12 million illegal aliens from American soil, or less than six months.

Third, the Federal government should also withhold all State-allocated Federal transportation highway funds from those States issuing illegal foreign nationals their state driver's licenses or vehicle registrations without first verifying their proof of citizenship utilizing state-issued and verified birth certificates. The Federal government Department of State should issue National Identification (NID) Cards to all legal citizens of this country, similar to the existing North American travel visas issued by the State Department. This would assist in verifying citizenship during Local, State, and Federal elections, and would prohibit illegal foreign nations from applying for state driver's licenses. All other foreign legal residents would possess a valid government-issued visa.

Fourth, I would also initiate the most comprehensive and thorough audit ever conducted by the United States to review all Social Security Numbers (SSN) by the Social Security Administration in cooperation with the Immigration and Naturalization Service (INS) and the Immigration and Customs Enforcement (ICE) to assist in the apprehension and deportation of all illegal immigrants, including those from Mexico. The Federal government should make mandatory utilization of the "eVerify" system for all employers of this country to check and verify citizenship and legal status of all the employees or face extremely stiff Federal fines and penalties greater than $25,000 for each illegal alien employee. The Federal government should also immediately verify the employee citizenship status of no less than the top 100 national employers having greater than 100,000 employees, and 100% employment of both the hospitality and food service industries. Fines and penalties would double for employers having more than 10 illegal alien employees.

Fifth, I would immediately suspend all foreign immigration and naturalization to the United States indefinitely, including those from Mexico until which time the national, or largest State unemployment percent rate falls below the unlawful immigrant population percentage rate.

Sixth, using Executive Order and Authoritative action of the President as provided by our United States Constitution, I would indefinitely suspend "habeas corpus" subject to the jurisdiction thereof for all matters relating to U.S. immigration law within the United States to enforce illegal alien deportation. Any legal action whatsoever attempting to prevent illegal immigrant deportation by any Plaintiff or Federal judge would result in the filing of Federal charges for both Obstruction of Justice and Treason.

Seventh, I would unconditionally command the Mexican government's immediate request for the repatriation and return of their country's native residents and citizens who are unlawfully residing within the borders of United States of America.

These seven objective goals will result in a net increase in job creation for black-Americans, military Veterans, and the youth of U.S. citizens. The number one greatest job creation action we as a nation can implement is enforcing our existing immigration and naturalization laws to actively and aggressively increase our foreign national deportation.

It will also increase our badly needed income tax revenue, install greater confidence in our economy, and reduce the overall effects of the related crime and drug trafficking resulting from illegal alien immigration from Mexico. My older brother Kevin would be alive today if our Federal government and corrupt Congress had enforced our existing immigration laws.

It disgusts me to know that every 22 seconds an American Veteran in desperate need of services and medical care commits suicide while our President and Federal government provides over $29 billion annually in Federal aid to illegal aliens, especially criminals from Mexico. Obviously our President prefers illegal aliens to our proud American veterans.

Over 12 million illegal aliens from all over the world are living within the borders of the United States having absolutely no allegiance nor patriotism to our great nation. They are illegally reaping the rewards and benefits paid for with the blood of our American Patriot forefathers and ancestors. It is also clearly obvious they have neither allegiance nor patriotism for there own country because they left. Having no national pride whatsoever in fighting for their own freedom and liberty to make their country a better place for their citizens, they have absolutely no intention of ever doing the same in America.

> "I want to restore our United States Citizenship back to a national privilege, not an unlawful entitlement to criminal foreign nationals." ~Marty Piatt, Architect

You are also invited to visit and join my anti-illegal immigration blog: "No Amnesty, No Immigration Reform" webpage on Facebook.

159

"They're afraid we're going to take over the governmental institutions and other institutions. They're right. We will take them over… We are here to stay." ~Richard Alatorre, Los Angeles City Council

"The American Southwest seems to be slowly returning to the jurisdiction of Mexico without firing a single shot."
~Excelsior, national newspaper of Mexico

"We have an aging white America. They are not making babies. They are dying. We are having babies. The explosion is in our population… I love it. They are shitting in their pants with fear. I love it."
~Jose Angel Gutierrez, Professor, University of Texas

"Remember 187--proposition to deny taxpayer funds for services to non-citizens--was the last gasp of white America in California."
~Art Torres, California Democratic Party Chairman

"We are politicizing every single one of these new citizens that are becoming citizens of this country… I gotta tell you that a lot of people are saying, "I'm going to go out there and vote because I want to pay them back." ~Gloria Molina, Los Angeles County Supervisor

"California is going to be a Hispanic state. Anyone who doesn't like it should leave." ~Mario Obledo, California Coalition of Hispanic Organizations and California State Secretary of Health, Education and Welfare under Governor Jerry Brown, also awarded the Presidential Medal of Freedom by President Bill Clinton

"We are practicing 'La Reconquista' in California"
~Jose Pescador Osuna, Mexican Consul General

"We need to avoid a white backlash by using codes understood by Latino"… ~Fernando Guerra, Professor, Loyola Marymount University

"Go back to Boston! Go back to Plymouth Rock, Pilgrims! Get out! We are the future. You are old and tired. Go on. We have beaten you. Leave like beaten rats. You old white people. It is your duty to die. Through our love of having children, we are going to take over."
~Augustin Cebada, Brown Berets

160

By Marty Piatt, Architect

RELIGION IN AMERICA

"That our civil rights have no dependence on our religious
opinions any more than our opinions in physics or geometry."
~Thomas Jefferson

With the 1559 Act of Uniformity in England, it became illegal not to attend official Church of England services, with a fine laid for each Sunday and holy day missed. The penalties for conducting unofficial services included larger fines in addition to imprisonment. A significant portion of the British population whom did not agree with this religious taxation would flee the country and separate themselves from the Church of England. They would later be known as Separatists, seeking religious freedom. Yet not all of the original American settlers of the British Colonies were men and women having deep religious convictions seeking religious freedom. Many of those who were not religious would flee the country seeking not to practice any form of religion. Refusing to compromise their religious beliefs and passionate convictions in the face of intense European religious persecution, many of the future Colonists would flee all parts of Europe to come to the American New World. This would include the French separatists.

My colonial Piatt ancestors actually originated from France. The Piatt Family (or Pyott), belonging to the French Protestant denomination, would flee France from the religious persecution of the Catholic Church and Vatican, settling in what would be known as the Province of New Jersey. Located between the Delaware and Hudson Rivers, New Jersey would soon become the "Crossroads of the American Revolution". The French Protestant separatists, widely known as the "French Huguenots", would flee the catholic nation beginning in the late 1500's seeking religious freedom in colonial America. Persecution of the Huguenots by the French Catholics would ultimately end in 1787 with the "Edict of Versailles", also known as the "Edict of Tolerance", when signed by Louis XVI, was the Declaration of the Rights of Man and Citizen of 1789 which granted French Protestants equal rights as citizens.

Many of my ancestors originally from New Jersey would later migrate to the great States of Kansas. From there some would migrate to the golden State of California, where my immediate relatives now reside.

The separatists, or Pilgrims as known a century later, became the name commonly applied to the early British settlers of the Plymouth Colony in what is now Plymouth, Massachusetts. The colony's leadership came from the religious congregations of Brownist English Dissenters, devout Separatist followers of Robert Browne. Established in late 1620, Plymouth Colony became the second permanent and most successful of the English settlements, later becoming the oldest continuously inhabited British settlement in American history.

The Pilgrims held "separatist" beliefs similar to the nonconforming movements led by religious activists Robert Browne, Henry Barrowe, and John Greenwood. Unlike the Puritan group who maintained membership and allegiance to the Church of England, the Pilgrim separatists held that their differences with the Church of England were not reconcilable. They believed that their worship should be organized independently of the trappings, traditions, and organization of a central English church. In an attempt to set up a separate Congregational Church in Norwich, Norfolk, England in 1580, Browne was arrested, but later released on the advice of his kinsman, William Cecil. Having become a leader in this movement, he and his followers were forced to leave England and emigrated to Middelburg in the Netherlands in 1581.

In 1593, under the policy of this time, Greenwood and Barrowe were executed for their religious sedition. Fleeing the volatile political environment in England for the relative calm and tolerance of the Netherlands, the congregation later arranged with English investors to establish a new colony in North America after having concerns of losing their cultural identity. The entire congregation was not able to depart as planned. Many members were unable to settle their affairs within the time needed. With a budget for travel and supplies limited, it was decided the younger and stronger members would undertake the initial voyage. The remainder of the congregation would follow at a later date if and when it was possible. With the congregation's personal and business matters agreed upon, a small ship and supplies were acquired. The first ship, the "Speedwell", was scheduled to transport a portion of the congregation from the Netherlands back to England, and then sail on to America. The Speedwell would then be kept for a fishing business with a crew hired for supporting services during the first year after reaching America. Her Master, John Chappell, captained the Speedwell, which was a 60-ton English galleon vessel.

By Marty Piatt, Architect

A second and much larger vessel, the "Mayflower", was later leased for transport and exploration services. Her Master, Christopher Jones, captained the Mayflower, a 180-ton Dutch cargo fluyt, with a contingent of between 25 and 35 crewmembers having an approximate 135 passenger capacity.

In July 1620, the Speedwell departed the Netherlands for England. Sailing back to England, they were to meet with the Mayflower and the additional colonists hired by the investors. In August, with final arrangements made, the two vessels set out for North America.

Soon thereafter, the Speedwell crew reported that their ship was leaking and taking on water. Both ships were diverted to Dartmouth, Devon. There the Speedwell was inspected for leaks, sealed and repaired, and made ready for sea. Now thought to be seaworthy, a second voyage by the Speedwell to depart to America was unsuccessful. The two ships having sailed only as far as Plymouth, Devon, the Speedwell was determined to be untrustworthy and sold.

It was later presumed that Speedwell's crewmembers had deliberately caused the ship to leak, allowing them to abandon their yearlong commitment. The ship's Master and some of the crew then transferred to Mayflower for the voyage to America. Of the original 121 total passengers of the two ships, only 102 were chosen to sail on the Mayflower with their supplies consolidated. Of these, about 28 of the adults were members of the congregation.

In September 1620, the greatly reduced contingent finally sailed successfully. Initially the voyage went smoothly. While under way, the Mayflower was met with strong winds and storms that caused a main beam to crack. Although they were more than half the way to their destination, the possibility of turning back was still a possible consideration. The crew was able to repair the ship sufficiently to continue using what was thought to be a "great iron screw" brought along by the colonist passengers.

During the voyage, one child was born, and one crewmember and one passenger died before reaching America. One passenger, John Howland, was thought washed overboard in the storm but managed to grab a topsail halyard that was trailing in the water and was hauled back aboard safely.

On November 9, 1620 land was finally sighted off the coast of Cape Cod. The passengers who had endured miserable conditions for about 65 days were lead by William Bruster in Psalm 100 as a prayer of "Thanksgiving". It was confirmed that the area of Cape Cod was within the New England territory. In an attempt to sail around the cape towards the Hudson River, also within the New England grant area, they encountered shoals and currents around a landmass formerly existing in the vicinity of what is known today as "Monomoy Island". With winter quickly approaching and provisions running dangerously low, the crew and passengers decided to return north and abandon their original landing plans.

On November 11, 1620, the Mayflower was anchored in what is today known as Provincetown Harbor, Massachusetts. Not having a patent to settle this area, some passengers questioned their right to land; their concern was that there was no legal authority to establish a colony at that location. To address this issue, a group of colonists, while still onboard as it lay anchored offshore, drafted the first governing document of the colony, known as the "Mayflower Compact". Promising cooperation among the settlers "for the general good of the Colony unto which we promise all due submission and obedience", it organized them into what was called a "civil Body Politick", in which issues would be decided by voting, the main ingredient of democracy.

The Mayflower Compact, referred to as America's, or the world's, first written Constitution, was the actual seed of our American democracy, and was not the seed of American theocracy as some would claim. The Mayflower Compact was ratified by majority rule, with 41 adult male passengers signing. The intent of the Mayflower Compact was to establish a means of governing the colony, which did little more than confirm that the colony would be governed like any other English town and served its original purpose of relieving the concerns of many of the settlers still on board the ship.

On November 13, 1620, the colonists finally set foot on land at what would later become Provincetown, Massachusetts. John Carver was chosen as the colony's first governor. It was Carver who had chartered the Mayflower, and being the most respected and affluent member of the group, his was the first signature on the Mayflower Compact.

By Marty Piatt, Architect

The location in Cape Cod Bay settled by the Plymouth Colony was outside the territory of the London Company, which had granted its patent. Having failed to secure a proper site for their settlement after three separate exploratory expeditions, the Mayflower left Provincetown Harbor and set sail for Plymouth Harbor. The northern coastal territory had been granted to the Plymouth Company, but this patent fell into disuse and was reorganized under a sea-to-sea charter under the Plymouth Council for New England. The actual Plymouth Colony would obtain land patents from the Plymouth Council in 1621 and 1630, and was governed independently from the Council under the Mayflower Compact.

On December 17, 1620 the Mayflower dropped anchor in Plymouth Harbor. Spending three days surveying for a settlement site, they rejected several sites, including one on Clark's Island and another at the mouth of the Jones River, in favor of a recently abandoned Native American settlement named Patuxet. The location was chosen largely for its defensive position; the settlement would be centered on two hills, Cole's Hill, where the village would be built, and Fort Hill, where a defensive cannon could be stationed. Another important factor in choosing the site was that prior Indian inhabitants had cleared much of the land, making agriculture much easier. Fresh water for the colony was provided by Town Brook and Billington Sea.

Although there are no contemporary accounts to verify the legend, Plymouth Rock is often hailed as the point where the colonists first set foot on their new homeland. The location of the colonists' settlement had been previously identified as "New Plymouth" in maps published by John Smith in 1614. The colonists decided to retain the name for their own settlement after their final point of departure from Plymouth, Devon, England. Settlement construction began immediately, with the first common structure nearly completed by January 1621. At that time, single men were ordered to join with families. Each extended family was assigned a plot and built its own dwelling. Supplies were brought ashore, and by early February 1621, the settlement was mostly complete.

Unfortunately, between the Mayflower landing and March 1621, only 47 colonists had survived. During this period, half the Mayflower crew also died. Upon the death of John Carver on April 5, 1621, William Bradford became governor serving for eleven consecutive years, and was elected to various other terms until his death in 1657.

Bradford surrendered the patent of Plymouth Colony to the freemen in 1640, less a small reserve of three parcels of land. When the Massachusetts Bay Colony was reorganized and issued a new charter as the Province of Massachusetts Bay in 1691, Plymouth Colony ended its history as a separate British colony.

The other colonies of New Jersey, Pennsylvania, and Maryland were conceived and established "as plantations of religion". Surges of ethnic groups from Europe and other parts of the world brought their traditional churches to the colonies. Some colonists, especially the English and the German, brought with them multiple Protestant denominations, in addition to Catholicism. The English Protestants, known as Puritans, wished to reform and purify the Church of England of what they considered to be unacceptable residues of Roman Catholicism. Zealous Puritans received savage punishments for their religious nonconformance in England.

Later in the 1620s, growing increasingly unsympathetic to Puritan demands, the leaders of the English state and church insisted that they conform to religious practices that they abhorred. Removing their ministers from office and threatening them with "extirpation from the earth", the Puritans did not acquiesce.

Beginning in 1630, as many as twenty thousand Puritans emigrated from England to the British colonies in America to gain the freedom to worship as they so chose, and most settled in New England.

The Puritan colonists were theologically "non-separating Congregationalists". Unlike the Separatist Pilgrims who previously ventured to Massachusetts ten years earlier, the Puritans believed that the "Church of England", however in need of major reforms, was their true church. Beholden to no hierarchy, each and every Congregational church in the Colonies was considered an independent entity. Several colonies had an "established" church, meaning that local tax revenues went to the established religious denomination. Generally speaking, even though the Colonial governments were not involved in religion, many of the religious denominations flourished.

Former Puritan leader Roger Williams, expelled from Massachusetts in the winter in 1636, issued an impassioned plea for freedom of conscience.

Williams wrote: "God requireth not an uniformity of Religion to be inacted and enforced in any civill state; which inforced uniformity [sooner or later] is the greatest occasion of civill Warre, ravishing of conscience, persecution of Christ Jesus in his servants, and of the hypocrisie and destruction of millions of souls." Williams, a Baptist theologian, is thought to have first used the phrase "a hedge or wall of separation between the garden of the church and the wilderness of the world". Williams later founded the colony Rhode Island on the principle of religious freedom, welcoming all people of religious belief, even those regarded as dangerously misguided; nothing could change his view believing "forced worship stinks in God's nostrils".

In 1682, William Penn, an English Quaker, drafted the first version of the Frame of Government of Pennsylvania, a Constitution for the Province of Pennsylvania, a proprietary colony granted to William Penn by Charles II of England. Penn, while still residing in England, sought to construct a new type of society in America with religious toleration and a great deal of freedom.

The Frame of Government of was created to supplement the colony's royal charter. Freedom of worship in the colony was to be absolute. All the traditional rights of Englishmen were also carefully safeguarded. Having lasting historical importance, The Frame of Government was yet another step in the future development of colonial American democracy. The colony's' legislature did not approve Penn's First Frame, but they finally accepted an amended version in 1693.

The Frame of Government incorporated very progressive ideas for its time period. The First Frame protected many rights and liberties including trial by jury, freedom of the press, and religious toleration. More so than any otherworld societies at the time, the use of the death penalty was much more limited in colonial Pennsylvania. Having four Frames, Penn drafted the Fourth Frame in 1701, also known as the Pennsylvania Charter of Privileges, or Charter of Liberties. The forging and making of our Liberty Bell was in response to the celebration of the fiftieth anniversary of the Fourth Frame of Government. Thereafter, freedom of religion became a basic American principle. The Separatists Pilgrims' and Protestant Puritans' stories and history of seeking religious freedom has become a central theme of the political and religious historical culture within the United States of America.

In 1777, Thomas Jefferson wrote within the Virginia Statute for Religious Freedom:

"That our civil rights have no dependence on our religious opinions any more than our opinions in physics or geometry".

This view has become a timeless cause for separating church and state. The Statute for Religious Freedom also supported the Establishment Clause and Free Exercise Clause of the First Amendment of our U.S. Constitution, and the freedom of conscience.

A treaty of peace and friendship between the United States and Tripoli that was approved by President George Washington explicitly stated:

"The government of the United States is not in any sense founded on the Christian religion."

American diplomat Joel Barlow negotiated this treaty during the administration of George Washington, although the senate did not ratify the treaty until John Adams had become President.

In 1802, during his first term as president, Thomas Jefferson declared his firm belief in the separation of church and state writing the following:

"Believing with you that religion is a matter which lies solely between man and his God, that he owes account to none other for his faith or his worship, that the legislative powers of government reach actions only and not opinions, I contemplate with sovereign reverence that act of the whole American people which declared that their legislature should 'make no law respecting an establishment of religion, or prohibiting the free exercise thereof,' thus building a wall of separation between church and state."

This reference by Thomas Jefferson in a letter to the Danbury, Conn. Baptists Association mirrored nearly an exact quote by Baptist theologian Roger Williams describing "a hedge or wall of separation between the garden of the church and the wilderness of the world". The heavy influx of immigration in the 19th and 20th century reinvigorated religion; and in many cases, the immigrants became much more religious than they had been in their native country asserting their new religious identities.

By Marty Piatt, Architect

As Europe became much more secularized in the twentieth century, our American society has largely resisted this trend and actually appears to be heading in the alternative opposite direction. So much so, that now in the twenty first century, the United States has become perhaps one of the most religious-persecuting of all the world's major nations, having religiously based moral issues, such as abortion and same-sex marriage, occupying the major two most socially-divisive topics in current American politics.

Having evolved from a prior historical era wanting to escape their religious persecution, it appears obvious to me that the far-right Christian conservative Republican Party is now leading the defiant and divisive trend of religious-persecuting. The far-right Christian conservatives call the far-right Muslims crazy fanatics, yet there is really no differentiating dissimilarity in their wanting to cede their religious beliefs into our American society, not unlike the Muslim extremists of Islam wanting a theocracy in Middle Eastern society. Equal to the Middle Eastern countries practicing the religion of Islam, I believe that the American Christian conservatives are nearly as zealous as their Middle Eastern Muslim counterparts.

The fundamentalist Muslim extremists would also prefer their Islam "Sharia" theocracy law in place in world societies. Sharia law is the moral code and religious law of Islam. Muslims believe Sharia is God's law dealing with crime, politics and economics, as well as personal matters such as sexual intercourse, hygiene, diet, prayer, and fasting; many of the same or similar topics addressed by secular, non-religious law. The reference to the Sharia law of Islam is traced directly to the Quran, wherein the adherents of Islam, the believers, are admonished by Allah [God] to follow the clear and right way, the path of Sharia: "Then we put thee on the [right] Way of religion so follow thou that [Way], and follow not the desires of those who know not." [Quran 45:18].

Because the religion of Islam, which is the only religion having no tolerance for non-believers or "Infidels", and imposes the threat of death for all those that do not believe, I would suggest that the practice of Islam in the United States of America should be unconstitutional. Our country's right to Freedom of Religion also protects Atheists and those who choose not to practice any form of religion whatsoever, including Islam.

The Christian conservatives would like prayer back in schools, the Ten Commandments posted in every Courthouse, amendments added to our Constitution prohibiting abortion and same-sex marriage, and to prohibit gay service members from joining the military wanting to defend a Constitution that grants us all personal liberties that do not protect their own 1st and 5th amendment rights, just to name just a few ideals.

We have fanatic Christian conservatives that bomb abortion clinics and kill doctors that perform abortions. The same like-minded parents who teach their children hate and intolerance of others perpetuating the civil injustice of discrimination. Unlike other human genetic attributes, hate and discrimination are taught, not inherited. I believe religion is the single most dividing aspect and factor in American society today. Instead of spreading love and tolerance as Jesus did, the far-right Christian conservatives are tearing at the fabric of our society that weaves us together as one unique and beautiful tapestry.

Before addressing the topics of women's reproductive rights and marriage equality, I would like to testify to my personal beliefs of religion, and how they relate to our American government, politics, and society.

I believe in a higher power, a divine entity and creator of our universe, the supreme Architect of all life. I believe in evolution; the world was not created in seven days.

I did not exist prior to birth, and I may not exist after death. I cannot honestly say for certainty that there is a heaven or a hell. I would like to believe that good people go to a better place we believe is heaven, and that bad people go to a terrible place we know as hell.

I do not know that, if hell does exist, it will be burning fire and brimstone of eternal damnation; or utter darkness and eternal solitude away from the light and love of God. I don't know if both heaven and hell are actually here on earth.

I believe that all energy is conserved; neither created nor lost, which is a fundamental law of physics and the universe.

I believe in karma; good things happen to good people, and bad things happen to bad people, a fundamental law of life and the universe.

I am Christian. Jesus Christ shed his blood on the cross giving his life for all so that we might have eternal salvation in his death. I believe in the holy trinity, God the father, God the son, and God the Holy Spirit. Unlike some religions, I believe this single defining aspect of the Holy Trinity is the basis and fundamental foundation of Christianity.

I am a sinner, yet saved through the blood of Jesus Christ, our savior. Not unlike other sinners, I have my transgressions that our heavenly Father and Jesus Christ has forgiven.

Judge me not on my actions or past, but rather on these words and the future I envision. A future we share together.

"For all have sinned and fall short of the glory of God."
~The Bible, [Romans 3:23]

"He that is without sin among you, let him cast the first stone."
~Jesus Christ, The Bible, [John 8:7]

"Judge not, lest you be judged."
~The Bible, [Matthew 7:1]

I have a fundamental tolerance of all world religions. However, I find it very interesting that the number one reason for war and death in our world's history is the result of our differences relating to religion, and the dividing aspects of religion.

Centuries of religious beliefs have not solved world hunger nor brought us world peace.

In Judaism, you are either Jew or gentile.

In Islam, you are either Muslim or infidel.

In Christianity, you are either a believer or a sinner.

There seems to be no middle ground or common understanding except that there is only one Creator; One entity with many names such as: YHWH (pronounced YA-WAY), God, Allah, Jehovah, Elaha, Gitche Manitou, Vishnu, etc.

171

Let me begin with the first topic, that of women's reproductive rights. The current legal standing of abortion is that the procedure is legal. Based upon the Supreme Court case of Roe v. Wade, 410 U.S. 113 [1973] concerning the issue of abortion, the ultimate landmark court ruling was an extremely controversial decision by the United States Supreme Court, debated even until this day. Writing for the majority, the opinion of Justice Harry Andrew Blackmun decided that a women's right to privacy under the due process clause in the Fourteenth Amendment to the United States Constitution extends to her decision to have an abortion.

But the Court also asserted that that right must be balanced against the state's two legitimate interests for regulating abortions: protecting prenatal life and protecting the woman's health. The Court resolved this balancing test by tying state regulations of abortion to the woman's current trimester of pregnancy, saying that these state interests become stronger over the course of a pregnancy. Later rejecting Roe's trimester framework, the Supreme Court, affirmed Roe's central holding that a person has a right to abortion up until viability. Deeming abortion a fundamental right under the United States Constitution, the Supreme Court thereby subjected all laws attempting to restrict abortion to the standard of "strict scrutiny".

In June 1969, Jane Roe, the alias given to Norma McCorvey, discovered that she was pregnant. This pregnancy would result in her having a third child. Her friends advised her to falsely claim that she had been raped. She would then be able to obtain a lawful abortion, with the understanding that Texas' anti-abortion laws allowed abortion in the cases of rape and incest. The ruling in Roe's favor on the merits of the case, the District Court declined to grant an injunction against the enforcement of the Texas laws barring abortion.

The District Court's decision was based upon the Ninth Amendment, relying on a concurring opinion in the 1965 Supreme Court case of Griswold v. Connecticut, regarding a right to use contraceptives.

Griswold v. Connecticut, 381 U.S. 479 [1965], was another landmark case which the Supreme Court ruled that the Ninth Amendment to the Constitution protected a women's right to privacy. Connecticut law had prohibited the use of contraceptives. By a vote of 7-2, the Supreme Court invalidated the law on the grounds that it violated the "right to marital privacy".

By Marty Piatt, Architect

Although the Bill of Rights does not explicitly mention "privacy", with the exception of the Fourth Amendment where I personally believe it is inferred, Justice William Douglas wrote for the majority that a person's right to privacy was found in the "penumbras" and "emanations" of other constitutional protections. A similar companion case, Doe v. Bolton, 410 U.S. 179 [1973], was yet another landmark decision of the Supreme Court overturning an abortion law of Georgia. The Supreme Court's decision was released on January 22, 1973, the very same day as the decision in the much better known case of Roe v. Wade. The same 7-2 majority that struck down a Texas abortion law in Roe v. Wade invalidated most of the remaining restrictions of the Georgia abortion law; also basing the ruling upon the violation of the Fourteenth Amendment.

A more recent case study, Stenberg v. Carhart, 530 U.S. 914 [2000], dealing with a Nebraska law which made performing partial-birth abortion illegal, except where necessary to save the life of the mother, was heard by the United States Supreme Court. This case dealt with pre-viability second trimester abortions; in which most abortions occur during the first trimester. Not unlike other states, Nebraska banned the procedure on the basis of public morality. Finding that the Nebraska statute criminalizing "partial birth abortion[s]" violated the due process clause of the Fourteenth Amendment, as interpreted in both the Planned Parenthood v. Casey and Roe v. Wade cases, the Supreme Court again struck down the law.

While defending another abortion case, Thornburgh v. American College of Obstetricians and Gynecologists, 476 U.S. 747 [1986], a Supreme Court case involving a challenge to Pennsylvania's Abortion Control Act of 1982, Justice Harry Andrew Blackmun wrote the following:

"Few decisions are more personal and intimate, more properly private, or more basic to individual dignity and autonomy, than a woman's decision – with the guidance of her physician and within the limits specified in Roe – whether to end her pregnancy. A woman's right to make that choice freely is fundamental..."

All these Supreme Court rulings are based on one common theme, a women's right to privacy; regardless of whether they are based on the Fourth, Ninth, or Fourteenth Amendment to the Constitution; affirming a women's right of choice.

I am personally against abortion. There is nothing more precious than life itself. I am particularly against late-term and partial-birth abortions. Partially birthing a baby, only to then evacuate its brain, when one additional vaginal push would deliver the child, is barbaric. However, that being said, I also lack the personal possession of a vagina. Therefore, my opinion means little. A woman's right to privacy and her right to reproductive choice far exceed my personal feelings and objections to this very divisive and private issue. So, I am equally both pro-life and pro-choice.

From a religious standpoint, the Bible states Adam was created by God from the dust of the earth and given life and a soul upon his first breathe. From the Old Testament of the Bible, the first book of Genesis, the second chapter, the seventh verse reads:

"Then the Lord God formed man of the dust of the ground, and breathed into his nostrils the breath of life; and man became a living soul." ~The Bible, [Genesis 2:7]

Based upon the Bible, the literal meaning of creation was that there was no "life or soul" prior to Adam's first breathe.

In addition, the actual conception of man and woman occurred in the previous first chapter of Genesis, verses 26 and 27 that both read:

"And God said: Let us make man in our image, after our likeness; and let them have dominion over the fish of the sea, and over the fowl of the air, and over the cattle, and over all the earth, and over every creeping thing that creepeth upon the earth."

"And God created man in His own image, in the image of God created He him; male and female created He them."

Based upon the Bible, the literal meaning of these verses is that there was no "life or soul" upon conceiving or conception. Yet, the Christian conservatives wish to believe that life begins at conception to perpetuate their unwavering moral objection to abortion. The very beginning of human life is also very subjective.

174

By Marty Piatt, Architect

What troubles me the most is that those opposing abortion unfortunately continue to persistently focus on the physical act of the abortion medical procedure itself, rather than the resulting actions and behavior that are actually responsible for the unwanted pregnancy. The Christian conservatives continually fail to address the matter of "abortive accountability", which I find to be an abomination.

I can think of no greater morally apprehensible and disgusting act, behavior, or circumstance than that of irresponsible heterosexual sexual relations leading to an unwanted pregnancy and abortion. In this day and age, pregnancy is absolutely preventable. To think that in the twenty-first century heterosexual couples have "chosen" to use abortion as birth control, is truly the only immoral abomination that exists in American society today. These are the same Christian conservatives that also appear to favor capital punishment, the taking of another life. I for one, support capital punishment; particularly in the case of parents murdering their own living children, those that rely solely on their parents for life, love, health, and security. Yet, no matter how heinous the crime, justifying the killing another human being is another profound and morally subjective situation.

"Thou shalt not kill." This commandment is stated twice in the Bible, both in Exodus 20:13 and Deuteronomy 5:17

As stated in many instances earlier, we possess a Constitution that specifically infers the separation of church and state, in any situation. Article VI of our Constitution also states: "no religious test shall ever be required…" implying yet another establishment of the separation of church and state in our Constitution. Any religious-based moral judgments and opinions with respect to abortion have absolutely no basis nor precedent in establishing justification for its prohibition, period.

Supreme Court Justice Hugo Black wrote in 1947 a majority opinion of the court:

"Neither [state nor federal government] can force nor influence a person to go to or to remain away from church against his will or force [them] to profess a belief or disbelief in any religion. No person can be punished for entertaining or professing religious beliefs or disbeliefs."

The issue of abortion cannot and must not be defined in any way that uses religious belief to punish those that are non-believers. This nation cannot justify taking any action or inflicting punishment upon any individual that may or may not have religious-based moral values.

Let me finish this chapter with the second and final topic of marriage equality. Many of the same justifications used against abortion are concurrently being indiscriminately applied by Christian conservatives in opposition to same-sex marriage, that of many religious moral beliefs.

To begin the discussion of marriage, the accepted definition of marriage should be established. Generally speaking, marriage is a legal or social contract between two consenting individuals creating an interpersonal union. Marriage can be either a civil or religious institution; in which the interpersonal relationship is acknowledged in numerous ways; usually being sexual and intimate in nature, depending on the culture or subculture in which it is established.

Marriage is generally recognized by both a religious authority and the State. Often viewed as a contract in accordance with marriage laws of the jurisdiction, civil marriage is the legal concept as a governmental institution irrespective of any religious affiliation, for Constitutional reasons. Individuals may marry for a variety of reasons including: legal, social, sexual, emotional, economic, religious, and spiritual purposes.

Individual's intentions for marriage may include a devote love of another, a public declaration of interpersonal commitment, legal protection of children, obligations establishing a traditional family unit, and even pre-arranged marriages. The act of marriage generally creates normative or legal obligations between the individuals involved. Some religions permit the dissolution of marriage through divorce or annulment.

As an institution, marriage has historically included restrictions; those being age, race, social status, consanguinity, or gender. Marriage restrictions are placed on society for numerous reasons that may benefit offspring, passing on a healthy genome to their children, maintaining distinctive cultural values, or as a result of discrimination based on fear, prejudice, and intolerance; the latter being the case for interracial and same-sex marriage.

By Marty Piatt, Architect

There is a history of discrimination in the United States having marriage restriction laws. Many of the states enacted miscegenation laws that were initially enacted in the slave-holding Colonies during the late 17th century. The legal prohibition of interracial marriage was first introduced in 1691 in Virginia, and in 1692 in Maryland, with marriage discrimination in these states lasting well into the 20th century until 1967.

Many of these states restricted many racial minorities from marrying white people. Most notably, Alabama, Arkansas, and Oklahoma banned blacks in particular. Other states including Mississippi and Missouri banned both blacks and Asians. North Carolina and South Carolina banned both blacks and Native American Indians. Georgia, South Carolina, and Virginia banned all non-white interracial marriage.

In the 1964 landmark case of McLaughlin v. Florida 379 U.S. 184, the United States Supreme Court unanimously ruled that a cohabitation law that was part of Florida's anti-miscegenation laws was unconstitutional. The Florida law prohibited habitual cohabitation by two unmarried people of opposite sex, if one is black, and the other is white. In its historic ruling, the Supreme Court thereby overturned the 1883 case of Pace v. Alabama, which had previously declared such discriminatory statutes as constitutional. Section 798.05 of Florida statute read:

"Any negro man and white woman, or any white man and negro woman, who are not married to each other, who shall habitually live in and occupy in the nighttime the same room shall each be punished by imprisonment not exceeding twelve months, or by fine not exceeding five hundred dollars."

This statute section was a part of the Adultery and Fornication laws of Florida, which were penalized by Chapter 798. While all the other sections of this chapter required proof that sexual intercourse took place, section 798.05 required only that cohabitation had occurred. Moreover, the law specifically prohibits a couple in which one is white and the other is black. It did not apply where one was black, and the other, for instance, was Native American. As such, it was part of Florida's anti-miscegenation laws, which prohibited marriage, cohabitation and extramarital sex between whites and blacks. Like all such state laws, it only concerned itself with relationships between whites and non-whites.

The Supreme Court found "That a general evil will be partially corrected may at times, and without more, serve to justify the limited application of a criminal law; but legislative discretion to employ the piecemeal approach stops short of permitting a State to narrow statutory coverage to focus on a racial group". Because the Florida law had not demonstrated any reason that made such race-specific prohibition necessary, the Supreme Court held the law had made a special case for couples of these two specific races.

The Florida law, which bore a "heavier burden of justification", resulted in the law having been held unconstitutional. However it must be noted, the Supreme Court in its decision did not overturn a related Florida statute that had prohibited interracial marriage between blacks and whites, which was not at issue or as a matter of fact in the case, even though the state had claimed that Section 798.05 was ancillary to it. The statute prohibiting marriage between whites and blacks was also part of Florida's anti-miscegenation laws [Fl. St. Ann. 741.11]. This and other similar state laws were later declared unconstitutional in yet another very important landmark Supreme Court decision involving the 1967 case of Loving v. Virginia.

The case of Loving v. Virginia, 388 U.S. 1 [1967] was a landmark civil rights case in which a unanimous decision by United States Supreme Court declared as unconstitutional Virginia's "Racial Integrity Act of 1924", an anti-miscegenation statute; thereby overturning the 1883 case of Pace v. Alabama in its entirety, thereby finally eliminating all legal race-based marriage restrictions in all of the United States of America.

In a unanimous decision dated June 12, 1967 the U.S. Supreme Court overturned the criminal convictions of Richard and Mildred Loving; dismissing the Commonwealth of Virginia's argument that their law forbidding both white and black persons from marrying persons of another race while providing identical penalties to both white and black violators, could not be construed as racially discriminatory. The plaintiffs, Mildred Delores Jeter, a woman of both African and Rappahannock Native American descent and Richard Perry Loving, a white man, were residents of Caroline County, within the Commonwealth of Virginia. In June 1958 the couple had married in the District of Columbia, having left Virginia to evade the Racial Integrity Act, a state law that banned interracial marriages between white persons and any non-white persons.

Upon their return to Virginia, the couple was charged with violating the interracial-marriage ban. The Loving's were found sleeping together in their bedroom by a group of police officers that had invaded their home in the hopes of finding them in the act of sexual intercourse; which was another crime within the ban. In their defense, Mrs. Loving had pointed to a marriage certificate on their bedroom wall. As a result, the marriage certificate became affirmative evidence that the police needed for a criminal charge to be filed, proving that they had been married in another state. The Loving's were specifically charged under Section 20-58 of the Virginia Code, which prohibited interracial couples from being married out of state and then returning to Virginia. Section 20-59, which classified "miscegenation" as a felony, was punishable by a prison sentence of between one and five years.

On January 6, 1959, the Loving's pled guilty and were sentenced to one year in prison, with the sentence suspended for 25 years on condition that the couple leave the State of Virginia. The trial judge in the Loving case, Leon M. Bazile, a devote "religious" and apparently bigoted man, proclaimed that:

"Almighty God created the races white, black, yellow, malay and red, and he placed them on separate continents. And but for the interference with his arrangement there would be no cause for such marriages. The fact that he separated the races shows that he did not intend for the races to mix." Judge Leon M. Bazile's discriminatory biased and racially motivated court ruling reflects a common religious moral rationale having similar precedent in others matters today. Judge Bazile's ruling mimicked an 18th-century statement of Johann Friedrich Blumenbach declaring:

"Finally, I am of opinion that after all these numerous instances I have brought together of negroes of capacity, it would not be difficult to mention entire well-known provinces of Europe, from out of which you would not easily expect to obtain off-hand such good authors, poets, philosophers, and correspondents of the Paris Academy; and on the other hand, there is no so-called savage nation known under the sun which has so much distinguished itself by such examples of perfectibility and original capacity for scientific culture, and thereby attached itself so closely to the most civilized nations of the earth, as the Negro."

The Loving's later moved to the District of Columbia.

On November 6, 1963, the American Civil Liberties Union filed a motion on their behalf in the state trial court asking Judge Bazile to vacate his judgment and set aside the sentence on the grounds that the violated statutes were unconstitutional according to the Fourteenth Amendment. They appealed when he refused. The Virginia Supreme Court of Appeals upheld the lower court's decision, and the case ultimately reached the Supreme Court of the United States.

The Supreme Court ultimately ruled that Virginia's anti-miscegenation statute violated both the Due Process Clause and the Equal Protection Clause of the Fourteenth Amendment.

In its historic decision, the Supreme Court wrote:

"Marriage is one of the 'basic civil rights of man', fundamental to our very existence and survival. To deny this fundamental freedom on so unsupportable a basis as the racial classifications embodied in these statutes, classifications so directly subversive of the principle of equality at the heart of the Fourteenth Amendment, is surely to deprive all the State's citizens of liberty without due process of law. The Fourteenth Amendment requires that the freedom of choice to marry not be restricted by invidious racial discrimination. Under our Constitution, the freedom to marry, or not marry, a person of another race resides with the individual and cannot be infringed by the State."

The Supreme Court also decided that state anti-miscegenation laws were racist and had been enacted to perpetuate "white supremacy".

The Supreme Court also declared in its decision that:

"There is patently no legitimate overriding purpose independent of invidious racial discrimination which justifies this classification. The fact that Virginia prohibits only interracial marriages involving white persons demonstrates that the racial classifications must stand on their own justification, as measures designed to maintain White Supremacy."

Forty-four years after the Loving v. Virginia ruling by the United States Supreme Court invalidating all anti-miscegenation laws, this country is now divided over another civil rights issue; that involving same-sex marriage.

The actual definition of "miscegenation" comes from the Latin words "miscere", meaning "to mix", and "genus", meaning "kind". Conversely, it must be distinguished that the word "gender" is actually derived from the Latin "genus", as is the root of "genre". Specifically, the meaning of "genus" more appropriately defines and refers to "gender", rather than race or nationality. Consequently, the realistic root meanings of "miscegenation" can have an inference of both racial- and gender-based meanings with either relating to marriage discrimination. The discrimination of gender-biased marriage also remains as anti-miscegenation in its basis and foundation as was racial-based marriage discrimination. Therefore, in this context, all laws prohibiting same-sex marriage should also be deemed unconstitutional under the very same precedent and legally disputed rationale used against racial anti-miscegenation marriage.

On May 20, 1996 in the landmark case of Romer v. Evans, 517 U.S. 620 [1996], an amendment to the Colorado state constitution entitled "Amendment 2" that was ruled to be unconstitutional. This was the first Supreme Court case to deal with same-sex civil rights. It would have prevented any city, town or county in the State of Colorado from taking any legislative, executive, or judicial action to recognize homosexual citizens as a "protected class". Voters in Colorado passed the referendum to their constitution. Rejecting the argument that "Amendment 2" blocked gay people from receiving "special rights", Justice Anthony Kennedy wrote for the court's majority:

"To the contrary, the amendment imposes a special disability upon those persons alone. Homosexuals are forbidden the safeguards that others enjoy or may seek without constraint."

The amendment was in violation of the equal protection clause of the Fourteenth Amendment to the U.S. Constitution. Kennedy also argued that protection offered by anti-discrimination laws were not "special rights" because they protected fundamental rights already enjoyed by all other citizens. This ruling set the stage for the Supreme Court ruling of Lawrence v. Texas involving anti-sodomy laws.

On June 26, 2003, in the landmark case of Lawrence v. Texas, 539 U.S. 558 [2003], the United States Supreme Court struck down a law that prohibited consensual same-sex sexual activity, specifically sodomy.

181

In a 6-3 ruling, by proxy, the court invalidated all remaining consensual same-sex sexual activity laws in the thirteen other states, thereby declaring same-sex sexual activity legal in every state and territory of the United States. This decision overruled an identical issue previously addressed the in the 1986 Bowers v. Hardwick case, where the Supreme Court upheld a challenge to the Georgia statute, not finding a constitutional protection of sexual privacy, declaring the court had previously viewed the liberty interest too narrowly. The majority now held that intimate consensual sexual conduct was part of the Liberty protected by substantive due process under the Fourteenth Amendment.

The case also had the effect of invalidating similar laws throughout the United States that purport to criminalize sodomy between consenting opposite-sex adults having consensual sexual activity in private.

In the case of Perry v. Schwarzenegger [also known as Perry v. Brown on appeal], a Federal lawsuit was filed in the United States District Court for the Northern District of California in which the constitutionality of "Proposition 8" was challenged. The suit seeks to strike down Proposition 8 as unconstitutional. The United States Supreme Court will eventually rule on the miscegenation issue of same-sex marriage in Perry v. Schwarzenegger originating from the State of California.

Proposition 8 was a November 4, 2008 ballot initiative and Constitutional amendment that was approved by California voters thereby amending the California Constitution to legally restrict marriage to opposite-sex couples only, in so doing prohibiting the State of California from recognizing all same-sex marriages performed on or after November 5, 2008.

The Proposition 8 ballot initiative was a result of the previous March 2000 ballot initiative known as "Proposition 22" that was invalidated by the Supreme Court of California in May 2008.

Proposition 22, also known as the California Defense of Marriage Act, was an initiative law enacted by voters in California to restrict marriages to only opposite-sex couples, thus prohibiting same-sex marriage. Numerous challenges to the constitutionality of the opposite-sex requirements found in California's marriage statutes, including Proposition 22, were brought before California courts.

Marriage as defined in Section 4100 of the California Civil Code prior to 1977, stated that marriage is: "a personal relation arising out of a civil contract, to which consent of the parties making that contract is necessary". The legal definition of marriage was later moved from the Civil Code to Section 300 of the Family Code in 1992 and the legislature amended the legal definition of marriage to remove any perceived ambiguity. A separate provision of the Family Code conversely governed recognition of marriages contracted elsewhere even though the definition governing who may marry in California explicitly precluded contracting a same-sex marriage.

Section 308 stated that a "marriage contracted outside this state that would be valid by the laws of the jurisdiction in which the marriage was contracted is valid in this state". In forcing California to recognize the validly of a same-sex marriage contracted in another state, advocates of Proposition 22 perceived Section 308 of the Family Code as a legal "loophole".

Prior to Proposition 22 being brought before California voters, marriage was defined in the Family Code as "a personal relation arising out of a civil contract between a man and a woman, to which the consent of the parties capable of making that contract is necessary." A San Francisco trial court later threw out all of the gender requirements on state constitutional grounds. On appeal, an intermediate court reversed the trial court's decision. Voting unanimously to review all six cases in December 2006, the California Supreme Court consolidated the cases as "In re Marriage Cases" and later on March 4, 2008 held oral arguments in the case.

On May 15, 2008, the California Supreme Court subsequently ruled that the Proposition 22 approved by California voters was in violation the Constitution of California and therefore was illegal and thus invalided.

Having a history of invalidating legislative discrimination in California, it must be noted that on October 1, 1948 in the case of Perez v. Sharp, the Supreme Court of California also recognized that interracial bans on marriage violated the Fourteenth Amendment of our Constitution. The court's opinion was the first of any state in the nation to strike down an anti-miscegenation law.

Proposition 8, which had the ballot title: Eliminates Rights of Same-Sex Couples to Marry, Initiative Constitutional Amendment; added the new provision, Section 7.5 of the Declaration of Rights, to the California Constitution, which provides that "only marriage between a man and a woman is valid or recognized in California". Its proponents also called the measure the "California Marriage Protection Act".

Proposition 8 voter approval overturned the California Supreme Court's ruling of "In re Marriage Cases" that same-sex couples have a constitutional right to marry in restricting the recognition of marriage to opposite-sex couples. As a Constitutional amendment, the wording of Proposition 8 was exactly the same that had been found in the previous Proposition 22, which was an ordinary statute. California's State Constitution put Proposition 8 into immediate effect the day after the election. Domestic partnerships in California and same-sex marriages performed prior to November 5, 2008 were left unaffected by the passage of Proposition 8.

After passage of Proposition 8, a legal challenge appealing the passage was filed with the Supreme Court of California.

The case of Strauss v. Horton was a consolidation of three separate lawsuits resulting from the passage of Proposition 8. Three of six suits filed by gay couples and government entities were accepted by the Supreme Court of California to be heard together.

On March 5, 2009, the Supreme Court of California in San Francisco heard the oral arguments of the case. Unprecedented in the history of the California Supreme Court, these cases would certainly set precedent as "no previous case had presented the question of whether an initiative could be used to take away fundamental rights", according to California Associate Supreme Court Justice Kathryn Mickle Werdegar.

Rendering its decision on May 26, 2009, the California Supreme Court held that Proposition 8 was in fact valid and enforceable from the moment it was passed. It could not however be applied to retroactively annul same-sex marriages that were performed while the practice was legal. This decision then resulted in the challenge to Proposition 8 in Federal Court with the filing of Perry v. Schwarzenegger, now titled Perry v. Brown in its appeal.

184

By Marty Piatt, Architect

On August 4, 2010, Judge Vaughn Walker ruled that Proposition 8 violated the Due Process and Equal Protection Clauses of the Fourteenth Amendment to the U.S. Constitution and had no rational basis or vested interest in denying gays and lesbians marriage licenses as follows:

"An initiative measure adopted by the voters deserves great respect. The considered views and opinions of even the most highly qualified scholars and experts seldom outweigh the determinations of the voters. When challenged, however, the voters' determinations must find at least some support in evidence. This is especially so when those determinations enact into law classifications of persons. Conjecture, speculation and fears are not enough. Still less will the moral disapprobation of a group or class of citizens suffice, no matter how large the majority that shares that view. The evidence demonstrated beyond serious reckoning that Proposition 8 finds support only in such disapproval. As such, Proposition 8 is beyond the constitutional reach of the voters or their representatives."

Judge Walker held that Proposition 8 was based on traditional notions of opposite-sex marriage and on moral disapproval of homosexuality, neither of which remains a legal basis for discrimination. He further noted also noted that gays and lesbians are exactly the type of minority that "strict scrutiny" was designed to protect:

"Proposition 8 fails to advance any rational basis in singling out gay men and lesbians for denial of a marriage license. Because California has no interest in discriminating against gay men and lesbians, and because Proposition 8 prevents California from fulfilling its constitutional obligation to provide marriages on an equal basis, the court concludes that Proposition 8 is unconstitutional."

The political campaigns both for and against Proposition 8 raised approximately $39.9 million "for" and $43.3 million "against", becoming the nation's all-time highest-funded political campaign in history on any state ballot surpassing all other campaigns in the country in campaign spending except for the Presidential candidates race. Over $83 billion dollars were spent to promote and defend hate, intolerance, and discrimination. How could $83 billion dollars have been better spent to greater benefit the precious lives of all our precious children, our senior citizens, and our brave veterans?

On August 16, 2010, the 9th U.S. Circuit Court of Appeals then ordered Judge Walker's ruling stayed pending its appeal.

On February 23, 2011 the Justice Department declared it would abandon all legal defense of the Defense of Marriage Act legislation.

On February 7, 2012, the 9th U.S. Circuit Court of Appeals ruled that the California ban on same-sex marriage as a result of the voter-approved passage of Proposition 8 was unconstitutional. The majority 2-1 decision ruled that California's Proposition 8 ban did not further "responsible procreation", which was at the heart of the argument by the ban's supporters. The ruling read: "Proposition 8 serves no purpose, and has no effect, other than to lessen the status and human dignity of gays and lesbians in California, and to officially reclassify their relationships as inferior to those of opposite-sex couples". In the ruling, Judge Stephen Reinhardt apparently focused on the very unique circumstances in California relating to Proposition 8, and whether voters legally had a valid reason for passing it. The backers of Proposition 8 had argued that it would advance better child-rearing, but Judge Reinhardt stated that the only effect of the measure was to deny same-sex couples the right to describe their relationship as a "marriage".

"Proposition 8 therefore could not have been enacted to advance California's interest in childrearing or responsible procreation", he wrote, "for it had no effect on the rights of same-sex couples to raise children or on the procreative practices of other couples." Having had the Defendant's request for an "en banc" review of the entire appeals court denied, the eventual outcome of Perry v. Brown rests with an appeal to the Supreme Court of United States.

On February 22, 2012 District Judge Jeffrey White, a George W. Bush appointee, found the Defense of Marriage Act (DOMA) unconstitutional violating the Constitution's equal protection clause because it denied benefits to gay and lesbian couples. Although those cases did not establish a binding precedent, justices on the 9th Circuit Court have previously ruled that DOMA is unconstitutional. Ruling in favor of a female Plaintiff who works for the appeals court that had been blocked from enrolling her wife in a family health insurance plan, Judge White asserted that the Office of Personnel Management (OPM) could not rely on the 1996 Defense of Marriage Act to deny the medical coverage.

On June 6, 2012, another Federal Judge Barbara Jones ruled that based on rational basis review, Section 3 of DOMA is unconstitutional and ordered that the plaintiff be paid the tax refund due to her.

On June 26, 2013, in the case of United States v. Windsor, the Supreme Court ruled that Section 3 of the DOMA to be unconstitutional.

Also on June 26, 2013, in the case of Brown v. Perry, the United States Supreme Court ruled that proponents of Proposition 8 did not possess legal standing to defend the law. The Supreme Court dismissed both the appeal and directed the Ninth Circuit to vacate its decision. The decision left intact the district court's 2010 ruling. Shortly thereafter, the Ninth Circuit lifted its stay of the district court's ruling, which enabled Governor Jerry Brown to order same-sex marriages to resume.

On June 26, 2015, in the case of Obergefell v. Hodges, the United States Supreme Court finally ruled that various State bans on same-sex marriages were to be unconstitutional. This date was also the anniversary of both the Windsor and Lawrence court rulings.

But what actually is at greater issue in the entire debate over marriage equality is plain and simply the religious belief that homosexuality is immoral; an unacceptable and intolerable behavior claimed by the Christian conservatives as a chosen lifestyle by gays and lesbians. I can no more agree that homosexuality is a chosen lifestyle than heterosexuality is a chosen lifestyle. I can only assume that the Christian conservatives were not born straight, but chose to live a heterosexual lifestyle. However repulsive or repugnant the homosexual lifestyle may be to some heterosexuals, it has been suggested by medical and physiological science that there may be a genetic predisposition or condition inherited from birth, rather than it being a direct product of someone's individual environment and upbringing.

The fact of the matter is, if homosexuality was a chosen lifestyle, the process of natural selection and evolution would have overridden the supposedly "chosen trait" and homosexuality would have ceased to exist and ended millennia ago. The mere fact that homosexuality still exists is clear and undeniable proof that there must be a human genetic factor involved perpetuating the continuation throughout our humanity's existence. One could question if homosexuality is normal or abnormal.

Yet that rhetorical question having no definitive answer would undoubtedly lead to a clearly subjective conjecture probably based upon an individual's religious moral and bias belief that it is abnormal, or another's unbiased and non-judgmental belief that it may actually be normal. The question remains: What is "normal"? What defines normality in terms of behavior in society? In my humble opinion, normality is defined as the conformance to the average, expected patterns of behavior studied within the context of human sociology.

"If you are a non-average, unique, and exceptional individual not bound by the restricting constraints of society marching to your own drum beat regardless of other average people's confining expectations, you are probably not normal." ~Marty Piatt

The next question remaining, what is "natural"? Are the definitions of "normal" and "natural" one in the same? Whether or not one believes homosexuality is normal or natural, or abnormal and unnatural is actually immaterial with respect to the debate over the civil rights pertaining to marriage equality.

The Supreme Court cases of Romer v. Evans in 1966, Living v. Virginia in 1967, and Lawrence v. Texas in 2003 affirmatively protecting the rights of American citizens within the equal protection and due process clauses of both the Fifth and Fourteenth Amendments to the United States Constitution. The Fifth Amendment applies to the laws enacted under the authority of Federal Government and the Fourteenth Amendment applies to the laws enacted under the authority of the several States.

Having been given a history of marriage injustice in the United States, the topic of marriage and Holy Matrimony should also be adequately addressed for better clarification. Not to confuse the two, marriage and Holy Matrimony are two very separate and distinctive ceremonies and rituals. Marriage can be either a religious ritual officiated by a representative of the church or religion, or it can be a civil union officiated by a governmental official having the authority to provide the wedding ceremony. Holy Matrimony may be considered marriage, however, marriage is not Holy Matrimony, two very exclusive wedding rituals. Holy Matrimony is absolutely exclusive to the church or religion. Conversely, marriage may be considered a civil union, yet a civil union is not considered marriage according to many State and Federal laws.

Having a separation of church and state, the government cannot, and should not, sanction any religious ceremony whatsoever. Herein lies the debate for all marriages. I cannot more fully understand and appreciate that the institution of any religion may have moral objections to performing the ritual of Holy Matrimony to same-sex couples; that is their right and belief as it may apply to their religion. I totally agree and have no issue with that circumstance. What I don't agree with is that religion in general believes it has a monopoly on the exclusive use and term of marriage, or defining the institution of marriage, and thereby justifying their biased position in terms of its "sanctity".

"Marriage is the union of two different surnames, in friendship and in love, in order to continue the posterity of the former sages, and to furnish those who shall preside at the sacrifices to heaven and earth, at those in the ancestral temple, and at those at the altars to the spirits of the land and grain." ~Confucius

"Sanctity", generally meaning Holy or Sacred in its religious definition, is a holiness of life and character: godliness. And yet the Republican Christian conservatives use the term: "protecting the sanctity of marriage" in justifying the prohibition of marriage to same-sex couples.

I beg to differ on that specific justification. The one and only situation threatening the institution of marriage including Holy Matrimony is divorce; predominately opposite-sex divorce. As most of us would agree, America has become a society permeated with divorce. Multiple marriages and divorces are not uncommon topics for ridicule and comedy in Hollywood movies, late night television, and scandalous magazine headlines describing the latest dirty and tawdry descriptive details of celebrity or politician separations.

Divorce statistics reveal very persuasive data involving the current state of the American family unit and the "sacred" institution of marriage. During past decade, the overall and commonly accepted American divorce rate has remained mostly unchanged for first-time marriages, having approximately 50% of marriages ending in divorce. For each successive marriage the statistical rate becomes even greater, having approximately 65% of second marriages ending in divorce, and even much higher rates for the third, fourth, fifth, and sixth (etc.) marriages.

American statistical divorce rates indicate that about 5% of marriages in this nation are ending every year, resulting in huge portion of society that has personally experienced divorce, or multiple divorces, at some point in their married lives. Yet, these are just divorce statistics, which may not correctly reflect the current state of the rampant infidelity in America. Almost all cultures that recognize marriage or Holy Matrimony also recognize adultery as a violation of the terms of marriage; in which the Christian conservatives also fail to fully recognize the matter of "adulterative accountability", perpetuating the unrealistic ideal defining what they believe is the "sanctity of marriage".

It can be estimated that roughly the same 50% rate of American divorces will equally apply to all married individuals in the United States engaging in infidelity and extra-marital sexual activities at some time during their marriage. These figures may also include a portion of both hetero- and homo-sexual infidelity activities within the marriage. Also occurring is heterosexual men, both married and single, seeking oral gratification having sexual encounters on the "down low" with homosexual men. These statistical numbers of marital infidelity are most likely on the conservative side, and are actually much greater. In addition, research statistics have also suggested and shown that nearly 3% of all babies born within marital relationships are the product and result of marital infidelity, with most of these children unknowingly being raised by husbands that are not the children's true biological fathers. More than 50% of all babies born to American women under the age of thirty occur outside of marriage.

The statistics of infidelity also do not account for agreed infidelity, or open marital relationships. It could easily be suggested that the remaining half of marriages have some percentage of non-monogamy, which may also include bi-sexual agreed infidelity within the marriage. It could therefore be very easily concluded that maybe less than one-quarter of all marriages in American society today maintain some sort of true loving devotion and mutual monogamy within their marriage vows.

The most common marital vows taken in marriage today in American society are actually based upon some form of the religious doctrine of the Church of England, written within the original 1662 Book of Common Prayer that was brought to the American colonies by both the Separatist Pilgrims and the Protestant Puritans in the early seventeenth century, including the Catholics that later followed to the new world.

As marital vows in the religious institution of both marriage and Holy Matrimony are stated ending with the covenant to God, oath to the Church, promise to one another, and in testament to the participating witnesses it is vowed:

"To have and to hold from this day forward, for better for worse, for richer for poorer, in sickness and in health, to love and to cherish, till death us do part", or "…as long as we both shall live".

"…til death do us part", or "…as long as we both shall live" is absolutely the defining religious clause representing the true sanctity of marriage.

> "…So they are no longer two, but one. Therefore what
> God has joined together, let man not separate."
> ~Jesus Christ, The Bible, [Matthew 19:6]

I can think of no greater morally apprehensible act, behavior, or circumstance, except abortion, which is a "chosen" lie and broken covenant with our almighty God. This is truly the most immoral and sacrilegious abomination relative to organized religion that exists in American society today.

So the Republican Christian conservatives want to protect the "sanctity of marriage" and Holy Matrimony?

It would seem quite apparent and obvious to me that to better protect the presumed "sanctity of marriage", one would not necessarily want to limit marriage utilizing unnecessary justifications based on hate, intolerance, and discrimination, but rather more importantly justifying the protective rationale with the total elimination and removal of divorce in our American society all together.

"Divorce and infidelity", not marriage equality, are the only defining causes threatening the "sanctity of marriage" and Holy Matrimony in American society today. Protecting the "sanctity of marriage" is really not the true goal of the Christian Conservatives and religion, but rather it is the perpetuation of hate, intolerance, and discrimination in the form of religious-persecuting, something that our religious founding fathers and Colonists were attempting to escape from in their coming to the America.

191

Morality is very subjective in this country today. The Republican Party and Christian conservatives are utilizing their religious-persecuting political methods to further achieve their goals of establishing what seems to be a mostly non-secular theocracy government all the while they are dividing and splintering our society and nation.

Having provided a historical and legal foundation in my opinions and thoughts on American religion, marriage, reproductive and civil rights, we need to acknowledge that the time has finally arisen for the United States of America to begin a conclusive end to the divisions separating our society regarding the politics of religion and government. It is extremely clear what our founding forefathers were trying to accomplish by creating what our nation has since defined as the "separation of church and state", were common goals to prevent divisions that bring unity to our country.

We as a society and a free people need to respect the blessed right of the First Amendment to our Constitution given to us by our founding forefathers; that being the right to freely worship, or not worship. In their infinite wisdom we need to be thankful there does not exist the establishment by our government of one exclusive national religion and official Church of the United States of America. Some of our religious founding forefathers and American colonists escaped the oppressive and persuasive tyranny of the official church of the government for very good reason and cause.

When we cease not to have the freedom of religion and belief, we have no real freedom. The good Lord gave us free conscience to love and worship of our own free will, so we as a nation should afford others the free conscience to not worship and believe. As stated by the seventeenth century Baptist theologian Roger Williams: "forced worship stinks in God's nostrils".

Our nation should put all personal and religious bias behind us, give thanks to our Creator for our life and prosperity, and wish well to others that may not share what we believe and perceive to be in our best interests as a people and as a nation.

> "That which we share in common far exceeds that
> which makes us unique." ~Marty Piatt, Architect

By Marty Piatt, Architect

With respect to freedom and liberty, I believe the sum of the parts far exceeds the sum of the whole. With our Declaration of Independence, both our nation and our people were given the blessed right to Life, Liberty, and the Pursuit of Happiness, whatever that may personally mean to us, which is also unique to us as individuals. Our freedom is not one-sided, and our religious beliefs come as a double-edged sword.

Our civil rights must have no dependence on our religious opinions or beliefs. Religion is a matter lying solely between an individual and their God and creator, and we owe no accountability to anyone for our faith and worship, and that the legislative powers of our government should pursue only actions, not opinions.

Neither our State nor our Federal government can force nor influence us to go to or to remain away from our church against our will, or force us to profess our belief or disbelief in any of our nation's religions. We should not be punished for entertaining or professing our religious beliefs or our disbeliefs.

We should realize that few decisions are more personal and intimate, more properly private, and more basic to individual dignity and autonomy, than a woman's decision having the guidance of her physician and her God, to end her pregnancy. A woman's right to make that choice freely is fundamental; a decision made without guilt, fear, or retribution.

Marriage is one of our basic civil rights, fundamental to our very existence and survival. To deny anyone this fundamental freedom on such unsupportable a basis and so directly subversive to the principle of equality at the heart of the Fourteenth Amendment, it will surely deprive all of us of our life, liberty, and happiness without our right of due process of law. Our Fourteenth Amendment requires that the freedom of our individual choice to marry shall not be restricted by invidious discrimination of others. Our Constitution gives us the freedom to marry, or not marry, another person of our choice and shall not be infringed by anyone.

In a rare public statement on June 12, 2007, Mildred Loving commented on the issue of same-sex marriage that was prepared for delivery on the fortieth anniversary of the Loving v. Virginia decision of the United States Supreme Court. Her following statement read as follows:

"Surrounded as I am now by wonderful children and grandchildren, not a day goes by that I don't think of Richard and our love, our right to marry, and how much it meant to me to have that freedom to marry the person precious to me, even if others thought he was the "wrong kind of person" for me to marry. I believe all Americans, no matter their race, no matter their sex, no matter their sexual orientation, should have that same freedom to marry. Government has no business imposing some people's religious beliefs over others. Especially if it denies people's civil rights. I am still not a political person, but I am proud that Richard's and my name is on a court case that can help reinforce the love, the commitment, the fairness, and the family that so many people, black or white, young or old, gay or straight seek in life. I support the freedom to marry for all. That's what Loving, and loving, are all about." ~Mildred Loving

"Bear in mind this sacred principle, that though the will of the majority is in all cases to prevail, that will to be rightful must be reasonable; that the minority possess their equal rights, which equal laws must protect, and to violate would be oppression." ~Thomas Jefferson

"It's time America realized that there was no gay exemption in the right to life, liberty, and the pursuit of happiness in the Declaration of Independence." ~Senator Barry M. Goldwater

"Millions of innocent men, women, and children, since the introduction of Christianity, have been burnt, tortured, fined, and imprisoned; yet we have not advanced one inch toward uniformity. What has been the effect of coercion? To make one-half the world fools and the other half hypocrites. To support roguery and error all over the earth."
~Thomas Jefferson

"We establish no religion in this country. We command no worship. We mandate no belief, nor will we ever. Church and state are and must remain separate." ~President Ronald Reagan

"We hold it for a fundamental and undeniable truth 'that religion, or the duty which we owe our Creator, and the manner of discharging it, can be directed only by reason and conviction, not by force or violence'. The religion, then, of every man must be left to the conviction and conscience of every man: and that it is the right of every man to exercise it as these may dictate." ~James Madison

"By the theory of our Government majorities rule, but this right is not an arbitrary or unlimited one. It is a right to be exercised in subornation to the Constitution and in conformity to it. One great object of the Constitution was to restrain majorities from oppressing minorities or encroaching upon their just rights. Minorities have a right to appeal to the Constitution as a shield against such oppression." ~James K. Polk

"To the corruptions of Christianity I am, indeed, opposed; but not to the genuine precepts of Jesus himself. I am a Christian, in the only sense in which he wished any one to be; sincerely attached to his doctrines, in preference to all others; ascribing to himself every human excellence..."
~Thomas Jefferson

"The purpose of separation of church and state is to keep forever from these shores the ceaseless strife that has soaked the soil of Europe in blood for centuries." ~James Madison

"The government of the United States is not, in any sense, founded on the Christian religion." ~John Adams, Treaty of Tripoli, 4 November 1796

"The day that this country ceases to be free for irreligion, it will cease to be free for religion." ~Herbert H. Jackson, Supreme Court Jurist

"Tolerance implies no lack of commitment on one's own beliefs.
Rather it condemns the oppression or persecution of others."
~John Fitzgerald Kennedy (JFK), former President

"Barry Goldwater exemplified honorable conservative principles such as respecting individual rights. Many of today's right-wing politicians, who mistakenly call themselves conservatives, can learn a lot about true conservatism by studying Barry Goldwater."
~Elizabeth Birch, Executive Director HRC

By Marty Piatt, Architect

EQUAL RIGHTS

"We have talked long enough in this country about equal rights.
We have talked for one hundred years of more. It is time now to
write the next chapter, and to write it in the books of Law."
~Lyndon B. Johnson, former President

The Equal Rights Amendment (ERA) was a proposed amendment to the United States Constitution. Originally written by Alice Paul in 1923, the ERA was introduced in Congress for the first time. Finally passing both houses of Congress in 1972, the ERA then went to the several state legislatures unfortunately failing to receive the requisite number of ratifications before the final June 30, 1982 deadline mandated by Congress expired. The ERA has since never been adopted nor ratified by the required State legislatures. Alice Paul, a suffragist leader, argued that although the 19th Amendment had prohibited the denial of the right to vote because of a person's sex, this right alone could not end the remaining legal discrimination vestiges based upon gender.

The text of the proposed ERA reads as follows:

Section 1. Equality of rights under the law shall not be denied or abridged by the United States or by any State on account of sex.

Section 2. The Congress shall have the power to enforce, by appropriate legislation, the provisions of this article.

Section 3. This amendment shall take effect two years after the date of ratification.

The ERA was presented as the "Lucretia Mott Amendment" during the celebration of the 75th anniversary of the 1848 Seneca Falls Convention and the Declaration of Sentiments. The Seneca Falls Convention was the first public meeting in the United States to debate and discuss women's rights. Lucretia Coffin Mott was most notably known to be an American Quaker, an abolitionist, an activist for women's rights, and a social reformer.

Beginning in 1940, the Republican Party included support of the ERA in its platform, renewing the plank every four years until 1980. Fearing that the amendment would invalidate protective labor legislation for women, the ERA was strongly opposed by the American Federation of Labor and other labor unions. Opposed by Eleanor Roosevelt and most New Dealers, they contended that women needed government protection and men did not. Because it would likely be a blow to labor unions and the movement for labor laws, opposition did not want the only labor protections abolished before they could be extended to men too. Aligning themselves with the anti-ERA labor unions, the amendment was opposed by most northern Democrats. Interestingly enough, the ERA was actually supported by the southern Democrats and almost all of the Republicans. Nevertheless, the ERA amendment kept true to the views of women's rights advocated by early feminists including Lucretia Mott, Elizabeth Cady Stanton, and Susan B. Anthony. Until the late 1960s, the main support base for the ERA was among wealthy, conservative women. After the Democrats decided to include the ERA in their platform in 1944, the Democratic Party did not however become united in favor of the ERA until the Congressional passage in 1972.

In 1966, at the Third National Conference on the Status of Women held in Washington, D.C., a group of activists including Betty Friedan frustrated with the lack of government action in enforcing Title VII of the Civil Rights Act formed the "National Organization for Women" (NOW), demanding full equality for all American women.

In 1967, at the urging of Alice Paul, NOW endorsed the ERA. Disagreeing with this endorsement, NOW's decision resulted in the formation of the "Women's Equity Action League" (WEAL) consisting of union Democrats and social conservatives that left NOW. Within a few years WEAL ultimately endorsed the ERA, and the move to support the amendment benefited NOW actually bolstering its membership.

By the late 1960s NOW had made significant political and legislative inroads and was gaining enough momentum to become a major lobbying force. Formerly known as the National American Woman Suffrage Association (NAWSA), the League of Women Voters, also fearing the loss of protective labor legislation, also opposed the Equal Rights Amendment up until 1972.

By Marty Piatt, Architect

The pace of ERA ratifications by the several state legislatures was initially quick. By the end of 1973 there were thirty ratifications, slowing down to just three ratifications in 1974, a single ratification in 1975, zero in 1976, and only one in 1977.

In proposing the ERA, the 92nd Congress had established a 7-year time limit for the ERA ratification and by the deadline on March 22, 1979, only 35 of the required 38 states had actually ratified the ERA. Congress jointly approved a controversial resolution in 1978 by a simple majority that extended the ERA ratification deadline to June 30, 1982. When asked to sign the joint resolution, President Carter indeed did, although expressing his doubt on purely procedural grounds as to the propriety of doing so. No additional states ratified or rescinded during this disputed time extension. Four state legislatures rescinded their ratifications before the original March 22, 1979 deadline.

While not going quite so far as to rescind their ERA ratification, a 5th state, South Dakota, adopted a resolution declaring that its ratification was not valid after the March 22, 1979 deadline. Of the twenty-one states have their own version of the ERA in their state constitutions, sixteen of those states ratified the ERA, while five did not.

As President, I will no longer wait for Congress or the States to take action. Following in the footsteps of Abraham Lincoln ending slavery with his "Emancipation Proclamation", I will issue the historic "Equal Rights Proclamation".

In addition, I will reconstitute the Supreme Court from the nine existing jurists to the proposed twelve jurists, consisting of 6 men jurists and 6 women jurists through the implementation of my proposed 28th amendment to the United States Constitution and the 2017 Articles of Federation, which creates a Federal Democracy within the United States of America based upon both freedom and equality.

"If I was President..."

By Marty Piatt, Architect

UNITED STATES CONSTITUTION

"The Constitution is not an instrument for the government to restrain the people; it is an instrument for the people to restrain the government - lest it come to dominate our lives and interests." ~Patrick Henry

The United States Constitution is by far one of the greatest documents written by mankind in the history of our human existence. It has become a living document that has for centuries guided one of the most powerful nations on earth to freedom, liberty, and prosperity. Our Constitution has also served as a role model document for many other international governments seeking to establish a nation of democracy and freedom.

Yet with all its greatness, the Constitution remains an imperfect document. It was debated, argued, agreed, and rushed into its existence vastly premature. I believe inherent flaws unforeseen at the time have actually contributed to the gradual decline of our country. Created at a time when only white men were created equal, women had very few rights if any, and black slaves represented only three-fifths of a "free" person as stated in our Constitution. It is my understanding that eight of our first founding United States Presidents owned slaves and worked them inside the historic walls of our nation's White House.

Our Constitution has a very dark and dishonorable history and was a shameful yet prudent attempt to establish a government based upon "freedom and democracy".

"We The People..." actually meant the ruling political elite, an educated Caucasian male group that was unrepresentative of the common founding settlers forming the original thirteen British colonies. An eighteenth-century document originally created and ratified by only thirteen of the now fifty States. Imperfect and incomplete for its time, it required amendments to be added extending the Constitution rights of its citizens. Blessings of Liberty included in our Bill of Rights, those being recognized as the first ten amendments to our Constitution.

The thirteenth amendment, including Lincoln's Emancipation Proclamation, abolished slavery ending a horrible injustice in our nation's history.

One portion of the fourteenth amendment granted by our forefathers gave birthright and citizenship to the newly freed slaves; never intended to be awarded to the unlawful illegal alien residents of this nation. The fifteenth amendment gave black males the right to vote; and for a short time black men had greater rights than white women. Later the nineteenth amendment would finally give women the right to vote; and yet women presently remain constitutionally unequal to men.

Still in this twenty-first century, laws that abridge the privileges and immunities of citizens of the United States depriving persons of life, liberty, and equal protection without due process of law guaranteed in our fourteenth amendment still exist today. Our current Constitution has served a useful purpose since its inception. However, a present juncture in our nation's history should make Americans reflect on this historical document and how it has fared the test of time, both good and bad.

Is there room for improvement achieving the original two main goals of the Constitution?

I believe the time has arisen for the United States of America to transform itself into a Federal Democracy, a government based upon all the positive attributes gained and experienced by our government since the earliest of time in our nation's history.

Just as the Committee of Detail was appointed to produce a first draft our Constitution, the 2017 Articles of Federation also refers to the several State constitutions, the existing Articles of Confederation, and other plans and materials.

There are equally both positive and negative aspects to our current Constitution, and its predecessor, our former Articles of Confederation.

"That whenever any Form of Government becomes destructive of these ends, it is the Right of the People to alter or to abolish it, and to institute new Government, laying its foundation on such principles and organizing its powers in such form, as to them shall seem most likely to effect their Safety and Happiness." ~The unanimous Declaration of the thirteen united States of America

Under my proposed **28**th amendment to our Constitution, the existing government would be transformed into a true Federal Democracy-based government with the following revisions and modifications:

Article I: The Federal legislature would consist of a unicameral Congress consisting of a House of Representatives and 'A Committee of the States' as first proposed in our Articles of Confederation;

Establish a Constitutional structure to the number of the House of Representatives.

Article II: Returning to our founding fathers original election process of selecting a separate President and Vice-President;

Replacing the Electoral College with a truly democratic non-partisan popular vote for Presidential elections;

Establishing uniformly occurring non-partisan primary and general elections;

Defining more clearly the Presidential powers and authority of executive actions including the provision of the line-item veto of Congressional budget legislation;

Remove the influence and expense of the Presidents' spouse or partner from Executive politics.

Article III: Reconstruct our Supreme Court with twelve Jurists; consisting equally of six men and six women member Jurists;

Establish a Constitutional structure to our Judicial Branch of government for the Supreme Court, District Courts (100), and Appellate Circuit Courts (11);

Establish Constitution clarification for Judicial Review of actions resulting from the Legislative and Executive Branches of government.

Provide a mechanism within the Constitution for the immediate removal and un-appointment of Federal and Supreme Court Judges.

Article IV: The United States shall guarantee to every sovereign State in this Union a "Federal Democratic" form of Government, and shall protect each of them against Invasion;

The several sovereign States comprising this Federal Democracy shall have the collective right to repeal any Federal law enacted by Congress whenever two-thirds deem it necessary;

The several sovereign States may enact laws relating to unlawful immigration not exceeding those uniform Federal Laws of Naturalization and Immigration; and shall be permitted to enforce all such laws preventing unlawful immigration.

Article V: The several State Legislatures, whenever two-thirds deem it necessary, shall propose amending Articles to this Constitution; shall call a Constitutional Convention for proposing amending Articles, when voted upon and ratified by three-fourths of the citizen People of the United States.

No amending Article shall abridge, negate, or otherwise undermine any previous enumerated Article of this Constitution hereafter.

The Constitution is not an instrument for the government to restrain the People; it is an instrument for the people to restrain the government; lest it come to dominate our lives and interests.

Article VI: Unchanged

Article VII: Unchanged

Article VIII – Bill of Rights: Our current Bill of Rights consisting of the former first ten amendments to our current Constitution would remain with minor modifications and clarifications. The practice of any religion or faith, which poses no threat of harm or death to all non-believers, may not be abridged.

Article IX – Equal Rights: The equal rights article consists of the modified preamble to our Declaration of Independence with the addition of the term "men and women" including the 14th amendment to current Constitution.

Article X – Birthright and Citizenship: Citizenship shall not be granted to children born to foreign nationals residing within the United States.

In line with the Constitution of Mexico, I would propose the following:

Immigrants to the United States of America must:

1. Have the means to sustain themselves economically;
2. Not be a financial burden whatsoever receiving no local, State, or Federal aid;
3. Be of economic and social benefit to the country;
4. Be of good character and have no criminal records at all;
5. Be contributors to the general well being of the nation.

United States Immigration law will ensure that:

1. Immigration authorities will have a record of each foreign visitor or immigrant;
2. Foreign visitors do not violate their visa status;
3. Foreign visitors are banned from interfering in the country's internal politics;
4. Foreign visitors who enter under false pretenses will be imprisoned and/or deported;
5. Foreign visitors violating the terms of their entry shall be imprisoned and/or deported, and shall forever be barred from the United States or receiving U.S. Citizenship;
6. Those who aid in illegal immigration will be fined and/or imprisoned, and permanently deported if illegally residing in the United States.

The two goals of our founding fathers in writing our original Constitution have also been met utilizing the same following rationale:

1. To insert essential principles only; lest the operations of government should be clogged by rendering those provisions permanent and unalterable, which ought to be accommodated to times and events; and,

2. To use simple and precise language, and general propositions, according to the example of the constitutions of the several states.

The 28th Constitutional amendment consisting of the new 2017 Articles of Federation that would transform the United States of America into a Federal Democracy consists of only 10 Articles; three less than the 13 articles within the 1778 Articles of Confederation; and 24 articles less than the 34 combined articles and amendments contained in our current U.S. Constitution.

I believe our new United States Constitution and 2017 Articles of Federation can have positive influence on both our county and the international community becoming a common template for real and lasting global freedom and democracy. We as a nation should realize that we cannot, and must not, spread democracy with armed force. We need not lead by our Imperialistic global crusades attempting to distill western values and beliefs with disregard for the local territorial customs and values.

This could be our nation's greatest opportunity and historic moment to lead the world and international communities by example. The United States can once again become a role model to all foreign governments seeking a secular-type of Federal Democracy respecting all religious beliefs, non-beliefs, and all personal values to inspire the world.

By Marty Piatt, Architect

JANUARY 20, 2017

"If by the mere force of numbers a majority should deprive a minority of any clearly written Constitutional right, it might, in a moral point of view, justify revolution."
~Abraham Lincoln

On January 20th, 2017, if elected to the Office the United States President, upon completing the Oath of Office, I would address the Nation as the 45th (or 55th) President announcing the historic convening of the Second Constitutional Convention on March 1st, 2017.

Coinciding with the 236th anniversary of the ratification of the original 1781 Articles of Confederation of the United States, delegates would meet at the Pennsylvania State House in Philadelphia, Pennsylvania to sign and ratify the historic 28th Amendment to our United States Constitution.

The 28th Amendment to our current U.S. Constitution would be the adoption and ratification of the 2017 Articles of Federation, consisting of the original Preamble and the Ten Articles of Federation, all comprising the 28th Amendment, and thus replacing the current U.S. Constitution.

The Second Constitutional Convention delegates would consist of representatives from the several State Legislatures. Ratification would require approval of three-quarter of the several States pursuant to Article VII of our current Constitution, and shall be sufficient for the establishment of this Constitution between the several States so ratifying the same.

And before the days' end, as President of the United States of America, I would issue the historic "Equal Rights Proclamation", which is based upon our nation's Declaration of Independence and U.S. Constitution as follows:

"I, Marty Piatt, President of the United States of America, do hereby proclaim: We hold these truths to be self-evident, that all Men and Woman are created equal, that they are endowed by their Creator with certain unalienable Rights, that among these are Life, Liberty, and the pursuit of Happiness."

"No State shall make or enforce any law which shall abridge the privileges or immunities of citizens of the United States; nor shall any State deprive any person of life, liberty, or property, without due process of law; nor deny to any person within its jurisdiction the equal protection of the laws."

"And unity within our country begins with equal rights for all men and women. Not until this great divide is bridged, this wound healed, can we as a nation move forward to pursue and achieve true happiness and prosperity."

THE FIRST ONE HUNDRED DAYS

On January 21st, I would initiate the first Executive Order providing "Conditional" Pardons to all Army, Navy, and Air Force warfighters convicted of any and all war crimes not committed against fellow United States warfighters while serving in Afghanistan and Iraq.

A second Executive Order would be issued for the establishment of a War Crimes Tribunal in cooperation with the International Criminal Court and the International Court of Justice, based in The Hague, Netherlands.

The Tribunal would investigate and prosecute war crimes allegedly committed by members of the George W. Bush Presidential administration, including but not limited to, the former President involving the invasion of Iraq.

The War Crimes Tribunal indictments would consist of the following allegations not unlike the war crimes of WWII:

1. Participation in a common plan or conspiracy for the accomplishment of a crime against peace;

2. Planning, initiating and waging wars of aggression and other crimes against peace;

3. War crimes; and Crimes against humanity.

Not one American warfighter shall remain in custody incarcerated for war crimes, which are ultimately the responsibility having been committed by George W. Bush, while the former President remains a free man.

A third Executive Order could be issued revoking each and every Executive Order, Directive, Memorandum, and Presidential Proclamation issued from January 20, 2000 forward, and proposing additional legislation repealing all Federal law signed into law by former President Bush, thus eliminating his Presidential legacy.

Other Executive Orders to be implemented are as follows:

Revoke the most recent Executive Order banning the deportation of certain illegal foreign nationals under the age of 30 brought into the United States illegally as children by their illegal immigrant parents;

Using Executive Order and Authoritative action of the President as provided by our United States Constitution, I would indefinitely suspend "habeas corpus" for all matters relating to existing U.S. immigration law to enforce illegal alien deportation of unlawful foreign nationals residing or entering this country illegally within the borders of the United States "subject to the jurisdiction thereof". Any legal action or court ruling whatsoever attempting to prevent illegal immigrant deportation by any Plaintiff or Federal judge would result in the immediate filing of Federal charges for both Obstruction of Justice and Treason to those offenders by the Office of the Attorney General under authority of the President;

Immediately abandon and remove all bi-lingual Federal government funding and communications, both verbal and written, within the United States borders and its sovereign territories;

Immediately require English language "only" spoken on all domestic military bases and installations excluding visiting foreign military personnel;

Immediately suspend all foreign immigration and naturalization to the United States indefinitely, including those from Mexico until which time the national, or largest State unemployment percent rate falls below the unlawful immigrant population percentage rate;

Immediately suspend all travel visas for foreign pregnant women entering this country;

Immediately suspend all foreign aid and domestic subsidies within our Federal budget, including all monies sent to Mexico;

Immediately normalize all government relations and trade with the country of Cuba.

Immediately normalize all government relations and trade with the country of Venezuela.

Immediately increase the import amounts of distilled ethanol and technology from the country of Brazil;

Immediately decrease the import amounts of foreign produced crude oil outside of the North and South American continents;

The list of Federal Laws I would like to REPEAL immediately within the first 100 days are as follows:

1.   Federal Reserve Act of 1913;

2.   Davis-Bacon Act of 1931;

3.   Fair Labor Standards Act of 1938;

4.   Hatch Act of 1939;

5.   Controlled Substance Act (CSA), Title II of the Comprehensive Drug Abuse Prevention and Control Act of 1970;

6.   Postal Reorganization Act of 1971;

7.   Federal Financing Bank Act of 1973;

8.   1983 amendments of the Social Security Act of 1935, which excludes the Social Security Trust Fund from the United States unified budget;

9.   Riegle-Neal Interstate Banking and Branching Efficiency Act of 1994 (IBBEA); thus restoring the Bank Holding Company Act of 1956;

10. Gramm–Leach–Bliley Act of 1999, also known as the Financial Services Modernization Act; thus restoring the Glass-Steagall Banking Act of 1933;

11. The USA PATRIOT Act of 2001 (also known as the "Patriot Act") Uniting (and) Strengthening America (by) Providing Appropriate Tools Required (to) Intercept (and) Obstruct Terrorism;

12. NASA Authorization Act of 2005;

13.   The Fair Minimum Wage Act of 2007;

14.   Patient Protection and Affordable Care Act of 2010 (also known as Obamacare) pending Supreme Court review;

15.   NASA Authorization Act of 2010;

16.   Don't Ask, Don't Tell Repeal Act of 2010; with reinstatement of Federal Judge Virginia A. Phillips ruling in the case of Log Cabin Republicans v. United States in favor of Plaintiff on the grounds that the military policy of "Don't ask, don't tell" is unconstitutional. The Constitutional rights of Americans do not require conditions, certification, or a waiting period.

On April 30, 2017 before the end of the first 100 days of my Presidency, I would hope to have accomplished the historic task of having my proposed 28th amendment to our Constitution consisting of the 2017 Articles of Federation to be completely ratified by three-quarters of the State legislatures of the United States of America.

By Marty Piatt, Architect

MY PRESIDENTIAL CANDIDACY

"Only those who attempt the absurd can achieve
the impossible." ~Robin Morgan

One of my earliest memories as a very, very young boy was sitting on the lap of my father's brother Richard, my Uncle Dick, and he asking me what I wanted to be when I grew up. With perfect recollection, my honest reply to him was that "I want to be President". I don't know what would have prompted me to speak that answer, but maybe even at an early age I knew that the Office of the President was a very important one.

My Uncle Dick, Richard Malcolm Piatt, a World War II veteran, proudly served our country and the United States Navy continuing in the Patriotic heritage of the Piatt family.

Surely this has been the dream of many young boys and girls in our country throughout our history. The roots of my answer were not necessarily the quest for power or financial gain, but rather the innocent and selfless desire of adolescence wishing to contribute to our nation's history and success. Ever since that early age in my life, I have pondered that young boy's wish during every Presidential election year since.

I began to have a great interest in politics and history as a teenager. As in life, we must understand our past to better understand our future. During my high school years Mr. John Lewin was one of my favorite American history teachers. Having initially studied law to become an attorney, Mr. Lewin would switch his major to education believing that as an attorney he would be hurting more people than he was to help. This decision would later benefit thousands of children throughout decades of his teaching at Marysville High School.

With these thoughts came ambitious goals of how our government could be improved and made much better. I believe each and every American citizen in this great nation, at one point in time, has pondered the very same thoughts of what we could do and accomplish if we became President of the United States. These very same Presidential ambitions have accumulated over the years, and finally, I had to pull these thoughts out of my head and put them down on paper.

213

As a registered Architect, one of my greatest assets is to have been blessed with the talent to express my visions of beauty, structure, and function, and transcribe them graphically onto paper. In this case, the results of my political visions have been in written form comprising the contents of this book.

Raised in a family of Republican parents, I had also been indoctrinated with the philosophies of the Republican Party, not unlike many children of political parents. I recall at the tender age of six years old the Presidential campaign of Barry Morris Goldwater in 1964, challenging the Democratic incumbent President Lyndon Baines Johnson (LBJ) who assumed the Office of the President after the unfortunate assassination of our former and late President John Fitzgerald Kennedy (JFK).

As a young Republican ineligible to vote, I recall Barry Goldwater, the five-term United States Senator from Arizona whose outstanding political career began in 1952. He was a truly progressive Republican that has been most often credited for sparking the resurgence of both the American conservative and libertarian political movements of the 1960's. The following (4) quotations are statements made by Senator Barry Goldwater:

"I don't have any respect for the religious right. There is no place in this country for practicing religion in politics. That goes for Falwell, Robertson and all the rest of these political preachers. They are a detriment to the country."

"The religious issues of these groups have little or nothing to do with conservative or liberal politics. The uncompromising position of these groups is a divisive element that could tear apart the very spirit of our representative system, if they gain sufficient strength."

"Government governs best when it governs least — and stays out of the impossible task of legislating morality."

"Mark my word, if and when these preachers get a hold of the [Republican] party, and they're sure trying to do so, it's going to be a terrible damn problem. Frankly these people frighten me. Politics and governing demand compromise. But these Christians believe they are acting in the name of God, so they can't and won't compromise. I know, I've tried to deal with them."

By Marty Piatt, Architect

After graduating Marysville High School at the age of seventeen in 1976, a bicentennial year celebrating the 200th anniversary of our county's Declaration of Independence, I was first eligible to vote in a Presidential election in 1980. I voted for Ronald Reagan, the former governor of California, and voted for him again in 1984.

The eighties were great for me professionally and personally. Having begun a life on my own, this decade shaped the individual I was to become. Becoming a free thinker, free from the indoctrination of my upbringing, I later realized that the Republican Party did not suit my personal and political beliefs.

I re-registered to the Democratic Party to vote for Jerry Brown for President in the primary, and sent him $100 dollars in his grass-roots campaign to lead our nation. I have not stopped hearing from him ever since. Jerry Brown, the former and now current Governor of California, had a great impact directing my political and moral compass. We do however greatly differ on immigration. Predominately, his flat-tax income tax proposal was of most interest to me. Not since the initial Revenue Act of 1861 has any politician suggested and enacted a flat income tax to fund the out-of-control spending of our Congress.

Having been an adamant supporter of President Ronald Reagan, I have since regretted my political support of our former President. Under the Republican leadership of President Ronald Reagan, our country had experienced a successful yet short-term prosperity, he ended the Cold War, brought the former Soviet Union to its knees and later destruction to what has become the reconstituted and successful Russian Federation, and finally gave our country a great and mighty military force to be reckoned with.

However, it was President Reagan's policies and directives in the 1980's that unfortunately resulted in the beginning of our economic disparity being experience between what has now been referred to as the 1% and 99% of our American population.

Under Reagan leadership, our national debt increased from approximately $994 billion in 1981, to approximately $2.867 trillion in 1989 when he left office. This was an increase of about 188%, nearly quadrupling our national debt under Republican leadership.

Under our next Republican President, George H. W. Bush, Reagan's Vice-president, our national debt then grew to $4.351 trillion, an increase of about 338% from the beginning of the Reagan era presidency. With our next Republican President, George W. Bush, our national debt grew from approximately $5.679 trillion to $10.413 trillion when he left office, an increase in excess of 83%.

Our current President has not fared much better to say the least, having been handed a national debt from his former Republican President in excess of $10+ trillion dollars, has accumulated addition national debt in excess of approximately $18+ trillion dollars. This was an increase of about 80%, an amount less than any of his Republican Presidential predecessors, yet still a very significant contribution to our national debt.

Neither Democrat nor Republican policies have ceased the borrow and spend cycle of our Federal government. Neither of our duopolistic system of political parties has earned or deserves the right to continued governance of our country. Hence my potential interest in the United States Presidency during our next election in November 2016.

On May 5, 2015 I re-registered in California as an independent voter. Believe it of not, George Washington, was an Independent having no party affiliation. Later that same day, I registered with the Federal Elections Commission (FEC) as a potential candidate in the 2016 Presidential election pending exploratory research. I did not register as a potential Presidential candidate for any partisan or independent party. My FEC candidate registration indicates my party affiliation as: "Unknown". I wish to keep my candidacy options open.

It's time to stop voting for both parties; they are each to blame for the destruction of our country. As long as the Democratic National Committee (DNC) and the Republican National Committee (RNC) are running and ruining our country, the status quo will remain. I hope Americans will come to their senses and vote for true Leader, and not just a party.

Out nation needs someone with independent vision that will empower and inspire all Americans to restore the respect and greatness of America.

I could conversely be elected to the Office of the President of the United States of America with a successful, yet unconventional "write-in" vote campaign of the American people, possibly receiving the greatest popular vote. But unfortunately popular vote means nothing in the Electoral College method of electing our United States President.

Unprecedented in American politics and election history, Senator Lisa Murkowski, a Republican from the State of Alaska, having failed to gain the Republican nomination in her State's primary election for Senator, mounted an unprecedented and historical challenge in 2010 with her "write-in" candidacy to regain her seat in the United States Senate, and actually succeeded in doing so.

However very unlikely it seemed at the time, facing astronomical odds against her reelection, Senator Lisa Murkowski's continued dedication and perseverance ultimately prevailed to win back her Senate seat in Alaska. Unprecedented in American politics and Presidential history, while facing astronomical odds of success, my potential Presidential "write-in" candidacy could become a creative grassroots alternative.

I am no one, yet I am someone. I am neither Democrat nor Republican. I am a native-born American citizen, over the age of 35, having been a resident of the United States of American since birth. I meet all the required conditions set forth in our United States Constitution to lead this great nation. There are no other requirements.

It should be noted that if elected to the Office of the President, I intend to donate one hundred percent of the entire $400,000 Executive salary of the Presidency equally to the charities of both the "St. Jude Children's Hospital" and the veteran's "Wounded Warrior Project". I will not accept compensation from the United States Treasury without first donating the sum to charity. I will not personally gain financially from our Unites States Treasury leading America. Americans should also know that every President in modern history has left office as a millionaire.

Should American voters decide in November 2016 that real change is necessary for our country to charter a new path to Constitutional democracy, sustained prosperity, and economic growth, their decision would determine the insurmountable odds I now face in winning the 2016 Presidential election.

The last Architect to serve in the White House was President Thomas Jefferson, our third President. He was also the principle Architect and author of our Declaration of Independence. I believe the time has come for another Architect to serve and provide vision in the White House. We do not need another corrupt political racketeer to become U.S. President.

The reality of the situation is, that in as much I believe the Electoral College is undemocratic and antiquated, it's currently the only game in town leading to the Oval Office of our nation's White House.

According to our election law, a Presidential candidate must acquire a minimum of 270 electoral votes of the total 538 electoral delegates to win the Presidential election. My 2016 Presidential election strategy would be to at least win and secure the following States electoral votes:

WEST COAST STATES (74):
California, 55
Oregon, 7
Washington, 12

SOUTHERN BORDER STATES (71):
Arizona, 11
New Mexico, 5
Texas, 55

GULF COAST STATES (50):
Louisiana, 8
Mississippi, 6
Alabama, 9
Florida, 27

NORTH EASTERN STATES (86):
New Jersey, 14
New York, 29
Pennsylvania, 20
Maryland, 10
Virginia, 13

GRAND TOTAL: 281 (+11)

By Marty Piatt, Architect

My political Presidential campaign strategy is based on the following assumptions:

1. The West coast will benefit from the construction of the new hybrid ethanol gasoline refinery built on the southern West coast. This will create surplus gasoline reserves throughout the United States substantially lowering all fuel prices in the entire country; in addition to my illegal immigration policies;

2. The Southern Border States will benefit most from my illegal immigration policies; in addition to my energy policies concerning solar energy

3. The Gulf Coast States will benefit from my future NASA mission goals and exploration to Mars which would also include Texas; in addition to my illegal immigration policies;

4. The North Eastern States of Virginia, and Maryland would also benefit from my future NASA mission goals and exploration to Mars.

5. The North Eastern States of New York and Pennsylvania are very important Democratic States.

The challenges to this strategy would be that the southern border and gulf coast States vote Republican more often than Democrat. My policies for a great NASA economy and firm illegal immigration enforcement may not be sufficient to win over those States voters. Hopefully my proposed NASA economy and illegal immigration policies will overcome any other negatively impacting policies.

The West coast, Northeast, Minnesota, Wisconsin, and Michigan have carried a Democrat in the last five Presidential elections since 1996.

New Hampshire, Iowa, and New Mexico have carried a Democrat in four out of five past Presidential elections.

Arizona, Louisiana, and Virginia have carried a Republican in three out of four past Presidential elections prior to 2012. Virginia carried a Democrat in 2012.

Florida has carried a Democrat in three of the past five Presidential elections.

Texas, Mississippi, and Alabama have carried a Republican in all five past Presidential elections.

With the election statistics having been researched, I still believe there must be a 2016 Presidential candidate that can win both Republican and Democratic votes uniting our country as one. I stand firm on my proposed political strategy.

And as for myself, this long shot Presidential candidacy still seems nearly impossible, to say the least.

The following are the executive endeavors I would like most to leave behind as my Presidential legacy:

1. A President remembered as the Equal Rights President that championed Women's and minority civil rights.

2. A President that lead our great nation into a new era of Federal Democracy and equality with the 2017 Articles of Federation.

3. A President that launched America back into outer space with the Saturn 2.0 rocket program with the Saturn C8 "Supernova" rocket becoming the world's "most powerful space launch vehicle".

4. A President that eliminated the current tax code and Internal Revenue Service (IRS) and instituted a Gross Income Tax (GIT).

5. A President that lead our nation forward with specific national energy policies benefiting all Americans.

6. A President that transformed our military into a defensive posture protecting our shorelines, borders, and airspaces.

7. A President that restored American citizenship to a national privilege, not an unlawful entitlement to illegal alien foreign nationals.

8. A President that rid our great country of illegal alien criminals.

9.   A President that balanced our national budget, reconciled and began the eliminating our national debt, and restored our nation's triple "A" credit rating (AAA) from Standard and Poor's (S&P).

10. A President that saved both the Social Security Administration and the United States Postal Service removing their "off-budget" financial status.

The Presidential legacies I hope to achieve are certainly ambitious goals worthy of an individual hoping to proudly occupy the Oval Office of the United States of America.

In the coming months, I hope I can persuade American voters to support my Presidential candidacy. In my hometown there is a term called "culling the peaches". When the peach tree has more fruit than it can support and will damage the tree and its branches, many of the green peaches are knocked off, or "culled", so the remaining fruit can ripen and sweeten without damage to the tree.

Right now, the Presidential candidates are culling themselves. They are debating their differences within their own parties, disparaging each other with crude rhetoric, and attacking one another with unnecessary insults about personal appearance, while revealing to all American voters their true colors as Presidential candidates, which are not red, white and blue.

I believe the actions of the Presidential candidates are truly disgraceful as well as embarrassing, to them and our nation.

As an independent Presidential candidate, the primaries do not impact me. I am biding my time for the right time, please be patient. The right time for America may well be worth waiting for.

By Marty Piatt, Architect

LEADERSHIP

In pondering my future candidacy, I wondered what type of person would make a great President. The title offers little in terms for the requirements of the position, only describing the presiding figurehead representing the United States government. Then I wondered, what type of President would make a great Leader? We would need to separate the type of leader from the style of leadership. A leader is described as one whom people follow or take direction. Leadership can be described as recruiting a group of people to achieve a mutual goal or task. Studies in leadership have provided many theories relating to the individual traits or qualities, in addition to a variety of leadership styles. Of the leadership styles recognized, I want only to focus on the four most basic of leadership styles, which are: Coercive, Authoritative, Affiliative, and Democratic.

COERCIVE: This leader takes command unilaterally inviting no opposing opinions, sometimes using fear and intimidation. This style of leadership is required when the group collective is in crisis. Once the crisis is resolved, leadership can potentially shift to another less-dictatorial leadership style.

AUTHORITATIVE: This leader has the powerful ability to communicate a mission while motivating others in the group. This style requires a clear vision for advancing forward empowering followers to succeed, and is significantly more effective for groups requiring a new vision or direction.

AFFILIATIVE: This leader excels at creating relationships. Followers having a sincere admiration for their leader build trust, loyalty, and cooperation within the communal group. This style provides greater harmony and improved morale, especially when an atmosphere where mistrust had previously existed, which lacked loyalty and dedication.

DEMOCRATIC: This leader builds consensus and popularity through group participation, which results in a much greater social commitment. This style remains very popular when a leader is uncertain what course of action to implement, permitting the group collective to provide important input in the decision making process.

My Presidential Leadership style will definitely be "Authoritative". Our country needs a leader with vision to empower and inspire Americans.

Research into Leadership and the focus of personal characteristics of people attributed to becoming leaders has provided the foundation for "Trait Theory of Leadership". Having completed the NAVFAC Executive Institute (NEI) 3-course leadership series, I wanted to know more about my personal traits and attributes for being a successful leader, potentially President. I investigated three very different Leadership Tendencies Assessment exams that provide a unique personality analysis for leadership potential. The individual exams were products of extensive research into personality traits conducted by Dale Carnegie, Thomas-Kilmann, and Myers-Briggs, which all are renowned in their specific fields of research. Without delving into the background of the assessments, I want to describe the results of these three leadership exams.

Dale Carnegie – As an American author, lecturer, and developer of the Dale Carnegie Training program founded in 1912, he believed it was possible to change other people's behavior by changing one's behavior toward them. Better known for his famous book: "How to Win Friends and Influence People", Dale Carnegie Training has since expanded the program to include Leadership Tendencies assessment training, which is similar in nature to a Personality Inventory assessment. Of the four types of Leadership Tendencies identified by Dale Carnegie, I ranked high as a Visionary and Analyzer, both equally having the same score, as opposed to the other remaining two tendencies identified as being an Achiever or Facilitator.

A VISIONARY is a forward thinker, is inspiring, has a sense of mission, anticipates problems, and focuses on outcomes; often a charismatic individual. One who looks at the big picture and guides the general direction of the group and processes. A Visionary can easily project the required sense of mission and direction that others are unable to provide. A Visionary empowers the Analyzer to examine the mission to ensure the common vision and purpose is maintained.

An ANALYZER is detail focused, decisive, keeps things on track, curious, knows what questions to ask, and assures results are appropriate. Someone who can become the conscience of the group providing the procedural and ethical compass to review group approaches and decisions required for mission success. The Analyzer cooperates with the Visionary to ensure the long-term common goals and purposes are achieved.

By Marty Piatt, Architect

Thomas-Kilmann – The Conflict Mode Instrument (**TKI**) assessment for conflict handling was developed to rank the behavior of an individual in conflict situations that appear to be incompatible with the concerns of other individuals. The ranking is based upon five categories of conflict modes having two scales in range, those being ASSERTIVENESS and COOPERATIVENESS.

Assertiveness can be described as an individual's attempt to satisfy their own concerns, while Cooperativeness can be described as an individual attempt to satisfy the concerns of all others, rather than their own.

My individual ranking was high in "Competing" on the scale of being Assertive, and very high in "Collaborative" on the scale of being Cooperative, having both scores above 80%, placing me in the upper 20 percentile. I received very-low rankings in the three remaining conflict-handling modes of Compromising, Avoiding, and Accommodating.

COMPETING is very assertive, and at times uncooperative. This can be a power-oriented mode used to defend a position believed to be correct. Competing individuals pursue their own concerns, sometimes at the expense of others using whatever methods are deemed appropriate. However, competing can also be described standing up for ideals that are inherently valuable to everyone.

A Competing mode is useful when:

1. Quick and decisive action is required, such as during an emergency;
2. Unpopular courses of action concerning important issues that require implementation;
3. Pursuing issues that are vital to the welfare of all others believed to be justified;
4. Protection against others that take advantage of non-competitive behavior.

COLLABORATING is both very assertive and very cooperative. A collaborating individual attempts to works with others endeavoring to find common solutions to fully satisfy the concerns of everyone without compromising or accommodating lesser outcomes. To fully explore the conflict and learn the insight of others, this individual can resolve the disagreement and creatively find solutions that are important to everyone.

A Collaborating mode is useful when:

1. An integral solution to all concerns becomes too important to compromise;
2. The objective is to learn, challenge assumptions, and understand the concerns of others;
3. Integrating the knowledge of others having differing perspectives on critical issues;
4. Gaining commitment and consensual decisions incorporating valid concerns of others.

Myers-Briggs – The Myers-Briggs Type Indicator (**MBTI**) assessment exam, developed by Isabel Briggs Myers and Katharine Cook Briggs, is a psychometric questionnaire based upon typological theories first proposed by Carl Gustav Jung in 1921. Also known as a Personality Inventory tool, the MBTI utilizes four principal psychological functions theorized by Jung to be: sensation, intuition, feeling, and thinking. These principal functions also correlate to four personality preferences, which are interests, needs, values, and motivation. From these, eight different personality traits were extrapolated in the MBTI consisting of: Extroversion (**E**), Introversion (**I**), Sensing (**S**), Intuition (**N**), Thinking (**T**), Feeling (**F**), Judging (**J**), and Perception (**P**), which has a total of sixteen psychometric combinations. The indicator questions used in the exam analyze the way an individual uses perception and judgment in the decision-making. Each combination of traits characterizes its own set of interests, values, and skills. The result of my MBTI Personality Inventory was scored as **I-N-F-J**, which implies Introversion, Intuition, Feeling, and Judging.

I N F J – The "**I**" for introversion likely indicates an individual relates more easily to internal ideals and concepts rather than external people and things. The "**N**" for intuition likely indicates an individual would prefer to look for possibilities and relationships rather than work with known facts and data. The "**F**" for feeling likely indicates an individual may base their judgments more on personal values or morals rather than on logic and analysis. The "**J**" for judging likely means an individual prefers a planned and orderly way of life more so than a flexible and spontaneous lifestyle. As a whole, **I N F J** individuals succeed by perseverance, originality, and the desire to accomplish whatever is needed or wanted. They are quietly forceful, conscientious, and genuinely concerned for others while endeavoring to put their best efforts into their work and achievements.

226

Respected for their firm beliefs and principles, **I N F J** individuals are likely to be honored and followed for their clear convictions in how to best serve the common good. These individuals focus their attention on possibilities handled with personal warmth towards others. With these traits, they tend to become enthusiastic and insightful while defining the scope of their abilities in understanding and communicating with others.

Minnesota Multiphasic Personality Inventory 2 – The Minnesota Multiphasic Personality Inventory 2 exam or **MMPI-2** for short, was first published and copyrighted in 1943 by the University of Minnesota, has since become the most widely used psychometric exam standardized for adult personality inventory assessment. The MMPI-2 test contains 567 very in-depth questions that are extremely broad reaching having ten clinical scales ranging from the following: 1-Hypochondria, 2-Depression, 3-Hysteria, 4-Anti-social, 5-Masculinity/Femininity, 6-Paranoia, 7-Anxiety, 8-Eccentric, 9-Manic, and 0-Social Introversion; where "0" represents the tenth scale. The MMPI-2 is the absolute gold standard for personality inventory assessment and is the third most frequently used exam in the field of psychology. Each of the clinical scales is scored in five levels, which are: Low, Modal, Moderate, High, and Very High. The raw test scores are then converted to a standardized metric known as T-scores, where the Mean or Average score is about 50, having a standard deviation of 10 points. The T-score category scale of "Modal" is considered to be the mean or average in psychological evaluations representing normal adult behavior.

Curious to know the psychological capacity I may have for Leadership, I voluntarily completed the MMPI-2 exam in early 2013, and had the test results of my personality inventory assessment analyzed having the assistance and supervision of a clinical psychologist. Of the ten clinical scales that were examined, six of my score results were "Modal" (normal), three were "Moderate", and only one score was considered "Low". Of the clinical scales in numerical order, the interpretive possibilities of my personal diagnosis suggest I am best described as being: 1). Realistic and insightful; 2). Emotionally well-balanced and modest; 3). Logical and levelheaded; 4). Sincere, trusting, persistent, and responsible; 5). Visionary, idealistic, and considerate; 6). Moralistic and watchful; 7). Orderly and perfectionist; 8). Adaptable and dependable; 9). Sociable, enthusiastic, and poised; and 0). Warm, self-confident, and assertive.

In a related examination, I took a generic online Intelligence Quotient (**IQ**) test achieving a score of **135**, and categorized as a "Visionary and Philosopher". A Genius IQ score generally begins within the range of 140 to 145. My IQ score classifies me in the "Gifted to Very Gifted" category. According to IQ statistical research, only about **1%** of the world population has an IQ of 135 or higher. On an intelligence level, becoming a Licensed Architect without the benefit of a formal college education majoring in Architecture has been a tremendous professional and personal accomplishment, for which I am extremely proud.

If I could pick six words to best describe my leadership personality traits based upon the preceding leadership assessments and examinations, they would include:

1. VISIONARY
2. EMPOWERING
3. COLLABORATIVE
4. INTUITIVE
5. INSIGHTFUL
6. COMMUNICATION

As Commander-in-Chief, the President also assumes command of our military, which consists of the Marine Corps, Navy, Army, and Air Force. However, Civilian leadership is considerably different than Military leadership. The Chain of Command in any military organization is absolutely paramount, and becomes the foundation of Military Leadership.

Related to the military command hierarchy, are the three C's or Command, Control, and Communications – "3C". For Military Leadership to be successful, it is very important that "communications" ensure that "command" actually results in "control". Communication is not just speaking, but more importantly listening. Basically, a metal chain itself cupped in your hands has no inherent strength, only weight. Yet when placed under tension, a chain has tremendous strength. Not unlike the interlocked arms of American Patriots holding the battle line, the Chain of Command is only as strong as its weakest link. Without adherence, the authority of the command structure becomes subverted and ineffective.

It is very important that any potential Presidential candidate completely understands the hierarchy of Military Leadership, which is not democratic.

As your Commander-in-Chief, I want to protect you and this country. I will not hesitate to smite those who wish to bring harm to Americans and our territories. I will defend our United States Constitution from all enemies, foreign and domestic, and enforce all laws protecting our borders.

As your President, I don't want to communicate and just speak to you, I want to equally listen to you. I don't want to control you, I want to empower you. I don't want to command you, I want to inspire you. The other Presidential candidates want to impress you; not me. I want to be a Presidential candidate that will empower and inspire you. I want to empower all Americans to do what they do best, and to encourage each other to do the same. Americans have proven they can achieve true greatness when working together having a single vision and goal.

As an Architect with vision, I want to inspire all Americans to be creative, and to dream of achieving tremendous personal accomplishments, what ever they may be. I don't want to impress you, I want you to impress yourselves and realize the great and wonderful talents you possess. I want to challenge all Americans to challenge themselves. If you can dream it, and believe it, you can do it. I want to enable all Americans to achieve great success in every facet of their life. Each and every American is a priceless human resource.

For a leader to empower Americans there must be motivation; empowerment alone is insufficient. Americans must be motivated and ambitious to become empowered. A leader cannot lead alone. For those to lead, there must be those that follow. And for those that follow, it will require others to manage and delegate, to successfully bring these goals into fruition. And within goals, there are milestones. Goals are not often accomplished as a single task. Goals may require multiple tasks, which in turn may require various milestones to be achieved. Successfully reaching individual tasks and milestones will determine the rate and future success in achieving the required goals. These tasks and milestones will require management. A manager will then delegate these critical tasks to those who possess specialized talents best suited to accomplish these tasks. And those that accomplish these tasks and milestones, become the priceless human resource a leader will rely on for success. A leader is not a manager. Americans should not confuse leadership with management. A leader does not delegate specific details, but rather provides vision for other to do so. A President does not manage Americans. A President leads America.

For a leader to inspire Americans there must be vision; inspiration alone is insufficient. A President must have vision and forethought to successfully express and communicate the goals necessary to be achieved. Without specific goals, vision alone is insufficient. I have previously discussed tasks I wish to achieve within the first one hundred days as President. I now want to describe more generally the specific goals I wish to accomplish. Listing only three of the most important goals I have as President in the order of their priority, they would include:

1. SECURE OUR BORDERS;

2. RESTRUCTURE THE FEDERAL RESERVE;

3. CREATE A FEDERAL DEMOCRACY.

Securing our borders is a matter of "National Security". A country has borders. A nation has citizens. Borders are not meant to keep citizens in, but rather to keep those who wish to bring harm to Americans and destruction to our nation out of the country. I want to protect America from enemies and forces outside of our country. Our government is secretly spying on each and every American believing the threat to our nation is actually from within. When our country has open borders that enable 12 million illegal aliens and possible Islamic terrorists to enter our country freely, of course the threat becomes internal. The unwarranted actions of our government and NSA against its own citizens results in American cynicism and paranoia, which then enables the potential threat of domestic terrorism, which then justifies the actions of our government, which then becomes a vicious cycle, and conundrum of unsecured borders.

Restructuring our Federal Reserve is a matter of "Financial Security". I hope to transform our nation's Federal Reserve system into an institution to protect the wealth and prosperity of American citizens while assisting the financing of our United States government, rather than the mechanism it has become to enable the greed and corruption of the American banking and lending industry. When the government no longer provides a security apparatus for banks and lenders to protect their fiscal irresponsibility at the great risk and cost of American taxpayers, their financial activities will then become their responsibility and liability, not Americans. A Federal Reserve Savings Banks will enable depositors to receive interest that will offset economic inflationary periods, while indirectly establishing and impacting the commercial lending interest rates of our banking system.

Creating a Federal Democracy is a matter of "Political Security". Our nation is not a democracy. The United States Constitution specifically states our country has a "Republican" form of government, not a "Democracy". The Legislative Branch of our government has become much too powerful and corrupt. I believe this disparity in Congressional power can be more equally reallocated to the several sovereign State legislatures that form our United States. The Electoral College detailed in our Constitution used to elect our President and Vice President is not at all democratic. It is an old mechanism created during a time of slavery and illiteracy in our nation that has become antiquated in need of replacement.

I believe neither the Democrat nor the Republican presidential candidates truly have the ability to unite our county, as it deserves to be united. The winning candidate for the Office of the President must not be the lesser of two evils. Neither the Democratic National Committee nor the Republican National Committee will dictate my political platform. I have my own soapbox to stand on, and will use my platform to speak my independent mind pursuing my vision to empower and inspire Americans while restoring Life, Liberty, Equality, and the pursuit of individual and personal Happiness to everyone in our great nation.

This country deserves a candidate that is central and independently focused on the important issues facing this great nation. Someone forging a common path to our enduring freedom and prosperity. A President that will empower and inspire Americans to make the United States a great country again. A President that has a plan to build American into a nation that will once again inspire the world. A Presidential candidate that has a blueprint for our future. When you vote for our next President, don't just vote for a candidate; cast your precious ballot for a great leader.

Our country is again at the crossroads of a new American Revolution. This time it is not in between the Hudson and Delaware Rivers in the Garden State of New Jersey. The revolutionary crossroad we face today is located at Main Street in Your Town, USA. The revolutionary issues that confronted our forefathers and my ancestors are no different today, than they were over two hundred years ago. Freedom, liberty, taxation, representation, and self-governance hindered by the status quo still remain worth fighting for. Our enemy is not the crown; our enemy is our bicameral Congress and the corrupt gang of racketeers than govern our Legislative Branch of Government.

231

"Instead of fighting with bullets, we shall fight with ballots."
~Marty Piatt, Architect

I wish to proudly follow in the Patriot footsteps of my family ancestors, the "Fighting Five Piatts" who bravely fought in our nation's American Revolutionary War. I believe my political endeavors and ambitions would make Major Daniel Piatt, and U.S. Civil War veteran Amos Daniel Piatt extremely proud. I am very honored and grateful to be one of many proud Piatt family descendants still fighting for our freedom.

If more than half of all American voters, believing that neither Democrats nor Republicans deserve the continued "privilege" to govern this great nation voted for me, I could win the Presidential election;

If more than half of all American voters, believing our current Republican form of national governance should be transformed into a Constitutional Federal Democracy voted for me, I could win the Presidential election;

If more than half of all American voters, believing that our antiquated 18th century Electoral College system of electing our President should be abolished and transformed into a Constitutional Federal Democracy of the 21st century, I could win the Presidential election;

If more than half of all American voters, believing that our existing Legislative Branch of Government consisting of a bicameral Congress has become a "corrupt gang of criminal racketeers" voted for me, I could win the Presidential election;

If more than half of all American voters, believing that all men and women are created equally voted for me, I could win the Presidential election;

If every woman and every minority, believing in a new Constitution instituted by our 28th amendment that will contain a Constitutional Article for Equal Rights voted for me, I could win the Presidential election;

By Marty Piatt, Architect

If 1/3 of all Democrats, and 1/3 of all Republicans, and 100% of all independent voters, believing that our current duopoly political system is in need of real change voted for me, I could win the Presidential election;

If every conservative Democrat, every liberal Republican, and every independent voter in the political center voted for me, I could win the Presidential election;

If more than half of Americans voters, believing that tax assessments levied on personal property unjustly penalizes a select portion of American citizens to finance Federal or State budget expenditures should become unconstitutional voted for me, I could win the Presidential election;

If more than half of Americans voters, believing than tax assessments levied by the Federal or State governments should only include personal income and/or consumption taxation voted for me, I could win the Presidential election;

If more than half of Americans voters, believing that we should venture into our universe and galaxy to explore, rather than venturing into unwanted war voted for me, I could win the Presidential election;

If 99% of American voters living on Main Street proudly occupying the United States of America voted for me, I could definitely win the next Presidential election in November 2016.

With my vision, I have drawn the plans to lead as your next President. This book is history. These pages have revisited our past, reaffirmed our present, and hopefully foretold our very bright future. I sincerely believe My Blueprint for American is our nation's way forward to begin a new era in American history, politics, and Presidential governance. As a nation, we must first take a step back, before we can take a leap of faith forward.

I am not a writer. I am an American Patriot attempting to follow in the historic footsteps of my proud ancestors who served our great country at a very critical and important time in our nation's rich history. Our nation is once again at a very critical time in American history. I sincerely hope this book and my optimistic political vision has provided not only information, but also more importantly inspiration. As Americans, I want you to reach for the stars, and travel to the stars; you can stand on my shoulders.

"Nothing changes until everything changes."
~Marty Piatt, Architect

"A house divided against itself cannot stand."
~The Bible, [Mark 3:25]

"United we stand, divided we fall."
~Author unknown

"America will never be destroyed from the outside. If we falter
and lose our freedoms, it will be because we destroyed ourselves."
~President Abraham Lincoln

"Lady Liberty has lost her way, and Lady Justice is blind,
and cannot help her." ~Marty Piatt, Architect

"Motivation is the art of getting people to do what you
want them to do because they want to do it."
~President and General Dwight D. Eisenhower

"Insight can only be truly obtained by delving past the facade
and illusory propaganda your own world feeds you."
~Josh M. Black

BIOGRAPHY

I was born Marty Eugene Piatt to Gale and Joana Piatt at 2:31 pm on Tuesday, the 21st of October 1958. I was the runt and last born in a set of newborn triplet babies weighing about 3 lbs. 15 oz. Having four older brothers, Christopher the oldest, Kevin the second oldest, Matthew (triplet #1), and Mark (triplet #2). Baby brother Kerry followed me thereafter. Kerry sadly passed away as a toddler at the age of 11 months from congenital heart and internal organ birth defects.

Brother Kevin died as a young adult at the age of 22; killed by a drunk driving illegal alien from Mexico that was charged with hit and run, leaving the scene of an accident, driving under the influence of alcohol, and vehicular manslaughter. The killer of my brother was sentenced to less than one year in county jail with his time served in the Sutter County Jail located in Yuba City, California.

After graduating from Marysville High School in June 1976, I later attended Yuba College and received an Associate of Science (AS) degree with a major in Architecture, and a minor in both Calculus and Physics in 1979. I later attended California State Polytechnic University at Pomona, California.

In 1980 I left northern California to seek architectural employment in southern California ending up in Orange County. I moved to Laguna Niguel in 1985.

From 1978 to 2005 I worked in the architecture and construction industries in both private practice and commercial employment.

I received my license as Registered Architect in the State of California in April 1988 after completing my 8-year minimum apprenticeship and having passed the 4-day, 32 1/2 hour Architects Registration Exam (ARE) without the benefit of a formal Bachelors Degree in Architecture.

I am among our nation's 5% of registered Architects licensed without a formal college education. Architects such as myself are referred to as "Maverick" architects in the industry, very similar to the term "Mustang" in the United States Navy.

I received my license as a Registered General Building Contractor in the State of California in March 1992.

I received my certification as a LEED Accredited Professional (LEED AP) in June 2009.

I received my certificate in our nation's Anti-Terrorism Force Protection (ATFP) from the Naval Facilities Engineering Service Center (NFESC) located in Port Hueneme, California in January 2010. As part of the Defense Acquisition Workforce Improvement Act (DAWIA) of 1990, I have earned and received the following six (6) DAWIA Career Field Certifications:

Facilities Engineering Level III in October 2009;
Financial Management Level I in August 2010;
Program Management Level I in September 2010;
Business Cost Estimating Level I in April 2011.

From October 2005 to the present, I have been employed by the Department of Defense within the Department of the Navy at Naval Facilities Engineering Command Southwest (NAVFAC SW) proudly serving my country currently working as a Construction Manager at the Resident Officer In Charge of Construction (ROICC), Marine Corps Base Camp Pendleton, California.

In 2006 I sold my Laguna Niguel property after nearly 22 years, and moved to Oceanside, California located in northern San Diego County, where I currently reside with my English Bulldog named Dozer.

You are also invited to visit and join my blog:
"Marty Piatt for U.S. President" webpage on Facebook.

APPENDIX

- Mayflower compact – 1620

- Frame of Government of Pennsylvania – 1682

- Declaration of Independence – 1776

- Articles of Confederation – 1778

- United States Constitution – 1787

- Amendments to the Constitution – 1791 to 1992

- 2017 Articles of Federation

MAYFLOWER COMPACT

In the name of God, Amen. We, whose names are underwritten, the loyal subjects of our dread Sovereign Lord King James, by the Grace of God, of Great Britain, France, and Ireland, King, defender of the Faith, etc.

Having undertaken, for the Glory of God, and advancements of the Christian faith and honor of our King and Country, a voyage to plant the first colony in the Northern parts of Virginia, do by these presents, solemnly and mutually, in the presence of God, and one another, covenant and combine ourselves together into a civil body politic; for our better ordering, and preservation and furtherance of the ends aforesaid; and by virtue hereof to enact, constitute, and frame, such just and equal laws, ordinances, acts, constitutions, and offices, from time to time, as shall be thought most meet and convenient for the general good of the colony; unto which we promise all due submission and obedience.

In witness whereof we have hereunto subscribed our names at Cape Cod the 11th of November, in the year of the reign of our Sovereign Lord King James, …1620.

FRAME OF GOVERNMENT FOR PENNSYLVANIA

The frame of the government of the province of Pennsylvania, in America: together with certain laws agreed upon in England, by the Governor and divers freemen of the aforesaid province. To be further explained and confirmed there, by the first provincial Council, that shall be held, if they see meet.

THE PREFACE

When the great and wise God had made the world, of all his creatures, it pleased him to choose man his Deputy to rule it: and to fit him for so great a charge and trust, he did not only qualify him with skill and power, but with integrity to use them justly. This native goodness was equally his honor and his happiness; and whilst he stood here, all went well; there was no need of coercive or compulsive means; the precept of divine love and truth, in his bosom, was the guide and keeper of his innocency. But lust prevailing against duty, made a lamentable breach upon it; and the law, that before had no power over him, took place upon him, and his disobedient posterity, that such as would not live comfortable to the holy law within, should fall under the reproof and correction of the just law without, in a judicial administration.

This the Apostle teaches in divers of his epistles: "The law (says he) was added because of transgression: "In another place, "Knowing that the law was not made for the righteous man; but for the disobedient and ungodly, for sinners, for unholy and profane, for murderers, for whoremongers, for them that defile themselves with mankind, and for man-stealers, for liars, for perjured persons," etc., but this is not all, he opens and carries the matter of government a little further: "Let every soul be subject to the higher powers; for there is no power but of God. The powers that be are ordained of God: whosoever therefore resists the power, resists the ordinance of God. For rulers are not a terror to good works, but to evil: wilt thou then not be afraid of the power? do that which is good, and thou shalt have praise of the same." "He is the minister of God to thee for good." "Wherefore ye must needs be subject, not only for wrath, but for conscience sake."

This settles the divine right of government beyond exception, and that for two ends: first, to terrify evil doers: secondly, to cherish those that do well; which gives government a life beyond corruption, and makes it as durable in the world, as good men shall be. So that government seems to me a part of religion itself, a thing sacred in its institution and end. For, if it does not directly remove the cause, it crushes the effects of evil, and is as such, (though a lower, yet) an emanation of the same Divine Power, that is both author and object of pure religion; the difference lying here, that the one is more free and mental, the other more corporal and compulsive in its operations: but that is only to evil doers; government itself being otherwise as capable of kindness, goodness and charity, as a more private society. They weakly err, that think there is no other use of government, than correction, which is the coarsest part of it: daily experience tells us, that the care and regulation of many other affairs, more soft, and daily necessary, make up much of the greatest part of government; and which must have followed the peopling of the world, had Adam never fell, and will continue among men, on earth, under the highest attainments they may arrive at, by the coming of the blessed Second Adam, the Lord from heaven. Thus much of government in general, as to its rise and end.

For particular frames and models, it will become me to say little; and comparatively I will say nothing. My reasons are:

First. That the age is too nice and difficult for it; there being nothing the wits of men are more busy and divided upon. It is true, they seem to agree to the end, to wit, happiness; but, in the means, they differ, as to divine, so to this human felicity; and the cause is much the same, not always want of light and knowledge, but want of using them rightly. Men side with their passions against their reason, and their sinister interests have so strong a bias upon their minds, that they lean to them against the good of the things they know.

Secondly, I do not find a model in the world, that time, place, and some singular emergences have not necessarily altered; nor is it easy to frame a civil government, that shall serve all places alike.

240

Thirdly. I know what is said by the several admirers of monarchy, aristocracy and democracy, which are the rule of one, a few, and many, and are the three common ideas of government, when men discourse on the subject. But I choose to solve the controversy with this small distinction, and it belongs to all three: Any government is free to the people under it (whatever be the frame) where the laws rule, and the people are a party to those laws, and more than this is tyranny, oligarchy, or confusion.

But, lastly, when all is said, there is hardly one frame of government in the world so ill designed by its first founders, that, in good hands, would not do well enough; and story tells us, the best, in ill ones, can do nothing that is great or good; witness the Jewish and Roman states. Governments, like clocks, go from the motion men give them; and as governments are made and moved by men, so by them they are ruined too. Wherefore governments rather depend upon men, than men upon governments. Let men be good, and the government cannot be bad; if it be ill, they will cure it. But, if men be bad, let the government be never so good, they will endeavor to warp and spoil it to their turn.

I know some say, let us have good laws, and no matter for the men that execute them: but let them consider, that though good laws do well, good men do better: for good laws may want good men, and be abolished or evaded [invaded in Franklin's print] by ill men; but good men will never want good laws, nor suffer ill ones. It is true, good laws have some awe upon ill ministers, but that is where they have not power to escape or abolish them, and the people are generally wise and good: but a loose and depraved people (which is the question) love laws and an administration like themselves. That, therefore, which makes a good constitution, must keep it, viz: men of wisdom and virtue, qualities, that because they descend not with worldly inheritances, must be carefully propagated by a virtuous education of youth; for which after ages will owe more to the care and prudence of founders, and the successive magistracy, than to their parents, for their private patrimonies.

These considerations of the weight of government, and the nice and various opinions about it, made it uneasy to me to think of publishing the ensuing frame and conditional laws, foreseeing both the censures, they will meet with, from men of differing humors and engagements, and the occasion they may give of discourse beyond my design.

But, next to the power of necessity, (which is a solicitor, that will take no denial) this induced me to a compliance, that we have (with reverence to God, and good conscience to men) to the best of our skill, contrived and composed the frame and laws of this government, to the great end of all government, viz: To support power in reverence with the people, and to secure the people from the abuse of power; that they may be free by their just obedience, and the magistrates honorable, for their just administration: for liberty without obedience is confusion, and obedience without liberty is slavery. To carry this evenness is partly owing to the constitution, and partly to the magistracy: where either of these fail, government will be subject to convulsions; but where both are wanting, it must be totally subverted; then where both meet, the government is like to endure. Which I humbly pray and hope God will please to make the lot of this of Pennsylvania. Amen.

WILLIAM PENN.

THE FRAME, ETC. - APRIL 25, 1682

I. To all Persons, to whom these presents may come. WHEREAS, king Charles the Second, by his letters patents, under the great seal of England, bearing date the fourth day of March in the Thirty and Third Year of the King, for divers considerations therein mentioned, hath been graciously pleased to give and grant unto me William Penn, by the name of William Penn, Esquire, son and heir of Sir William Penn, deceased, and to my heirs and assigns forever, all that tract of land, or Province, called Pennsylvania, in America, with divers great powers, pre-eminences, royalties, jurisdictions, and authorities, necessary for the well-being and government thereof: Now know ye, that for the well-being and government of the said province, and for the encouragement of all the freemen and planters that may be therein concerned, in pursuance of the powers aforementioned, I, the said William Penn, have declared, granted, and confirmed, and by these presents, for me, my heirs and assigns, do declare, grant, and confirm unto all the freemen, planters and adventurers of, in and to the said province, these liberties, franchises, and properties, to be held, enjoyed and kept by the freemen, planters, and inhabitants of the said province of Pennsylvania for ever.

By Marty Piatt, Architect

Imprimis. That the government of this province shall, according to the powers of the patent, consist of the Governor and freemen of the said province, in form of a provincial Council and General Assembly, by whom all laws shall be made, officers chosen, and public affairs transacted, as is hereafter respectively declared, that is to say--

II. That the freemen of the said province shall, on the twentieth day of the twelfth month, which shall be in this present year one thousand six hundred eighty and two, meet and assemble in some fit place, of which timely notice shall be before hand given by the Governor or his Deputy; and then, and there, shall choose out of themselves seventy-two persons of most note for their wisdom, virtue and ability, who shall meet, on the tenth day of the first month next ensuing, and always be called, and act as, the provincial Council of the said province.

III. That, at the first choice of such provincial Council, one-third part of the said provincial Council shall be chosen to serve for three years, then next ensuing; one-third part, for two years then next ensuing; and one-third part, for one year then next ensuing such election, and no longer; and that the said third part shall go out accordingly: and on the twentieth day of the twelfth month, as aforesaid, yearly for ever afterwards, the freemen of the said province shall, in like manner, meet and assemble together, and then choose twenty-four persons, being one-third of the said number, to serve in provincial Council for three years: it being intended, that one-third part of the whole provincial Council (always consisting, and to Consist, of seventy-two persons, as aforesaid) falling off yearly, it shall be yearly supplied by such new yearly elections, as aforesaid; and that no one person shall continue therein longer than three years: and, in case any member shall decease before the last election during his time, that then at the next election ensuing his decease, another shall be chosen to supply his place, for the remaining time, he was to have served, and no longer.

IV. That, after the first seven years, every one of the said third parts, that goes yearly off, shall be incapable of being chosen again for one whole year following: that so all may be fitted for government, and have experience of the care and burden of it.

V. That the provincial Council, in all cases and matters of moment, as their arguing upon bills to be passed into laws, erecting courts of justice, giving judgment upon criminals impeached, and choice of officers, in such

243

manner as is hereinafter mentioned, not less than two-thirds of the whole provincial Council shall make a quorum, and that the consent and approbation of two-thirds of such quorum shall be had in all such cases and matters of moment.

And moreover that, in all cases and matters of lesser moment, twenty-four Members of the said provincial Council shall make a quorum, the majority of which twenty-four shall, and may, always determine in such cases and causes of lesser moment.

VI. That, in this provincial Council, the Governor or his Deputy, shall or may, always preside, and have a treble voice; and the said provincial Council shall always continue, and sit upon its own adjournments and committees.

VII. That the Governor and provincial Council shall prepare and propose to the General Assembly, hereafter mentioned, all bills, which they shall, at any time, think fit to be passed into laws, within the said province; which bills shall be published and affixed to the most noted places, in the inhabited parts thereof, thirty days before the meeting of the General Assembly, in order to the passing them into laws or rejecting of them, as the General Assembly shall see meet.

VIII. That the Governor and provincial Council shall take care, that all laws, statutes and ordinances, which shall at any time be made within the said province, be duly and diligently executed.

IX. That the Governor and provincial Council shall, at all times, have the care of the peace and safety of the province, and that nothing be by any person attempted to the subversion of this frame of government.

X. That the Governor and provincial Council shall, at all times, settle and order the situation of all cities, ports, and market towns in every county, modelling therein all public buildings, streets, and market places, and shall appoint all necessary roads, and high-ways in the province.

XI. That the Governor and provincial Council shall, at all times, have power to inspect the management of the public treasury, and punish those who shall convert any part thereof to any other use, than what hath been agreed upon by the Governor, provincial Council, and General Assembly.

XII. That the Governor and provincial Council, shall erect and order all public schools, and encourage and reward the authors of useful sciences and laudable inventions in the said province.

XIII. That, for the better management of the powers and trust aforesaid, the provincial Council shall, from time to time, divide itself into four distinct and proper committees, for the more easy administration of the affairs of the Province, which divides the seventy-two into four eighteens, every one of which eighteens shall consist of six out of each of the three orders, or yearly elections, each of which shall have a distinct portion of business, as followeth: First, a committee of plantations, to situate and settle cities, ports, and market towns, and high-ways, and to hear and decide all suits and controversies relating to plantations. Secondly, a committee of justice and safety, to secure the peace of the Province, and punish the mal-administration of those who subvert justice to the prejudice of the public, or private, interest. Thirdly, a committee of trade and treasury, who shall regulate all trade and commerce, according to law, encourage manufacture and country growth, and defray the public charge of the Province. And, Fourthly, a committee of manners, education, and arts, that all wicked and scandalous living may be prevented, and that youth may be successively trained up in virtue and useful knowledge and arts: the quorum of each of which committees being six, that is, two out of each of the three orders, or yearly elections, as aforesaid, make a constant and standing Council of twenty-four, which will have the power of the provincial Council, being the quorum of it, in all cases not excepted in the fifth article; and in the said committees, and standing Council of the Province, the Governor, or his Deputy, shall, or may preside, as aforesaid; and in the absence of the Governor, or his Deputy, if no one is by either of them appointed, the said committees or Council shall appoint a President for that time, and not otherwise; and what shall be resolved at such committees, shall be reported to the said Council of the province, and shall be by them resolved and confirmed before the same shall be put in execution; and that these respective committees shall not sit at one and the same time, except in cases of necessity.

XIV. And, to the end that all laws prepared by the Governor and provincial Council aforesaid, may yet have the more full concurrence of the freemen of the province, it is declared, granted and confirmed, that, at the time and place or places, for the choice of a provincial Council, as aforesaid, the said freemen shall yearly choose Members to serve in a

General Assembly, as their representatives, not exceeding two hundred persons, who shall yearly meet on the twentieth day of the second month, which shall be in the year one thousand six hundred eighty and three following, in the capital town, or city, of the said province, where, during eight days, the several Members may freely confer with one another; and, if any of them see meet, with a committee of the provincial Council (consisting of three out of each of the four committees aforesaid, being twelve in all) which shall be, at that time, purposely appointed to receive from any of them proposals, for the alterations or amendment of any of the said proposed and promulgated bills: and on the ninth day from their so meeting, the said General Assembly, after reading over the proposed bills by the Clerk of the provincial Council, and the occasions and motives for them being opened by the Governor or his Deputy, shall give their affirmative or negative, which to them seems best, in such manner as hereinafter is expressed. But not less than two-thirds shall make a quorum in the passing of laws, and choice of such officers as are by them to be chosen.

XV. That the laws so prepared and proposed, as aforesaid, that are assented to by the General Assembly, shall be enrolled as laws of the Province, with this stile: By the Governor, with the assent and approbation of the freemen in provincial Council and General Assembly.

XVI. That, for the establishment of the government and laws of this province, and to the end there may be an universal satisfaction in the laying of the fundamentals thereof: the General Assembly shall, or may, for the first year, consist of all the freemen of and in the said province; and ever after it shall be yearly chosen, as aforesaid; which number of two hundred shall be enlarged as the country shall increase in people, so as it do not exceed five hundred, at any time; the appointment and proportioning of which, as also the laying and methodizing of the choice of the provincial Council and General Assembly, in future times, most equally to the divisions of the hundreds and counties, which the country shall hereafter be divided into, shall be in the power of the provincial Council to propose, and the General Assembly to resolve.

XVII. That the Governor and the provincial Council shall erect, from time to time, standing courts of justice, in such places and number as they shall judge convenient for the good government of the said province. And that the provincial Council shall, on the thirteenth day of the first month, yearly, elect and present to the Governor, or his Deputy, a double number of persons, to serve for Judges, Treasurers, Masters of Rolls, within the said province, for the year next ensuing; and the freemen of the said province, in the county courts, which they shall be erected, and till then, in the General Assembly, shall, on the three and twentieth day of the second month, yearly, elect and present to the Governor, or his Deputy, a double member of persons, to serve for Sheriffs, Justices of the Peace, and Coroners, for the year next ensuing; out of which respective elections and presentments, the Governor or his Deputy shall nominate and commission the proper number for each Officer, the third day after the said presentments, or else the first named in such presentment, for each office, shall stand and serve for that office the year ensuing.

XVIII. But forasmuch as the present condition of the province requires some immediate settlement, and admits not of so quick a revolution of officers; and to the end the said Province may, with all convenient speed, be well ordered and settled, I, William Penn, do therefore think fit to nominate and appoint such persons for Judges, Treasurers, Masters of the Rolls, Sheriffs, Justices of the Peace, and Coroners, as are most fitly qualified for those employments; to whom I shall make and grant commissions for the said offices, respectively, to hold to them, to whom the same shall be granted, for so long time as every such person shall well behave himself in the office, or place, to him respectively granted, and no longer. And upon the decease or displacing of any of the said officers, the succeeding officer, or officers, shall be chosen, as aforesaid.

XIX. That the General Assembly shall continue so long as may be needful to impeach criminals, fit to be there impeached, to pass bills into laws, that they shall think fit to pass into laws, and till such time as the Governor and provincial Council shall declare that they have nothing further to propose unto them, for their assent and approbation: and that declaration shall be a dismiss to the General Assembly for that time; which General Assembly shall be, notwithstanding, capable of assembling together upon the summons of the provincial Council, at any time during that year, if the said provincial Council shall see occasion for their so assembling.

XX. That all the elections of members, or representatives of the people, to serve in provincial Council and General Assembly, and all questions to be determined by both, or either of them, that relate to passing of bills into laws, to the choice of officers, to impeachments by the General Assembly, and judgment of criminals upon such impeachments by the provincial Council, and to all other cases by them respectively judged of importance, shall be resolved and determined by the ballot; and unless on sudden and indispensable occasions, no business in provincial Council, or its respective committees, shall be finally determined the same day that it is moved.

XXI. That at all times when, and so often as it shall happen that the Governor shall or may be an infant, under the age of one and twenty years, and no guardians or commissioners are appointed in writing, by the father of the said infant, or that such guardians or commissioners, shall be deceased; that during such minority, the provincial Council shall, from time to time, as they shall see meet, constitute and appoint guardians or commissioners, not exceeding three; one of which three shall preside as deputy and chief guardian, during such minority, and shall have and execute, with the consent of the other two, all the power of a Governor, in all the public affairs and concerns of the said province.

XXII. That, as often as any day of the month, mentioned in any article of this charter, shall fall upon the first day of the week, commonly called the Lord's Day, the business appointed for that day shall be deferred till the next day, unless in case of emergency.

XXIII. That no act, law, or ordinance whatsoever, shall at any time hereafter, be made or done by the Governor of this province, his heirs or assigns, or by the freemen in the provincial Council, or the General Assembly, to alter, change, or diminish the form, or effect, of this charter, or any part, or clause thereof, without the consent of the Governor, his heirs, or assigns, and six parts of seven of the said freemen in provincial Council and General Assembly.

XXIV. And lastly, that I, the said William Penn, for myself, my heirs and assigns, have solemnly declared, granted and confirmed, and do hereby solemnly declare, grant and confirm, that neither I, my heirs, nor assigns, shall procure or do anything or things, whereby the liberties, in this charter contained and expressed, shall be infringed or broken; and if anything be procured by any person or persons contrary to these premises, it shall be held of no force or effect. In witness whereof, I, the said William Penn, have unto this present character of liberties set my hand and broad seal, this five and twentieth day of the second month, vulgarly called April, in the year of our Lord one thousand six hundred and eighty-two.

WILLIAM PENN.

LAWS AGREED UPON IN ENGLAND, ETC.

I.   That the charter of liberties, declared, granted and confirmed the five and twentieth day of the second month, called April, 1682, before divers witnesses, by William Penn, Governor and chief Proprietor of Pennsylvania, to all the freemen and planters of the said province, is hereby declared and approved, and shall be forever held for fundamental in the government thereof, according to the limitations mentioned in the said charter.

II.   That every inhabitant in the said province, that is or shall be, a purchaser of one hundred acres of land, or upwards, his heirs and assigns, and every person who shall have paid his passage, and taken up one hundred acres of land, at one penny an acre, and have cultivated ten acres thereof, and every person, that hath been a servant, or bonds-man, and is free by his service, that shall have taken up his fifty acres of land, and cultivated twenty thereof, and every inhabitant, artificer, or other resident in the said province, that pays scot and lot to the government; shall be deemed and accounted a freeman of the said province: and every such person shall, and may, be capable of electing, or being elected, representatives of the people, in provincial Council, or General Assembly, in the said province.

III.   That all elections of members, or representatives of the people and freemen of the province of Pennsylvania, to serve in provincial Council, or General Assembly, to be held within the said province, shall be free and voluntary: and that the elector, that shall receive any reward or gift, in meat, drink, monies, or otherwise, shall forfeit his right to elect; and such person as shall directly or indirectly give, promise, or bestow any such reward as aforesaid, to be elected, shall forfeit his election, and be thereby incapable to serve as aforesaid: and the provincial Council and General Assembly shall be the sole judges of the regularity, or irregularity of the elections of their own respective Members.

IV. That no money or goods shall be raised upon, or paid by, any of the people of this province by way of public tax, custom or contribution, but by a law, for that purpose made; and whoever shall levy, collect, or pay any money or goods contrary thereunto, shall be held a public enemy to the province and a betrayer of the liberties of the people thereof.

V. That all courts shall be open, and justice shall neither be sold, denied nor delayed.

VI. That, in all courts all persons of all persuasions may freely appear in their own way, and according to their own manner, and there personally plead their own cause themselves; or, if unable, by their friends: and the first process shall be the exhibition of the complaint in court, fourteen days before the trial; and that the party, complained against, may be fitted for the same, he or she shall be summoned, no less than ten days before, and a copy of the complaint delivered him or her, at his or her dwelling house. But before the complaint of any person be received, he shall solemnly declare in court, that he believes, in his conscience, his cause is just.

VII. That all pleadings, processes and records in courts, shall be short, and in English, and in an ordinary and plain character, that they may be understood, and justice speedily administered.

VIII. That all trials shall be by twelve men, and as near as may be, peers or equals, and of the neighborhood, and men without just exception; in cases of life, there shall be first twenty-four returned by the sheriffs, for a grand inquest, of whom twelve, at least, shall find the complaint to be true; and then the twelve men, or peers, to be likewise returned by the sheriff, shall have the final judgment. But reasonable challenges shall be always admitted against the said twelve men, or any of them.

IX. That all fees in all cases shall be moderate, and settled by the provincial Council, and General Assembly, and be hung up in a table in every respective court; and whosoever shall be convicted of taking more, shall pay twofold, and be dismissed his employment; one moiety of which shall go to the party wronged.

X. That all prisons shall be work-houses, for felons, vagrants, and loose and idle persons; whereof one shall be in every county.

XI. That all prisoners shall be bailable by sufficient sureties, unless for capital offenses, where the proof is evident, or the presumption great.

XII. That all persons wrongfully imprisoned, or prosecuted at law, shall have double damages against the informer, or prosecutor.

XIII. That all prisons shall be free, as to fees, food and lodging.

XIV. That all lands and goods shall be liable to pay debts, except where there is legal issue, and then all the goods, and one-third of the land only.

XV. That all wills, in writing, attested by two witnesses, shall be of the same force as to lands, as other conveyances, being legally proved within forty days, either within or without the said province.

XVI. That seven years quiet possession shall give an unquestionable right, except in cases of infants, lunatics, married women, or persons beyond the seas.

XVII. That all briberies and extortion whatsoever shall be severely punished.

XVIII. That all fines shall be moderate, and saving men's contenements, merchandize, or wainage.

XIX. That all marriages (not forbidden by the law of God, as to nearness of blood and affinity by marriage) shall be encouraged; but the parents, or guardians, shall be first consulted, and the marriage shall be published before it be solemnized; and it shall be solemnized by taking one another as husband and wife, before credible witnesses; and a certificate of the whole, under the hands of parties and witnesses, shall be brought to the proper register of that county, and shall be registered in his office.

XX. And, to prevent frauds and vexatious suits within the said province, that all charters, gifts, grants, and conveyances of and (except leases for a year or under) and all bills, bonds, and specialties above five pounds, and not under three months, made in the said province, shall be enrolled, or registered in the public enrolment office of the said province, within the space of two months next after the making thereof, else to be void in law, and all deeds, grants, and conveyances of land (except as aforesaid) within the said province, and made out of the said province, shall be enrolled or registered, as aforesaid, within six months next after the making thereof, and settling and constituting an enrolment office or registry within the said province, else to be void in law against all persons whatsoever.

XXI. That all defacer or corrupters of charters, gifts, grants, bonds, bills, wills, contracts, and conveyances, or that shall deface or falsify any enrolment, registry or record, within this province, shall make double satisfaction for the same; half whereof shall go to the party wronged, and they shall be dismissed of all places of trust, and be publicly disgraced as false men.

XXII. That there shall be a register for births, marriages, burials, wills, and letters of administration, distinct from the other registry.

XXIII. That there shall be a register for all servants, where their names, time, wages, and days of payment shall be registered.

XXIV. That all lands and goods of felons shall be liable, to make satisfaction to the party wronged twice the value; and for want of lands or goods, the felons shall be bondmen to work in the common prison, or work-house, or otherwise, till the party injured be satisfied.

XXV. That the estates of capital offenders, as traitors and murderers, shall go, one-third to the next of kin to the sufferer, and the remainder to the next of kin to the criminal.

XXVI. That all witnesses, coming, or called, to testify their knowledge in or to any matter or thing, in any court, or before any lawful authority, within the said province, shall there give or deliver in their evidence, or testimony, by solemnly promising to speak the truth, the whole truth, and nothing but the truth, to the matter, or thing in question. And in case any person so called to evidence, shall be convicted of wilful falsehood, such person shall suffer and undergo such damage or penalty, as the person, or persons, against whom he or she bore false witness, did, or should, undergo; and shall also make satisfaction to the party wronged, and be publicly exposed as a false witness, never to be credited in any court, or before any Magistrate, in the said province.

XXVII. And, to the end that all officers chosen to serve within this province, may, with more care and diligence, answer the trust reposed in them, it is agreed, that no such person shall enjoy more than one public office, at one time.

XXVIII. That all children, within this province, of the age of twelve years, shall be taught some useful trade or skill, to the end none may be idle, but the poor may work to live, and the rich, if they become poor, may not want.

XXIX. That servants be not kept longer than their time, and such as are careful, be both justly and kindly used in their service, and put in fitting equipage at the expiration thereof, according to custom.

XXX. That all scandalous and malicious reporters, backbiters, defamers and spreaders of false news, whether against Magistrates, or private persons, shall be accordingly severely punished, as enemies to the peace and concord of this province.

XXXI. That for the encouragement of the planters and traders in this province, who are incorporated into a society, the patent granted to them by William Penn, Governor of the said province, is hereby ratified and confirmed.

XXXII. * * *

XXXIII. That all factors or correspondents in the said province, wronging their employers, shall make satisfaction, and one-third over, to their said employers: and in case of the death of any such factor or correspondent, the committee of trade shall take care to secure so much of the deceased party's estate as belongs to his said respective employers.

XXXIV. That all Treasurers, Judges, Masters of the Rolls, Sheriffs, Justices of the Peace, and other officers and persons whatsoever, relating to courts, or trials of causes, or any other service in the government; and all Members elected to serve in provincial Council and General Assembly, and all that have right to elect such Members, shall be such as possess faith in Jesus Christ, and that are not convicted of ill fame, or unsober and dishonest conversation, and that are of one and twenty years of age, at least; and that all such so qualified, shall be capable of the said several employments and privileges, as aforesaid.

XXXV. That all persons living in this province, who confess and acknowledge the one Almighty and eternal God, to be the Creator, Upholder and Ruler of the world; and that hold themselves obliged in conscience to live peaceably and justly in civil society, shall, in no ways, be molested or prejudiced for their religious persuasion, or practice, in matters of faith and worship, nor shall they be compelled, at any time, to frequent or maintain any religious worship, place or ministry whatever.

XXXVI. That, according to the good example of the primitive Christians, and the case of the creation, every first day of the week, called the Lord's day, people shall abstain from their common daily labor, that they may the better dispose themselves to worship God according to their understandings.

XXXVII. That as a careless and corrupt administration of justice draws the wrath of God upon magistrates, so the wildness and looseness of the people provoke the indignation of God against a country: therefore, that all such offenses against God, as swearing, cursing, lying, profane talking, drunkenness, drinking of healths, obscene words, incest, sodomy, rapes, whoredom, fornication, and other uncleanness (not to be repeated) all treasons, misprisions, murders, duels, felony, seditions, maims, forcible entries, and other violence, to the persons and estates of the inhabitants within this province; all prizes, stage-plays, cards, dice, May-games, gamesters, masques, revels, bull-baitings, cock-fightings, bear-baitings, and the like, which excite the people to rudeness, cruelty, looseness, and irreligion, shall be respectively discouraged, and severely punished, according to the appointment of the Governor and freemen in provincial Council and General Assembly; as also all proceedings contrary to these laws, that are not here made expressly penal.

XXXVIII. That a copy of these laws shall be hung up in the provincial Council, and in public courts of justice: and that they shall be read yearly at the opening of every provincial Council and General Assembly, and court of justice; and their assent shall be testified, by their standing up after the reading thereof.

By Marty Piatt, Architect

XXXIX. That there shall be, at no time, any alteration of any of these laws, without the consent of the Governor, his heirs, or assigns, and six parts of seven of the freemen, met in provincial Council and General Assembly.

XL. That all other matters and things not herein provided for, which shall, and may, concern the public justice, peace or safety of the said province; and the raising and imposing taxes, customs, duties, or other charges whatsoever, shall be, and are, hereby referred to the order, prudence and determination of the Governor and freemen, in provincial Council and General Assembly, to be held, from time to time, in the said province.

Signed and sealed by the Governor and freemen aforesaid, the fifth day of the third month, called May, one thousand six hundred and eighty-two.

"If I was President…"

DECLARATION OF INDEPENDENCE

When in the Course of human events, it becomes necessary for one people to dissolve the political bands which have connected them with another, and to assume among the powers of the earth, the separate and equal station to which the Laws of Nature and of Nature's God entitle them, a decent respect to the opinions of mankind requires that they should declare the causes which impel them to the separation.

We hold these truths to be self-evident, that all men are created equal, that they are endowed by their Creator with certain unalienable Rights, that among these are Life, Liberty and the pursuit of Happiness. — That to secure these rights, Governments are instituted among Men, deriving their just powers from the consent of the governed, — That whenever any Form of Government becomes destructive of these ends, it is the Right of the People to alter or to abolish it, and to institute new Government, laying its foundation on such principles and organizing its powers in such form, as to them shall seem most likely to effect their Safety and Happiness. Prudence, indeed, will dictate that Governments long established should not be changed for light and transient causes; and accordingly all experience hath shewn, that mankind are more disposed to suffer, while evils are sufferable, than to right themselves by abolishing the forms to which they are accustomed. But when a long train of abuses and usurpations, pursuing invariably the same Object evinces a design to reduce them under absolute Despotism, it is their right, it is their duty, to throw off such Government, and to provide new Guards for their future security.

Such has been the patient sufferance of these Colonies; and such is now the necessity which constrains them to alter their former Systems of Government. The history of the present King of Great Britain is a history of repeated injuries and usurpations, all having in direct object the establishment of an absolute Tyranny over these States. To prove this, let Facts be submitted to a candid world.

He has refused his Assent to Laws, the most wholesome and necessary for the public good.

He has forbidden his Governors to pass Laws of immediate and pressing importance, unless suspended in their operation till his Assent should be obtained; and when so suspended, he has utterly neglected to attend to them.

He has refused to pass other Laws for the accommodation of large districts of people, unless those people would relinquish the right of Representation in the Legislature, a right inestimable to them and formidable to tyrants only.

He has called together legislative bodies at places unusual, uncomfortable, and distant from the depository of their public Records, for the sole purpose of fatiguing them into compliance with his measures.

He has dissolved Representative Houses repeatedly, for opposing with manly firmness his invasions on the rights of the people.

He has refused for a long time, after such dissolutions, to cause others to be elected; whereby the Legislative powers, incapable of Annihilation, have returned to the People at large for their exercise; the State remaining in the mean time exposed to all the dangers of invasion from without, and convulsions within.

He has endeavoured to prevent the population of these States; for that purpose obstructing the Laws for Naturalization of Foreigners; refusing to pass others to encourage their migrations hither, and raising the conditions of new Appropriations of Lands.

He has obstructed the Administration of Justice, by refusing his Assent to Laws for establishing Judiciary powers.

He has made Judges dependent on his Will alone, for the tenure of their offices, and the amount and payment of their salaries.

He has erected a multitude of New Offices, and sent hither swarms of Officers to harrass our people, and eat out their substance.

He has kept among us, in times of peace, Standing Armies without the Consent of our legislatures.

By Marty Piatt, Architect

He has affected to render the Military independent of and superior to the Civil power.

He has combined with others to subject us to a jurisdiction foreign to our constitution, and unacknowledged by our laws; giving his Assent to their Acts of pretended Legislation:

For Quartering large bodies of armed troops among us:

For protecting them, by a mock Trial, from punishment for any Murders which they should commit on the Inhabitants of these States:

For cutting off our Trade with all parts of the world:

For imposing Taxes on us without our Consent:

For depriving us in many cases, of the benefits of Trial by Jury:

For transporting us beyond Seas to be tried for pretended offences:

For abolishing the free System of English Laws in a neighbouring Province, establishing therein an Arbitrary government, and enlarging its Boundaries so as to render it at once an example and fit instrument for introducing the same absolute rule into these Colonies:

For taking away our Charters, abolishing our most valuable Laws, and altering fundamentally the Forms of our Governments:

For suspending our own Legislatures, and declaring themselves invested with power to legislate for us in all cases whatsoever.

He has abdicated Government here, by declaring us out of his Protection and waging War against us.

He has plundered our seas, ravaged our Coasts, burnt our towns, and destroyed the lives of our people.

He is at this time transporting large Armies of foreign Mercenaries to compleat the works of death, desolation and tyranny, already begun with circumstances of Cruelty & perfidy scarcely paralleled in the most barbarous ages, and totally unworthy the Head of a civilized nation.

He has constrained our fellow Citizens taken Captive on the high Seas to bear Arms against their Country, to become the executioners of their friends and Brethren, or to fall themselves by their Hands.

He has excited domestic insurrections amongst us, and has endeavoured to bring on the inhabitants of our frontiers, the merciless Indian Savages, whose known rule of warfare, is an undistinguished destruction of all ages, sexes and conditions.

In every stage of these Oppressions We have Petitioned for Redress in the most humble terms: Our repeated Petitions have been answered only by repeated injury. A Prince whose character is thus marked by every act which may define a Tyrant, is unfit to be the ruler of a free people.

Nor have We been wanting in attentions to our British brethren. We have warned them from time to time of attempts by their legislature to extend an unwarrantable jurisdiction over us. We have reminded them of the circumstances of our emigration and settlement here. We have appealed to their native justice and magnanimity, and we have conjured them by the ties of our common kindred to disavow these usurpations, which, would inevitably interrupt our connections and correspondence. They too have been deaf to the voice of justice and of consanguinity. We must, therefore, acquiesce in the necessity, which denounces our Separation, and hold them, as we hold the rest of mankind, Enemies in War, in Peace Friends.

We, therefore, the Representatives of the united States of America, in General Congress, Assembled, appealing to the Supreme Judge of the world for the rectitude of our intentions, do, in the Name, and by Authority of the good People of these Colonies, solemnly publish and declare, That these United Colonies are, and of Right ought to be Free and Independent States; that they are Absolved from all Allegiance to the British Crown, and that all political connection between them and the State of Great Britain, is and ought to be totally dissolved; and that as Free and Independent States, they have full Power to levy War, conclude Peace, contract Alliances, establish Commerce, and to do all other Acts and Things which Independent States may of right do. And for the support of this Declaration, with a firm reliance on the protection of divine Providence, we mutually pledge to each other our Lives, our Fortunes and our sacred Honor.

"If I was President..."

THE ARTICLES OF CONFEDERATION

Agreed to by Congress November 15, 1777; ratified and in force, March 1, 1781.

PREAMBLE

To all to whom these Presents shall come, we the undersigned Delegates of the States affixed to our Names send greeting.

Whereas the Delegates of the United States of America in Congress assembled did on the fifteenth day of November in the Year of our Lord One Thousand Seven Hundred and Seventy seven, and in the Second Year of the Independence of America, agree to certain articles of Confederation and perpetual Union between the States of New Hampshire, Massachusetts-bay, Rhode Island and Providence Plantations, Connecticut, New York, New Jersey, Pennsylvania, Delaware, Maryland, Virginia, North Carolina, South Carolina and Georgia, in the words following, viz:

Articles of Confederation and perpetual Union between the States of New Hampshire, Massachusetts-bay, Rhode Island and Providence Plantations, Connecticut, New York, New Jersey, Pennsylvania, Delaware, Maryland, Virginia, North Carolina, South Carolina and Georgia.

Article I. The Stile of this Confederacy shall be "The United States of America."

Article II. Each state retains its sovereignty, freedom, and independence, and every Power, Jurisdiction, and right, which is not by this confederation expressly delegated to the United States, in Congress assembled.

Article III. The said States hereby severally enter into a firm league of friendship with each other, for their common defense, the security of their liberties, and their mutual and general welfare, binding themselves to assist each other, against all force offered to, or attacks made upon them, or any of them, on account of religion, sovereignty, trade, or any other pretense whatever.

Article IV. The better to secure and perpetuate mutual friendship and intercourse among the people of the different States in this union, the free inhabitants of each of these States, paupers, vagabonds, and fugitives from justice excepted, shall be entitled to all privileges and immunities of free citizens in the several States; and the people of each State shall have free ingress and regress to and from any other State, and shall enjoy therein all the privileges of trade and commerce, subject to the same duties, impositions, and restrictions as the inhabitants thereof respectively, provided that such restrictions shall not extend so far as to prevent the removal of property imported into any State, to any other State, of which the owner is an inhabitant; provided also that no imposition, duties or restriction shall be laid by any State, on the property of the united States, or either of them.

If any person guilty of, or charged with, treason, felony, or other high misdemeanor in any State, shall flee from justice, and be found in any of the united States, he shall, upon demand of the Governor or executive power of the State from which he fled, be delivered up and removed to the State having jurisdiction of his offense.

Full faith and credit shall be given in each of these States to the records, acts, and judicial proceedings of the courts and magistrates of every other State.

Article V. For the most convenient management of the general interests of the united States, delegates shall be annually appointed in such manner as the legislatures of each State shall direct, to meet in Congress on the first Monday in November, in every year, with a power reserved to each State to recall its delegates, or any of them, at any time within the year, and to send others in their stead for the remainder of the year.

No State shall be represented in Congress by less than two, nor more than seven members; and no person shall be capable of being a delegate for more than three years in any term of six years; nor shall any person, being a delegate, be capable of holding any office under the united States, for which he, or another for his benefit, receives any salary, fees or emolument of any kind.

Each State shall maintain its own delegates in a meeting of the States, and while they act as members of the committee of the States.

In determining questions in the united States, in Congress assembled, each State shall have one vote.

Freedom of speech and debate in Congress shall not be impeached or questioned in any court or place out of Congress, and the members of Congress shall be protected in their persons from arrests or imprisonments, during the time of their going to and from, and attendance on Congress, except for treason, felony, or breach of the peace.

Article VI. No State, without the consent of the united States in Congress assembled, shall send any embassy to, or receive any embassy from, or enter into any conference, agreement, alliance or treaty with any King, Prince or State; nor shall any person holding any office of profit or trust under the united States, or any of them, accept any present, emolument, office or title of any kind whatever from any King, Prince or foreign State; nor shall the United States in congress assembled, or any of them, grant any title of nobility.

No two or more States shall enter into any treaty, confederation or alliance whatever between them, without the consent of the united States in congress assembled, specifying accurately the purposes for which the same is to be entered into, and how long it shall continue.

No State shall lay any imposts or duties, which may interfere with any stipulations in treaties, entered into by the united States in congress assembled, with any King, Prince or State, in pursuance of any treaties already proposed by congress, to the courts of France and Spain.

No vessel of war shall be kept up in time of peace by any State, except such number only, as shall be deemed necessary by the united States in congress assembled, for the defense of such State, or its trade; nor shall any body of forces be kept up by any State in time of peace, except such number only, as in the judgment of the united States, in congress assembled, shall be deemed requisite to garrison the forts necessary for the defense of such State; but every State shall always keep up a well-regulated and disciplined militia, sufficiently armed and accoutered, and shall provide and constantly have ready for use, in public stores, a due number of field pieces and tents, and a proper quantity of arms, ammunition and camp equipage.

No State shall engage in any war without the consent of the united States in congress assembled, unless such State be actually invaded by enemies, or shall have received certain advice of a resolution being formed by some nation of Indians to invade such State, and the danger is so imminent as not to admit of a delay till the united States in congress assembled can be consulted; nor shall any State grant commissions to any ships or vessels of war, nor letters of marque or reprisal, except it be after a declaration of war by the united States in congress assembled, and then only against the kingdom or State and the subjects thereof, against which war has been so declared, and under such regulations as shall be established by the united States in congress assembled, unless such State be infested by pirates, in which case vessels of war may be fitted out for that occasion, and kept so long as the danger shall continue, or until the united States in congress assembled shall determine otherwise.

Article VII. When land forces are raised by any State for the common defense, all officers of or under the rank of colonel, shall be appointed by the legislature of each State respectively, by whom such forces shall be raised, or in such manner as such State shall direct, and all vacancies shall be filled up by the State which first made the appointment.

Article VIII. All charges of war, and all other expenses that shall be incurred for the common defense or general welfare, and allowed by the united States in congress assembled, shall be defrayed out of a common treasury, which shall be supplied by the several States in proportion to the value of all land within each State, granted or surveyed for any person, as such land and the buildings and improvements thereon shall be estimated according to such mode as the united States in congress assembled, shall from time to time direct and appoint.

The taxes for paying that proportion shall be laid and levied by the authority and direction of the legislatures of the several States within the time agreed upon by the united States in congress assembled.

Article IX. The united States in congress assembled, shall have the sole and exclusive right and power of determining on peace and war, except in the cases mentioned in the sixth article – of sending and receiving ambassadors – entering into treaties and alliances, provided that no treaty of commerce shall be made whereby the legislative power of the respective States shall be restrained from imposing such imposts and duties on foreigners, as their own people are subjected to, or from prohibiting the exportation or importation of any species of goods or commodities whatsoever — of establishing rules for deciding in all cases, what captures on land or water shall be legal, and in what manner prizes taken by land or naval forces in the service of the United States shall be divided or appropriated — of granting letters of marque and reprisal in times of peace — appointing courts for the trial of piracies and felonies committed on the high seas and establishing courts for receiving and determining finally appeals in all cases of captures, provided that no member of Congress shall be appointed a judge of any of the said courts.

The United States in Congress assembled shall also be the last resort on appeal in all disputes and differences now subsisting or that hereafter may arise between two or more States concerning boundary, jurisdiction or any other causes whatever; which authority shall always be exercised in the manner following. Whenever the legislative or executive authority or lawful agent of any State in controversy with another shall present a petition to Congress stating the matter in question and praying for a hearing, notice thereof shall be given by order of Congress to the legislative or executive authority of the other State in controversy, and a day assigned for the appearance of the parties by their lawful agents, who shall then be directed to appoint by joint consent, commissioners or judges to constitute a court for hearing and determining the matter in question: but if they cannot agree, Congress shall name three persons out of each of the United States, and from the list of such persons each party shall alternately strike out one, the petitioners beginning, until the number shall be reduced to thirteen; and from that number not less than seven, nor more than nine names as Congress shall direct, shall in the presence of Congress be drawn out by lot, and the persons whose names shall be so drawn or any five of them, shall be commissioners or judges, to hear and finally determine the controversy, so always as a major part of the judges who shall hear the cause shall agree in the determination: and if either party shall neglect to attend at the day appointed, without showing reasons, which Congress shall judge sufficient, or being present shall refuse to strike, the Congress shall proceed to nominate three persons out of each State, and the secretary of Congress shall strike in behalf of such party absent or refusing; and the judgment and sentence of the court to be appointed, in the manner before prescribed, shall be final and conclusive; and if any of the parties shall refuse to submit to the authority of such court, or to appear or defend their claim or cause, the court shall nevertheless proceed to pronounce sentence, or judgment, which shall in like manner be final and decisive, the judgment or sentence and other proceedings being in either case transmitted to Congress, and lodged among the acts of Congress for the security of the parties concerned: provided that every commissioner, before he sits in judgment, shall take an oath to be administered by one of the judges of the supreme or superior court of the State, where the cause shall be tried, 'well and truly to hear and determine the matter in question, according to the best of his judgment, without favor, affection or hope of reward': provided also, that no State shall be deprived of territory for the benefit of the United States.

All controversies concerning the private right of soil claimed under different grants of two or more States, whose jurisdictions as they may respect such lands, and the States which passed such grants are adjusted, the said grants or either of them being at the same time claimed to have originated antecedent to such settlement of jurisdiction, shall on the petition of either party to the Congress of the United States, be finally determined as near as may be in the same manner as is before prescribed for deciding disputes respecting territorial jurisdiction between different States.

The United States in Congress assembled shall also have the sole and exclusive right and power of regulating the alloy and value of coin struck by their own authority, or by that of the respective States — fixing the standards of weights and measures throughout the United States — regulating the trade and managing all affairs with the Indians, not members of any of the States, provided that the legislative right of any State within its own limits be not infringed or violated — establishing or regulating post offices from one State to another, throughout all the United States, and exacting such postage on the papers passing through the same as may be requisite to defray the expenses of the said office – appointing all officers of the land forces, in the service of the United States, excepting regimental officers — appointing all the officers of the naval forces, and commissioning all officers whatever in the service of the United States — making rules for the government and regulation of the said land and naval forces, and directing their operations.

The United States in Congress assembled shall have authority to appoint a committee, to sit in the recess of Congress, to be denominated 'A Committee of the States', and to consist of one delegate from each State;

and to appoint such other committees and civil officers as may be necessary for managing the general affairs of the United States under their direction — to appoint one of their members to preside, provided that no person be allowed to serve in the office of president more than one year in any term of three years; to ascertain the necessary sums of money to be raised for the service of the United States, and to appropriate and apply the same for defraying the public expenses — to borrow money, or emit bills on the credit of the United States, transmitting every half-year to the respective States an account of the sums of money so borrowed or emitted — to build and equip a navy — to agree upon the number of land forces, and to make requisitions from each State for its quota, in proportion to the number of white inhabitants in such State; which requisition shall be binding, and thereupon the legislature of each State shall appoint the regimental officers, raise the men and cloath, arm and equip them in a solid- like manner, at the expense of the United States; and the officers and men so cloathed, armed and equipped shall march to the place appointed, and within the time agreed on by the United States in Congress assembled. But if the United States in Congress assembled shall, on consideration of circumstances judge proper that any State should not raise men, or should raise a smaller number of men than the quota thereof, such extra number shall be raised, officered, cloathed, armed and equipped in the same manner as the quota of each State, unless the legislature of such State shall judge that such extra number cannot be safely spread out in the same, in which case they shall raise, officer, cloath, arm and equip as many of such extra number as they judge can be safely spared. And the officers and men so cloathed, armed, and equipped, shall march to the place appointed, and within the time agreed on by the united States in congress assembled.

The united States in congress assembled shall never engage in a war, nor grant letters of marque or reprisal in time of peace, nor enter into any treaties or alliances, nor coin money, nor regulate the value thereof, nor ascertain the sums and expenses necessary for the defense and welfare of the United States, or any of them, nor emit bills, nor borrow money on the credit of the united States, nor appropriate money, nor agree upon the number of vessels of war, to be built or purchased, or the number of land or sea forces to be raised, nor appoint a commander in chief of the army or navy, unless nine States assent to the same: nor shall a question on any other point, except for adjourning from day to day be determined, unless by the votes of the majority of the united States in congress assembled.

The congress of the united States shall have power to adjourn to any time within the year, and to any place within the united States, so that no period of adjournment be for a longer duration than the space of six months, and shall publish the journal of their proceedings monthly, except such parts thereof relating to treaties, alliances or military operations, as in their judgment require secrecy; and the yeas and nays of the delegates of each State on any question shall be entered on the journal, when it is desired by any delegates of a State, or any of them, at his or their request shall be furnished with a transcript of the said journal, except such parts as are above excepted, to lay before the legislatures of the several States.

Article X. The committee of the States, or any nine of them, shall be authorized to execute, in the recess of congress, such of the powers of congress as the united States in congress assembled, by the consent of the nine States, shall from time to time think expedient to vest them with; provided that no power be delegated to the said Committee, for the exercise of which, by the articles of confederation, the voice of nine States in the Congress of the United States assembled be requisite.

Article XI. Canada acceding to this confederation, and adjoining in the measures of the united States, shall be admitted into, and entitled to all the advantages of this union; but no other colony shall be admitted into the same, unless such admission be agreed to by nine States.

Article XII. All bills of credit emitted, monies borrowed, and debts contracted by, or under the authority of congress, before the assembling of the united States, in pursuance of the present confederation, shall be deemed and considered as a charge against the United States, for payment and satisfaction whereof the said united States, and the public faith are hereby solemnly pledged.

Article XIII. Every State shall abide by the determination of the united States in congress assembled, on all questions which by this confederation are submitted to them. And the Articles of this confederation shall be inviolably observed by every State, and the union shall be perpetual; nor shall any alteration at any time hereafter be made in any of them; unless such alteration be agreed to in a congress of the united States, and be afterwards confirmed by the legislatures of every State.

By Marty Piatt, Architect

And Whereas it hath pleased the Great Governor of the World to incline the hearts of the legislatures we respectively represent in Congress, to approve of, and to authorize us to ratify the said articles of confederation and perpetual union. Know Ye that we the undersigned delegates, by virtue of the power and authority to us given for that purpose, do by these presents, in the name and in behalf of our respective constituents, fully and entirely ratify and confirm each and every of the said articles of confederation and perpetual union, and all and singular the matters and things therein contained: And we do further solemnly plight and engage the faith of our respective constituents, that they shall abide by the determinations of the united States in congress assembled, on all questions, which by the said confederation are submitted to them. And that the articles thereof shall be inviolably observed by the States we respectively represent, and that the union shall be perpetual.

In Witness whereof we have hereunto set our hands in Congress. Done at Philadelphia in the State of Pennsylvania the ninth Day of July in the Year of our Lord one thousand seven Hundred and Seventy-eight, and in the Third Year of the independence of America.

"If I was President…"

UNITED STATES CONSTITUTION

We the People of the United States, in Order to form a more perfect Union, establish Justice, insure domestic Tranquility, provide for the common defence, promote the general Welfare, and secure the Blessings of Liberty to ourselves and our Posterity, do ordain and establish this Constitution for the United States of America.

ARTICLE I.

Section. 1.

All legislative Powers herein granted shall be vested in a Congress of the United States, which shall consist of a Senate and House of Representatives.

Section. 2.

The House of Representatives shall be composed of Members chosen every second Year by the People of the several States, and the Electors in each State shall have the Qualifications requisite for Electors of the most numerous Branch of the State Legislature.

No Person shall be a Representative who shall not have attained to the Age of twenty five Years, and been seven Years a Citizen of the United States, and who shall not, when elected, be an Inhabitant of that State in which he shall be chosen.

Representatives and direct Taxes shall be apportioned among the several States which may be included within this Union, according to their respective Numbers, which shall be determined by adding to the whole Number of free Persons, including those bound to Service for a Term of Years, and excluding Indians not taxed, three fifths of all other Persons. The actual Enumeration shall be made within three Years after the first Meeting of the Congress of the United States, and within every subsequent Term of ten Years, in such Manner as they shall by Law direct. The Number of Representatives shall not exceed one for every thirty Thousand, but each State shall have at Least one Representative; and until such enumeration shall be made, the State of New Hampshire shall be entitled to chuse three, Massachusetts eight, Rhode-Island and Providence Plantations one, Connecticut five, New-York six, New Jersey four, Pennsylvania eight, Delaware one, Maryland six, Virginia ten, North Carolina five, South Carolina five, and Georgia three.

When vacancies happen in the Representation from any State, the Executive Authority thereof shall issue Writs of Election to fill such Vacancies.

The House of Representatives shall chuse their Speaker and other Officers; and shall have the sole Power of Impeachment.

Section. 3.

The Senate of the United States shall be composed of two Senators from each State, chosen by the Legislature thereof for six Years; and each Senator shall have one Vote.

Immediately after they shall be assembled in Consequence of the first Election, they shall be divided as equally as may be into three Classes. The Seats of the Senators of the first Class shall be vacated at the Expiration of the second Year, of the second Class at the Expiration of the fourth Year, and of the third Class at the Expiration of the sixth Year, so that one third may be chosen every second Year; and if Vacancies happen by Resignation, or otherwise, during the Recess of the Legislature of any State, the Executive thereof may make temporary Appointments until the next Meeting of the Legislature, which shall then fill such Vacancies.

No Person shall be a Senator who shall not have attained to the Age of thirty Years, and been nine Years a Citizen of the United States, and who shall not, when elected, be an Inhabitant of that State for which he shall be chosen.

The Vice President of the United States shall be President of the Senate, but shall have no Vote, unless they be equally divided.

The Senate shall chuse their other Officers, and also a President pro tempore, in the Absence of the Vice President, or when he shall exercise the Office of President of the United States.

The Senate shall have the sole Power to try all Impeachments. When sitting for that Purpose, they shall be on Oath or Affirmation. When the President of the United States is tried, the Chief Justice shall preside: And no Person shall be convicted without the Concurrence of two thirds of the Members present.

Judgment in Cases of Impeachment shall not extend further than to removal from Office, and disqualification to hold and enjoy any Office of honor, Trust or Profit under the United States: but the Party convicted shall nevertheless be liable and subject to Indictment, Trial, Judgment and Punishment, according to Law.

Section. 4.

The Times, Places and Manner of holding Elections for Senators and Representatives, shall be prescribed in each State by the Legislature thereof; but the Congress may at any time by Law make or alter such Regulations, except as to the Places of chusing Senators.

The Congress shall assemble at least once in every Year, and such Meeting shall be on the first Monday in December, unless they shall by Law appoint a different Day.

Section. 5.

Each House shall be the Judge of the Elections, Returns and Qualifications of its own Members, and a Majority of each shall constitute a Quorum to do Business; but a smaller Number may adjourn from day to day, and may be authorized to compel the Attendance of absent Members, in such Manner, and under such Penalties as each House may provide.

Each House may determine the Rules of its Proceedings, punish its Members for disorderly Behaviour, and, with the Concurrence of two thirds, expel a Member.

Each House shall keep a Journal of its Proceedings, and from time to time publish the same, excepting such Parts as may in their Judgment require Secrecy; and the Yeas and Nays of the Members of either House on any question shall, at the Desire of one fifth of those Present, be entered on the Journal.

Neither House, during the Session of Congress, shall, without the Consent of the other, adjourn for more than three days, nor to any other Place than that in which the two Houses shall be sitting.

Section. 6.

The Senators and Representatives shall receive a Compensation for their Services, to be ascertained by Law, and paid out of the Treasury of the United States. They shall in all Cases, except Treason, Felony and Breach of the Peace, be privileged from Arrest during their Attendance at the Session of their respective Houses, and in going to and returning from the same; and for any Speech or Debate in either House, they shall not be questioned in any other Place.

No Senator or Representative shall, during the Time for which he was elected, be appointed to any civil Office under the Authority of the United States, which shall have been created, or the Emoluments whereof shall have been encreased during such time; and no Person holding any Office under the United States, shall be a Member of either House during his Continuance in Office.

Section. 7.

All Bills for raising Revenue shall originate in the House of Representatives; but the Senate may propose or concur with Amendments as on other Bills.

Every Bill which shall have passed the House of Representatives and the Senate, shall, before it become a Law, be presented to the President of the United States: If he approve he shall sign it, but if not he shall return it, with his Objections to that House in which it shall have originated, who shall enter the Objections at large on their Journal, and proceed to reconsider it. If after such Reconsideration two thirds of that House shall agree to pass the Bill, it shall be sent, together with the Objections, to the other House, by which it shall likewise be reconsidered, and if approved by two thirds of that House, it shall become a Law. But in all such Cases the Votes of both Houses shall be determined by yeas and Nays, and the Names of the Persons voting for and against the Bill shall be entered on the Journal of each House respectively. If any Bill shall not be returned by the President within ten Days (Sundays excepted) after it shall have been presented to him, the Same shall be a Law, in like Manner as if he had signed it, unless the Congress by their Adjournment prevent its Return, in which Case it shall not be a Law.

Every Order, Resolution, or Vote to which the Concurrence of the Senate and House of Representatives may be necessary (except on a question of Adjournment) shall be presented to the President of the United States; and before the Same shall take Effect, shall be approved by him, or being disapproved by him, shall be repassed by two thirds of the Senate and House of Representatives, according to the Rules and Limitations prescribed in the Case of a Bill.

Section. 8.

The Congress shall have Power To lay and collect Taxes, Duties, Imposts and Excises, to pay the Debts and provide for the common Defence and general Welfare of the United States; but all Duties, Imposts and Excises shall be uniform throughout the United States;

To borrow Money on the credit of the United States;

To regulate Commerce with foreign Nations, and among the several States, and with the Indian Tribes;

To establish an uniform Rule of Naturalization, and uniform Laws on the subject of Bankruptcies throughout the United States;

To coin Money, regulate the Value thereof, and of foreign Coin, and fix the Standard of Weights and Measures;

To provide for the Punishment of counterfeiting the Securities and current Coin of the United States;

To establish Post Offices and post Roads;

To promote the Progress of Science and useful Arts, by securing for limited Times to Authors and Inventors the exclusive Right to their respective Writings and Discoveries;

To constitute Tribunals inferior to the supreme Court;

To define and punish Piracies and Felonies committed on the high Seas, and Offences against the Law of Nations;

To declare War, grant Letters of Marque and Reprisal, and make Rules concerning Captures on Land and Water;

To raise and support Armies, but no Appropriation of Money to that Use shall be for a longer Term than two Years;

To provide and maintain a Navy;

To make Rules for the Government and Regulation of the land and naval Forces;

To provide for calling forth the Militia to execute the Laws of the Union, suppress Insurrections and repel Invasions;

To provide for organizing, arming, and disciplining, the Militia, and for governing such Part of them as may be employed in the Service of the United States, reserving to the States respectively, the Appointment of the Officers, and the Authority of training the Militia according to the discipline prescribed by Congress;

To exercise exclusive Legislation in all Cases whatsoever, over such District (not exceeding ten Miles square) as may, by Cession of particular States, and the Acceptance of Congress, become the Seat of the Government of the United States, and to exercise like Authority over all Places purchased by the Consent of the Legislature of the State in which the Same shall be, for the Erection of Forts, Magazines, Arsenals, dock-Yards, and other needful Buildings;--And

To make all Laws which shall be necessary and proper for carrying into Execution the foregoing Powers, and all other Powers vested by this Constitution in the Government of the United States, or in any Department or Officer thereof.

Section. 9.

The Migration or Importation of such Persons as any of the States now existing shall think proper to admit, shall not be prohibited by the

Congress prior to the Year one thousand eight hundred and eight, but a Tax or duty may be imposed on such Importation, not exceeding ten dollars for each Person.

The Privilege of the Writ of Habeas Corpus shall not be suspended, unless when in Cases of Rebellion or Invasion the public Safety may require it.

No Bill of Attainder or ex post facto Law shall be passed.

No Capitation, or other direct, Tax shall be laid, unless in Proportion to the Census or enumeration herein before directed to be taken.

No Tax or Duty shall be laid on Articles exported from any State.

No Preference shall be given by any Regulation of Commerce or Revenue to the Ports of one State over those of another; nor shall Vessels bound to, or from, one State, be obliged to enter, clear, or pay Duties in another.

No Money shall be drawn from the Treasury, but in Consequence of Appropriations made by Law; and a regular Statement and Account of the Receipts and Expenditures of all public Money shall be published from time to time.

No Title of Nobility shall be granted by the United States: And no Person holding any Office of Profit or Trust under them, shall, without the Consent of the Congress, accept of any present, Emolument, Office, or Title, of any kind whatever, from any King, Prince, or foreign State.

Section. 10.

No State shall enter into any Treaty, Alliance, or Confederation; grant Letters of Marque and Reprisal; coin Money; emit Bills of Credit; make any Thing but gold and silver Coin a Tender in Payment of Debts; pass any Bill of Attainder, ex post facto Law, or Law impairing the Obligation of Contracts, or grant any Title of Nobility.

No State shall, without the Consent of the Congress, lay any Imposts or Duties on Imports or Exports, except what may be absolutely necessary for executing it's inspection Laws: and the net Produce of all Duties and Imposts, laid by any State on Imports or Exports, shall be for the Use of the Treasury of the United States; and all such Laws shall be subject to the Revision and Controul of the Congress.

No State shall, without the Consent of Congress, lay any Duty of Tonnage, keep Troops, or Ships of War in time of Peace, enter into any Agreement or Compact with another State, or with a foreign Power, or engage in War, unless actually invaded, or in such imminent Danger as will not admit of delay.

ARTICLE II.

Section. 1.

The executive Power shall be vested in a President of the United States of America. He shall hold his Office during the Term of four Years, and, together with the Vice President, chosen for the same Term, be elected, as follows:

Each State shall appoint, in such Manner as the Legislature thereof may direct, a Number of Electors, equal to the whole Number of Senators and Representatives to which the State may be entitled in the Congress: but no Senator or Representative, or Person holding an Office of Trust or Profit under the United States, shall be appointed an Elector.

The Electors shall meet in their respective States, and vote by Ballot for two Persons, of whom one at least shall not be an Inhabitant of the same State with themselves. And they shall make a List of all the Persons voted for, and of the Number of Votes for each; which List they shall sign and certify, and transmit sealed to the Seat of the Government of the United States, directed to the President of the Senate. The President of the Senate shall, in the Presence of the Senate and House of Representatives, open all the Certificates, and the Votes shall then be counted. The Person having the greatest Number of Votes shall be the President, if such Number be a Majority of the whole Number of Electors appointed; and if there be more than one who have such Majority, and have an equal Number of Votes, then the House of Representatives shall immediately chuse by Ballot one of them for President; and if no Person have a Majority, then from the five highest on the List the said House shall in like

Manner chuse the President. But in chusing the President, the Votes shall be taken by States, the Representation from each State having one Vote; A quorum for this purpose shall consist of a Member or Members from two thirds of the States, and a Majority of all the States shall be necessary to a Choice. In every Case, after the Choice of the President, the Person having the greatest Number of Votes of the Electors shall be the Vice President. But if there should remain two or more who have equal Votes, the Senate shall chuse from them by Ballot the Vice President.

The Congress may determine the Time of chusing the Electors, and the Day on which they shall give their Votes; which Day shall be the same throughout the United States.

No Person except a natural born Citizen, or a Citizen of the United States, at the time of the Adoption of this Constitution, shall be eligible to the Office of President; neither shall any Person be eligible to that Office who shall not have attained to the Age of thirty five Years, and been fourteen Years a Resident within the United States.

In Case of the Removal of the President from Office, or of his Death, Resignation, or Inability to discharge the Powers and Duties of the said Office, the Same shall devolve on the Vice President, and the Congress may by Law provide for the Case of Removal, Death, Resignation or Inability, both of the President and Vice President, declaring what Officer shall then act as President, and such Officer shall act accordingly, until the Disability be removed, or a President shall be elected.

The President shall, at stated Times, receive for his Services, a Compensation, which shall neither be increased nor diminished during the Period for which he shall have been elected, and he shall not receive within that Period any other Emolument from the United States, or any of them.

Before he enter on the Execution of his Office, he shall take the following Oath or Affirmation:--"I do solemnly swear (or affirm) that I will faithfully execute the Office of President of the United States, and will to the best of my Ability, preserve, protect and defend the Constitution of the United States."

Section. 2.

The President shall be Commander in Chief of the Army and Navy of the United States, and of the Militia of the several States, when called into the actual Service of the United States; he may require the Opinion, in writing, of the principal Officer in each of the executive Departments, upon any Subject relating to the Duties of their respective Offices, and he shall have Power to grant Reprieves and Pardons for Offences against the United States, except in Cases of Impeachment.

He shall have Power, by and with the Advice and Consent of the Senate, to make Treaties, provided two thirds of the Senators present concur; and he shall nominate, and by and with the Advice and Consent of the Senate, shall appoint Ambassadors, other public Ministers and Consuls, Judges of the supreme Court, and all other Officers of the United States, whose Appointments are not herein otherwise provided for, and which shall be established by Law: but the Congress may by Law vest the Appointment of such inferior Officers, as they think proper, in the President alone, in the Courts of Law, or in the Heads of Departments.

The President shall have Power to fill up all Vacancies that may happen during the Recess of the Senate, by granting Commissions which shall expire at the End of their next Session.

Section. 3.

He shall from time to time give to the Congress Information of the State of the Union, and recommend to their Consideration such Measures as he shall judge necessary and expedient; he may, on extraordinary Occasions, convene both Houses, or either of them, and in Case of Disagreement between them, with Respect to the Time of Adjournment, he may adjourn them to such Time as he shall think proper; he shall receive Ambassadors and other public Ministers; he shall take Care that the Laws be faithfully executed, and shall Commission all the Officers of the United States.

Section. 4.

The President, Vice President and all civil Officers of the United States, shall be removed from Office on Impeachment for, and Conviction of, Treason, Bribery, or other high Crimes and Misdemeanors.

ARTICLE III.

Section. 1.

The judicial Power of the United States shall be vested in one supreme Court, and in such inferior Courts as the Congress may from time to time ordain and establish. The Judges, both of the supreme and inferior Courts, shall hold their Offices during good Behaviour, and shall, at stated Times, receive for their Services a Compensation, which shall not be diminished during their Continuance in Office.

Section. 2.

The judicial Power shall extend to all Cases, in Law and Equity, arising under this Constitution, the Laws of the United States, and Treaties made, or which shall be made, under their Authority;--to all Cases affecting Ambassadors, other public Ministers and Consuls;--to all Cases of admiralty and maritime Jurisdiction;--to Controversies to which the United States shall be a Party;--to Controversies between two or more States;-- between a State and Citizens of another State,--between Citizens of different States,--between Citizens of the same State claiming Lands under Grants of different States, and between a State, or the Citizens thereof, and foreign States, Citizens or Subjects.

In all Cases affecting Ambassadors, other public Ministers and Consuls, and those in which a State shall be Party, the supreme Court shall have original Jurisdiction. In all the other Cases before mentioned, the supreme Court shall have appellate Jurisdiction, both as to Law and Fact, with such Exceptions, and under such Regulations as the Congress shall make.

The Trial of all Crimes, except in Cases of Impeachment, shall be by Jury; and such Trial shall be held in the State where the said Crimes shall have been committed; but when not committed within any State, the Trial shall be at such Place or Places as the Congress may by Law have directed.

Section. 3.

Treason against the United States, shall consist only in levying War against them, or in adhering to their Enemies, giving them Aid and Comfort. No Person shall be convicted of Treason unless on the Testimony of two Witnesses to the same overt Act, or on Confession in open Court.

The Congress shall have Power to declare the Punishment of Treason, but no Attainder of Treason shall work Corruption of Blood, or Forfeiture except during the Life of the Person attainted.

ARTICLE IV.

Section. 1.

Full Faith and Credit shall be given in each State to the public Acts, Records, and judicial Proceedings of every other State. And the Congress may by general Laws prescribe the Manner in which such Acts, Records and Proceedings shall be proved, and the Effect thereof.

Section. 2.

The Citizens of each State shall be entitled to all Privileges and Immunities of Citizens in the several States.

A Person charged in any State with Treason, Felony, or other Crime, who shall flee from Justice, and be found in another State, shall on Demand of the executive Authority of the State from which he fled, be delivered up, to be removed to the State having Jurisdiction of the Crime.

No Person held to Service or Labour in one State, under the Laws thereof, escaping into another, shall, in Consequence of any Law or Regulation therein, be discharged from such Service or Labour, but shall be delivered up on Claim of the Party to whom such Service or Labour may be due.

Section. 3.

New States may be admitted by the Congress into this Union; but no new State shall be formed or erected within the Jurisdiction of any other State; nor any State be formed by the Junction of two or more States, or Parts of States, without the Consent of the Legislatures of the States concerned as well as of the Congress.

The Congress shall have Power to dispose of and make all needful Rules and Regulations respecting the Territory or other Property belonging to the United States; and nothing in this Constitution shall be so construed as to Prejudice any Claims of the United States, or of any particular State.

Section. 4.

The United States shall guarantee to every State in this Union a Republican Form of Government, and shall protect each of them against Invasion; and on Application of the Legislature, or of the Executive (when the Legislature cannot be convened), against domestic Violence.

ARTICLE V.

The Congress, whenever two thirds of both Houses shall deem it necessary, shall propose Amendments to this Constitution, or, on the Application of the Legislatures of two thirds of the several States, shall call a Convention for proposing Amendments, which, in either Case, shall be valid to all Intents and Purposes, as Part of this Constitution, when ratified by the Legislatures of three fourths of the several States, or by Conventions in three fourths thereof, as the one or the other Mode of Ratification may be proposed by the Congress; Provided that no Amendment which may be made prior to the Year One thousand eight hundred and eight shall in any Manner affect the first and fourth Clauses in the Ninth Section of the first Article; and that no State, without its Consent, shall be deprived of its equal Suffrage in the Senate.

ARTICLE VI.

All Debts contracted and Engagements entered into, before the Adoption of this Constitution, shall be as valid against the United States under this Constitution, as under the Confederation.

This Constitution, and the Laws of the United States which shall be made in Pursuance thereof; and all Treaties made, or which shall be made, under the Authority of the United States, shall be the supreme Law of the Land; and the Judges in every State shall be bound thereby, any Thing in the Constitution or Laws of any State to the Contrary notwithstanding.

The Senators and Representatives before mentioned, and the Members of the several State Legislatures, and all executive and judicial Officers, both of the United States and of the several States, shall be bound by Oath or Affirmation, to support this Constitution; but no religious Test shall ever be required as a Qualification to any Office or public Trust under the United States.

ARTICLE VII.

The Ratification of the Conventions of nine States, shall be sufficient for the Establishment of this Constitution between the States so ratifying the Same.

The Word, "the," being interlined between the seventh and eighth Lines of the first Page, the Word "Thirty" being partly written on an Erazure in the fifteenth Line of the first Page, The Words "is tried" being interlined between the thirty second and thirty third Lines of the first Page and the Word "the" being interlined between the forty third and forty fourth Lines of the second Page.

Attest William Jackson Secretary

done in Convention by the Unanimous Consent of the States present the Seventeenth Day of September in the Year of our Lord one thousand seven hundred and Eighty seven and of the Independance of the United States of America the Twelfth In witness whereof We have hereunto subscribed our Names

AMENDMENTS TO THE CONSTITUTION

Amendment 1 - Freedom of Religion, Press, Expression. Ratified 12/15/1791

Congress shall make no law respecting an establishment of religion, or prohibiting the free exercise thereof; or abridging the freedom of speech, or of the press; or the right of the people peaceably to assemble, and to petition the Government for a redress of grievances.

Amendment 2 - Right to Bear Arms. Ratified 12/15/1791

A well regulated Militia, being necessary to the security of a free State, the right of the people to keep and bear Arms, shall not be infringed.

Amendment 3 - Quartering of Soldiers. Ratified 12/15/1791

No Soldier shall, in time of peace be quartered in any house, without the consent of the Owner, nor in time of war, but in a manner to be prescribed by law.

Amendment 4 - Search and Seizure. Ratified 12/15/1791

The right of the people to be secure in their persons, houses, papers, and effects, against unreasonable searches and seizures, shall not be violated, and no Warrants shall issue, but upon probable cause, supported by Oath or affirmation, and particularly describing the place to be searched, and the persons or things to be seized.

Amendment 5 - Trial and Punishment, Compensation for Takings. Ratified 12/15/1791

No person shall be held to answer for a capital, or otherwise infamous crime, unless on a presentment or indictment of a Grand Jury, except in cases arising in the land or naval forces, or in the Militia, when in actual service in time of War or public danger; nor shall any person be subject for the same offense to be twice put in jeopardy of life or limb; nor shall be compelled in any criminal case to be a witness against himself, nor be deprived of life, liberty, or property, without due process of law; nor shall private property be taken for public use, without just compensation.

Amendment 6 - Right to Speedy Trial, Confrontation of Witnesses. Ratified 12/15/1791

In all criminal prosecutions, the accused shall enjoy the right to a speedy and public trial, by an impartial jury of the State and district wherein the crime shall have been committed, which district shall have been previously ascertained by law, and to be informed of the nature and cause of the accusation; to be confronted with the witnesses against him; to have compulsory process for obtaining witnesses in his favor, and to have the Assistance of Counsel for his defence.

Amendment 7 - Trial by Jury in Civil Cases. Ratified 12/15/1791

In Suits at common law, where the value in controversy shall exceed twenty dollars, the right of trial by jury shall be preserved, and no fact tried by a jury, shall be otherwise re-examined in any Court of the United States, than according to the rules of the common law.

Amendment 8 - Cruel and Unusual Punishment. Ratified 12/15/1791

Excessive bail shall not be required, nor excessive fines imposed, nor cruel and unusual punishments inflicted.

Amendment 9 - Construction of Constitution. Ratified 12/15/1791

The enumeration in the Constitution, of certain rights, shall not be construed to deny or disparage others retained by the people.

Amendment 10 - Powers of the States and People. Ratified 12/15/1791

The powers not delegated to the United States by the Constitution, nor prohibited by it to the States, are reserved to the States respectively, or to the people.

Amendment 11 - Judicial Limits. Ratified 2/7/1795

The Judicial power of the United States shall not be construed to extend to any suit in law or equity, commenced or prosecuted against one of the United States by Citizens of another State, or by Citizens or Subjects of any Foreign State.

Amendment 12 - Choosing the President, Vice-President. Ratified 6/15/1804

The Electors shall meet in their respective states, and vote by ballot for President and Vice-President, one of whom, at least, shall not be an inhabitant of the same state with themselves; they shall name in their ballots the person voted for as President, and in distinct ballots the person voted for as Vice-President, and they shall make distinct lists of all persons voted for as President, and of all persons voted for as Vice-President and of the number of votes for each, which lists they shall sign and certify, and transmit sealed to the seat of the government of the United States, directed to the President of the Senate;

The President of the Senate shall, in the presence of the Senate and House of Representatives, open all the certificates and the votes shall then be counted;

The person having the greatest Number of votes for President, shall be the President, if such number be a majority of the whole number of Electors appointed; and if no person have such majority, then from the persons having the highest numbers not exceeding three on the list of those voted for as President, the House of Representatives shall choose immediately, by ballot, the President. But in choosing the President, the votes shall be taken by states, the representation from each state having one vote; a quorum for this purpose shall consist of a member or members from two-thirds of the states, and a majority of all the states shall be necessary to a choice. And if the House of Representatives shall not choose a President whenever the right of choice shall devolve upon them, before the fourth day of March next following, then the Vice-President shall act as President, as in the case of the death or other constitutional disability of the President.

The person having the greatest number of votes as Vice-President, shall be the Vice-President, if such number be a majority of the whole number of Electors appointed, and if no person have a majority, then from the two highest numbers on the list, the Senate shall choose the Vice-President; a quorum for the purpose shall consist of two-thirds of the whole number of Senators, and a majority of the whole number shall be necessary to a choice. But no person constitutionally ineligible to the office of President shall be eligible to that of Vice-President of the United States.

Amendment 13 - Slavery Abolished. Ratified 12/6/1865

1. Neither slavery nor involuntary servitude, except as a punishment for crime whereof the party shall have been duly convicted, shall exist within the United States, or any place subject to their jurisdiction.

2. Congress shall have power to enforce this article by appropriate legislation.

Amendment 14 - Citizenship Rights. Ratified 7/9/1868

1. All persons born or naturalized in the United States, and subject to the jurisdiction thereof, are citizens of the United States and of the State wherein they reside. No State shall make or enforce any law which shall abridge the privileges or immunities of citizens of the United States; nor shall any State deprive any person of life, liberty, or property, without due process of law; nor deny to any person within its jurisdiction the equal protection of the laws.

2. Representatives shall be apportioned among the several States according to their respective numbers, counting the whole number of persons in each State, excluding Indians not taxed. But when the right to vote at any election for the choice of electors for President and Vice-President of the United States, Representatives in Congress, the Executive and Judicial officers of a State, or the members of the Legislature thereof, is denied to any of the male inhabitants of such State, being twenty-one years of age, and citizens of the United States, or in any way abridged, except for participation in rebellion, or other crime, the basis of representation therein shall be reduced in the proportion which the number of such male citizens shall bear to the whole number of male citizens twenty-one years of age in such State.

3. No person shall be a Senator or Representative in Congress, or elector of President and Vice-President, or hold any office, civil or military, under the United States, or under any State, who, having previously taken an oath, as a member of Congress, or as an officer of the United States, or as a member of any State legislature, or as an executive or judicial officer of any State, to support the Constitution of the United States, shall have engaged in insurrection or rebellion against the same, or given aid or comfort to the enemies thereof. But Congress may by a vote of two-thirds of each House, remove such disability.

4. The validity of the public debt of the United States, authorized by law, including debts incurred for payment of pensions and bounties for services in suppressing insurrection or rebellion, shall not be questioned. But neither the United States nor any State shall assume or pay any debt or obligation incurred in aid of insurrection or rebellion against the United States, or any claim for the loss or emancipation of any slave; but all such debts, obligations and claims shall be held illegal and void.

5. The Congress shall have power to enforce, by appropriate legislation, the provisions of this article.

Amendment 15 - Race No Bar to Vote. Ratified 2/3/1870

1. The right of citizens of the United States to vote shall not be denied or abridged by the United States or by any State on account of race, color, or previous condition of servitude.

2. The Congress shall have power to enforce this article by appropriate legislation.

Amendment 16 - Status of Income Tax Clarified. Ratified 2/3/1913

The Congress shall have power to lay and collect taxes on incomes, from whatever source derived, without apportionment among the several States, and without regard to any census or enumeration.

Amendment 17 - Senators Elected by Popular Vote. Ratified 4/8/1913

The Senate of the United States shall be composed of two Senators from each State, elected by the people thereof, for six years; and each Senator shall have one vote. The electors in each State shall have the qualifications requisite for electors of the most numerous branch of the State legislatures.

When vacancies happen in the representation of any State in the Senate, the executive authority of such State shall issue writs of election to fill such vacancies: Provided, That the legislature of any State may empower the executive thereof to make temporary appointments until the people fill the vacancies by election as the legislature may direct.

This amendment shall not be so construed as to affect the election or term of any Senator chosen before it becomes valid as part of the Constitution.

Amendment 18 - Liquor Abolished. Ratified 1/16/1919. Repealed by Amendment 21, 12/5/1933

1. After one year from the ratification of this article the manufacture, sale, or transportation of intoxicating liquors within, the importation thereof into, or the exportation thereof from the United States and all territory subject to the jurisdiction thereof for beverage purposes is hereby prohibited.

2. The Congress and the several States shall have concurrent power to enforce this article by appropriate legislation.

3. This article shall be inoperative unless it shall have been ratified as an amendment to the Constitution by the legislatures of the several States, as provided in the Constitution, within seven years from the date of the submission hereof to the States by the Congress.

Amendment 19 - Women's Suffrage. Ratified 8/18/1920

The right of citizens of the United States to vote shall not be denied or abridged by the United States or by any State on account of sex.

Congress shall have power to enforce this article by appropriate legislation.

Amendment 20 - Presidential, Congressional Terms. Ratified 1/23/1933

1. The terms of the President and Vice President shall end at noon on the 20th day of January, and the terms of Senators and Representatives at noon on the 3d day of January, of the years in which such terms would have ended if this article had not been ratified; and the terms of their successors shall then begin.

2. The Congress shall assemble at least once in every year, and such meeting shall begin at noon on the 3d day of January, unless they shall by law appoint a different day.

3. If, at the time fixed for the beginning of the term of the President, the President elect shall have died, the Vice President elect shall become President. If a President shall not have been chosen before the time fixed for the beginning of his term, or if the President elect shall have failed to qualify, then the Vice President elect shall act as President until a President shall have qualified; and the Congress may by law provide for the case wherein neither a President elect nor a Vice President elect shall have qualified, declaring who shall then act as President, or the manner in which one who is to act shall be selected, and such person shall act accordingly until a President or Vice President shall have qualified.

4. The Congress may by law provide for the case of the death of any of the persons from whom the House of Representatives may choose a President whenever the right of choice shall have devolved upon them, and for the case of the death of any of the persons from whom the Senate may choose a Vice President whenever the right of choice shall have devolved upon them.

5. Sections 1 and 2 shall take effect on the 15th day of October following the ratification of this article.

6. This article shall be inoperative unless it shall have been ratified as an amendment to the Constitution by the legislatures of three-fourths of the several States within seven years from the date of its submission.

Amendment 21 - Amendment 18 Repealed. Ratified 12/5/1933

1. The eighteenth article of amendment to the Constitution of the United States is hereby repealed.

2. The transportation or importation into any State, Territory, or possession of the United States for delivery or use therein of intoxicating liquors, in violation of the laws thereof, is hereby prohibited.

3. The article shall be inoperative unless it shall have been ratified as an amendment to the Constitution by conventions in the several States, as provided in the Constitution, within seven years from the date of the submission hereof to the States by the Congress.

Amendment 22 - Presidential Term Limits. Ratified 2/27/1951

1. No person shall be elected to the office of the President more than twice, and no person who has held the office of President, or acted as President, for more than two years of a term to which some other person was elected President shall be elected to the office of the President more than once. But this Article shall not apply to any person holding the office of President, when this Article was proposed by the Congress, and shall not prevent any person who may be holding the office of President, or acting as President, during the term within which this Article becomes operative from holding the office of President or acting as President during the remainder of such term.

2. This article shall be inoperative unless it shall have been ratified as an amendment to the Constitution by the legislatures of three-fourths of the several States within seven years from the date of its submission to the States by the Congress.

Amendment 23 - Presidential Vote for District of Columbia. Ratified 3/29/1961

1. The District constituting the seat of Government of the United States shall appoint in such manner as the Congress may direct: A number of electors of President and Vice President equal to the whole number of Senators and Representatives in Congress to which the District would be entitled if it were a State, but in no event more than the least populous State; they shall be in addition to those appointed by the States, but they shall be considered, for the purposes of the election of President and Vice President, to be electors appointed by a State; and they shall meet in the District and perform such duties as provided by the twelfth article of amendment.

2. The Congress shall have power to enforce this article by appropriate legislation.

Amendment 24 - Poll Tax Barred. Ratified 1/23/1964

1. The right of citizens of the United States to vote in any primary or other election for President or Vice President, for electors for President or Vice President, or for Senator or Representative in Congress, shall not be denied or abridged by the United States or any State by reason of failure to pay any poll tax or other tax.

2. The Congress shall have power to enforce this article by appropriate legislation.

Amendment 25 - Presidential Disability and Succession. Ratified 2/10/1967

1. In case of the removal of the President from office or of his death or resignation, the Vice President shall become President.

2. Whenever there is a vacancy in the office of the Vice President, the President shall nominate a Vice President who shall take office upon confirmation by a majority vote of both Houses of Congress.

3. Whenever the President transmits to the President pro tempore of the Senate and the Speaker of the House of Representatives his written declaration that he is unable to discharge the powers and duties of his office, and until he transmits to them a written declaration to the contrary, such powers and duties shall be discharged by the Vice President as Acting President.

4. Whenever the Vice President and a majority of either the principal officers of the executive departments or of such other body as Congress may by law provide, transmit to the President pro tempore of the Senate and the Speaker of the House of Representatives their written declaration that the President is unable to discharge the powers and duties of his office, the Vice President shall immediately assume the powers and duties of the office as Acting President.

Thereafter, when the President transmits to the President pro tempore of the Senate and the Speaker of the House of Representatives his written declaration that no inability exists, he shall resume the powers and duties of his office unless the Vice President and a majority of either the principal officers of the executive department or of such other body as Congress may by law provide, transmit within four days to the President pro tempore of the Senate and the Speaker of the House of Representatives their written declaration that the President is unable to discharge the powers and duties of his office. Thereupon Congress shall decide the issue, assembling within forty eight hours for that purpose if not in session. If the Congress, within twenty one days after receipt of the latter written declaration, or, if Congress is not in session, within twenty one days after Congress is required to assemble, determines by two thirds vote of both Houses that the President is unable to discharge the powers and duties of his office, the Vice President shall continue to discharge the same as Acting President; otherwise, the President shall resume the powers and duties of his office.

Amendment 26 - Voting Age Set to 18 Years. Ratified 7/1/1971

1. The right of citizens of the United States, who are eighteen years of age or older, to vote shall not be denied or abridged by the United States or by any State on account of age.

By Marty Piatt, Architect

2. The Congress shall have power to enforce this article by appropriate legislation.

Amendment 27 - Limiting Changes to Congressional Pay. Ratified 5/7/1992

No law, varying the compensation for the services of the Senators and Representatives, shall take effect, until an election of Representatives shall have intervened.

2017 ARTICLES OF FEDERATION

CONSTITUTION PREAMBLE

We The People of the United States, in Order to form a more perfect Union, establish Justice, insure domestic Tranquility, provide for the common Defense, promote the general Welfare, and secure the Blessings of Liberty to ourselves and our Posterity, do ordain and establish this Constitution and Articles of Federation for the United States of America.

ARTICLE I – LEGISLATIVE BRANCH OF GOVERNMENT

Section 1 – The Legislature

The Legislative Power herein granted shall be vested in a non-partisan unicameral Congress of the United States, which shall consist of a House of Representatives.

Section 2 – The House of Representatives

The House of Representatives shall be composed of Members chosen every fourth year by the citizen People of the United States within the State they shall represent, with half its members elected every second year.

The terms of the Representatives shall end at noon on the 3rd day of January. No member shall be elected more than two terms.

No Person shall be a Representative who shall not have attained to the Age of twenty five Years, and been seven Years a Citizen of the United States, and who shall not, when elected, be an Inhabitant of that State in which he shall be chosen.

The total Number of Representatives shall be equal to tenfold the number of the several States apportioned to the States. Representatives shall be apportioned among the United States, which may be included within this Union, according to their respective Numbers, which shall be determined by the Number of Persons.

Representatives shall be apportioned among the several States according to their respective numbers, counting the whole number of persons in each State, excluding Indians not taxed.

But when the right to vote at any election for President of the United States, Representatives in Congress, the Executive and Judicial officers of a State, or the members of the Legislature thereof, is denied to any of the citizen inhabitants of such State, being eighteen years of age, and citizens of the United States, or in any way abridged, except for participation in rebellion, or other crime, the basis of representation therein shall be reduced in the proportion which the number of citizens shall bear to the whole number of citizens eighteen years of age in such State.

When vacancies happen in the Representation from any State, the Executive Authority thereof shall issue Writs of Election to fill such Vacancies.

The House of Representatives shall choose their Speaker and other Officers; and shall have the sole Power of Impeachment. The Vice President of the United States shall be President of the House of Representatives, but shall have no Vote, unless they be equally divided.

When sitting for that Purpose, they shall be on Oath or Affirmation. When the President of the United States is tried, the Chief Justice shall preside; and no Person shall be convicted without the Concurrence of two thirds of the Members present.

Judgment in Cases of Impeachment shall not extend further than to removal from Office, and disqualification to hold and enjoy any Office of honor, Trust or Profit under the United States, but the Party convicted shall nevertheless be liable and subject to Indictment, Trial, Judgment and Punishment, according to Law.

Section 3 – Elections, Meetings

The Times, Places and Manner of holding Elections for Representatives, shall be prescribed in each State by the Legislature thereof; but the Congress may at any time by Law make or alter such Regulations, except as to the Places of choosing Senators.

The Congress shall assemble at least once in every year, and such meeting shall begin at noon on the 3rd day of January, unless they shall by law appoint a different day.

Section 4 – Memberships, Rules, Journals

Congress shall be the Judge of the Elections, Returns and Qualifications of its own Members, and a Majority of each shall constitute a Quorum to do Business; but a smaller Number may adjourn from day to day, and may be authorized to compel the Attendance of absent Members, in such Manner, and under such Penalties as each House may provide.

Congress may determine the Rules of its Proceedings, punish its Members for disorderly Behavior, and, with the Concurrence of two thirds, expel a Member. All members shall be accountable to Federal law.

Congress shall keep a Journal of its Proceedings, and publish the same; and the Yeas and Nays of the Members of Congress on any question shall, at the Desire of one-fifth of those Present, be entered on the Journal.

During the Session of Congress, shall not adjourn for more than three days, nor to any other Place than that in which Congress shall be sitting.

Section 5 - Compensation

The Representatives shall receive a sole Compensation for their Services, to be ascertained by Law applicable to all those under Federal servitude, and paid out of the Treasury of the United States.

Representatives may enact no Law determining their own special Compensation and benefits in excess of those for Federal servitude administered by the Federal office of personnel management.

Representatives shall receive no additional compensation from any other entity or source whatsoever for whom they may owe allegiance other than the Unites States for whom they serve and the state they represent.

No law, varying the compensation for the services of the Representatives, shall take effect, until an election of Representatives shall have intervened.

They shall in all Cases, except Treason, Felony and Breach of the Peace, be privileged from Arrest during their Attendance at the Session of Congress, and in going to and returning from the same; and for any Speech or Debate; they shall not be questioned in any other Place.

No Representative shall, during the Time for which they were elected, be appointed to any civil Office under the Authority of the United States, which shall have been created, or the Emoluments whereof shall have been increased during such time; and no Person holding any Office under the United States, shall be a Member of Congress during his Continuance in Office.

Section 6 - Revenue Bills, Legislative Process, Presidential Veto

All Bills for raising Revenue shall originate in the House of Representatives. Every Bill which shall have passed the House of Representatives by simple majority, shall, before it become a Law, be presented to the President of the United States; If the President approves, it shall be signed, but if not shall return it, with Objections, who shall enter the Objections at large on the Journal, and proceed to reconsider it.

If after such Reconsideration two-thirds of Congress shall agree to pass the Bill, it shall become a Law. But in all such Cases the Votes shall be determined by Yeas and Nays, and the Names of the Persons voting for and against the Bill shall be entered on the Journal.

If any Bill shall not be returned by the President within ten Days after it shall have been presented to the President, the same shall be a Law, in like Manner as if the President had signed it, unless the Congress by their Adjournment prevent its Return, in which Case it shall not be a Law.

A Committee of the States, consisting of one Representative-delegate from each of the several States shall review and debate all proposed legislation; not on its merit, but rather on its Constitutionality; for adherence to the Constitution prior to submission to the President for approval.

The Committee may approve by simple majority vote, or reject the proposed legislation and return it to the House members for Reconsideration.

A Committee of States shall approve all Executive appointees by simple majority vote, or reject the proposed appointee and return the request to the President for Reconsideration.

Every Order, Resolution, or Vote (except on a question of Adjournment) shall be presented to the President of the United States; and before the Same shall take Effect, shall be approved by the President, or being disapproved by the President, shall be repassed by two-thirds of the House of Representatives, according to the Rules and Limitations prescribed in the Case of a Bill.

Section 7 – Powers of Congress

The Congress shall have Power To lay and collect Taxes, Duties, Imposts and Excises, to pay the Debts and provide for the common Defense and general Welfare of the United States; but all Duties, Imposts and Excises shall be uniform throughout the United States;

The Congress shall have power to lay and collect taxes on all gross incomes, or consumption of goods and services, from whatever source derived, without apportionment among the several States, and without regard to any census or enumeration. No non-governmental income receiving entity, foreign or domestic, including but not limited to: a person, group, organization, committee, corporation, religious institution, political party, campaign, referendum, initiative, lobby, etc; shall be exempt from income taxation.

To regulate Commerce with foreign Nations, and among the several States, and with the Indian Tribes;

To establish uniform Laws of Naturalization and Immigration, and with the willing assistance of the several States, shall enforce said laws preventing unlawful immigration;

To establish uniform Laws on the subject of Bankruptcies throughout the United States;

To coin Money, regulate the Value thereof, and of foreign Coin, and fix the Standard of Weights and Measures;

To provide for the Punishment of counterfeiting the Securities and current Coin of the United States;

To regulate political campaign financing;

To establish Post Offices and Post Roads;

To promote the Progress of Science and useful Arts, by securing for limited Times to Authors and Inventors the exclusive Right to their respective Writings and Discoveries;

To define and punish Piracies and Felonies committed on the high Seas, and Offenses against the Law of Nations;

To declare War, grant Letters of Marque and Reprisal, and make Rules concerning Captures on Land and Water;

To provide and maintain an Army, Navy, and Air Force for National Defense protecting the borders, shores, and airspace of the Unites States and its sovereign territories.

To make Rules for the Government and Regulation of the National Defense;

To provide for calling forth the Militia to execute the Laws of the Union, suppress Insurrections and repel Invasions;

To provide for organizing, arming, and disciplining, the Militia, and for governing such Part of them as may be employed in the Service of the United States, reserving to the States respectively, the Appointment of the Officers, and the Authority of training the Militia according to the discipline prescribed by Congress;

To exercise exclusive Legislation in all Cases whatsoever, over such District (not exceeding ten Miles square) as may, by Cession of particular States, and the Acceptance of Congress, become the Seat of the Government of the United States, and to exercise like Authority over all Places purchased by the Consent of the Legislature of the State in which the Same shall be, for the Erection of Forts, Magazines, Arsenals, Dockyards, and other needful Buildings;

To make all Laws which shall be necessary and proper for carrying into Execution the foregoing Powers, and all other Powers vested by this Constitution in the Government of the United States, or in any Department or Officer thereof.

Section 8 – Limits on Congress

The Privilege of the Writ of Habeas Corpus shall not be suspended, unless when in Cases of Rebellion or Invasion the public Safety may require it.

Congress shall enact no law that applies to the Citizens of the United States that does not apply equally to its members; and, Congress shall enact no law that applies to its members that does not apply equally to the citizens of the United States;

No Bill of Attainder or Ex Post Facto Law shall be passed retroactively changing the legal consequences, standing, or status of judicial rulings of constitutional authority, actions committed, or relationships that existed prior to the enactment of the law.

No Capitation, or other direct, Tax shall be laid, unless in Proportion to the Census or enumeration herein before directed to be taken.

No Tax or Duty shall be laid on Articles exported from any State.

No Preference shall be given by any Regulation of Commerce or Revenue to the Ports of one State over those of another; nor shall Vessels bound to, or from, one State, be obliged to enter, clear, or pay Duties in another.

No Money shall be drawn from the Treasury, but in Consequence of Appropriations made by Law; and a regular Statement and Account of the Receipts and Expenditures of all public Money shall be published.

No Money, in excess of Money available from the United States Treasury, shall be drawn or dispersed; or borrowed from any other foreign country, entity, or source for expenditure.

No Title of Nobility shall be granted by the United States; And no Person holding any Office of Profit or Trust under them, shall, without the Consent of the Congress, accept of any present, Emolument, Office, or Title, of any kind whatever, from any King, Prince, or foreign State.

Section 9 - Powers prohibited of States

No State shall enter into any Treaty, Alliance, or Confederation; grant Letters of Marque and Reprisal; coin Money; emit Bills of Credit; make any Thing but gold and silver Coin a Tender in Payment of Debts; pass any Law impairing the Obligation of Contracts, or grant any Title of Nobility.

No State shall pass a Bill of Attainder or Ex Post Facto Law retroactively changing the legal consequences, standing, or status of Judicial rulings of constitutional authority, actions committed, or relationships that existed prior to the enactment of the law.

No State shall, without the Consent of the Congress, lay any Imposts or Duties on Imports or Exports, except what may be absolutely necessary for executing it's inspection Laws, and the net Produce of all Duties and Imposts, laid by any State on Imports or Exports, shall be for the Use of the Treasury of the United States; and all such Laws shall be subject to the Revision and Control of Congress.

No State shall, without the Consent of Congress, lay any Duty of Tonnage, keep Troops, or Ships of War in time of Peace, enter into any Agreement or Compact with another State, or with a foreign Power, or engage in War, unless actually invaded, or in such imminent Danger as will not admit of delay.

No State shall enact or enforce Laws in excess of those enacted by Congress to establish uniform Laws of Naturalization and Immigration, but shall have the right to enforce all such Laws.

No state may impose taxation on property, and may only impose taxation on income and/or consumption.

By Marty Piatt, Architect

ARTICLE II – EXECUTIVE BRANCH OF GOVERNMENT

Section 1 – The President

The Executive Power shall be vested in a President of the United States of America. The President shall hold his Office during the Term of four Years, and, together with the Vice President, chosen for the same Term, be elected by the citizen People of the United States. The terms of the President and Vice President shall end at noon on the 20th day of January.

The Presidential candidate having the greatest Number of Votes of the People exceeding fifty percent in the Primary election shall be the President. In every Case, after the Choice of the President, the candidate having the greatest number of votes of the People shall be the Vice President.

But if there should remain two or more candidates having equal votes, or votes less than fifty percent, three Presidential candidates receiving the greatest number of votes shall be decided in the General election.

A non-partisan Primary election shall occur on the first Tuesday after the first Monday in the month of June. A non-partisan General election shall occur on the first Tuesday after the first Monday in the month of November; and the election day of each election shall be the same throughout the United States.

The right of citizens of the United States, who are eighteen years of age or older, to vote shall not be denied or abridged by the United States or by any State on account of race, color, sex, or age, and shall provide proof of citizenship to vote.

The right of citizens of the United States to vote in any primary, general, or other election shall not be denied or abridged by the United States or any State by reason of failure to pay any poll tax or other tax.

No Person except a natural born Citizen, or a Citizen of the United States, shall be eligible to the Office of President; neither shall any Person be eligible to that Office who shall not have attained to the Age of thirty-five Years, and been fourteen Years a Resident within the United States.

In Case of the Removal of the President from Office, or of his Death, Resignation, or Inability to discharge the Powers and Duties of the said Office, the Same shall devolve on the Vice President, and for the Case of Removal, Death, Resignation or Inability, both of the President and Vice President, the Speaker of the House shall then act as President; and for the Case of Removal, Death, Resignation or Inability, of the Speaker of the House, the Supreme Court Chief Justice shall then act as President; and all shall act accordingly, until the Disability be removed, or a President shall be elected.

The President shall, at stated Times, receive for his Services, a Compensation, which shall neither be increased nor diminished during the Period for which he shall have been elected, and he shall not receive within that Period any other Emolument from the United States, or any of them.

The President's spouse, domestic partner, or cohabitant, being an unelected person, shall not receive any compensation or Emolument paid from the United States Treasury, benefits, appointments, executive or Federal servitude, nor special privileges; that would otherwise be granted or bestowed to any member of Nobility.

Before the President enter on the Execution of his Office, the President shall take the following Oath or Affirmation: "I do solemnly swear [or affirm] that I will faithfully execute the Office of President of the United States, and will to the best of my ability, preserve, protect and defend the Constitution of the United States."

Section 2 - Civilian Power over Military, Cabinet, Pardon Power, Appointments

The President shall be Commander in Chief of the Armed Forces of the United States, and of the Militia of the several States, when called into the actual Service of the United States; may require the Opinion, in writing, of the principal Officer in each of the executive Departments, upon any Subject relating to the Duties of their respective Offices, and shall have the Power to grant Reprieves and Pardons for Offences against the United States, except in Cases of Impeachment.

The President shall have the Power, by and with the Advice and Consent of Congress, to make Treaties, provided two-thirds of the Representatives present concur; and shall nominate, and by and with the Advice and Consent of Congress, shall appoint Ambassadors, other public Ministers and Consuls, Jurors of the Supreme Court, and all other Officers of the United States, whose Appointments are not herein otherwise provided for, and which shall be established by Law: but the Congress may by Law vest the Appointment of such inferior Officers, as they think proper, in the President alone, in the Courts of Law, or in the Heads of Departments.

The President shall have Power to fill all Vacancies that may happen during the Recess of the Congress, by granting Commissions, which shall expire at the End of their next Session.

The President shall have the power to submit for Legislative review and approval proposed government spending budgets; maintaining an executive option of a line-item veto of all Legislative spending bills.

The President shall have the power to issue Executive Orders, Directives, Memorandums, or Presidential Proclamations to clarify, enforce, or act to further law put forth by the Congress or the Constitution; and shall, in a national emergency created by an attack upon the United States, its territories or possessions, or its armed forces, issue orders to repel attacks against the United States as Commander and Chief of the Armed Forces of the United States.

No Executive department or personnel shall intervene in any matter relating to Legislative or Judicial rulings, proceedings, or involvement in matters undermining Constitutional authority that would otherwise compromise the Separation of Powers between the Branches of Government as set forth in this Constitution.

Section 3 - State of the Union, Convening Congress

The President shall from time to time give to the Congress Information of the State of the Union, and recommend to their Consideration such Measures as he shall judge necessary and expedient; and may, on extraordinary Occasions, convene Congress, and in Case of Disagreement, with Respect to the Time of Adjournment, may adjourn Congress to such Time as he shall think proper; shall receive Ambassadors and other public Ministers; shall take Care that the Laws be faithfully executed, and shall Commission all the Officers of the United States.

Section 4 - Disqualification

The President, Vice President and all civil Officers of the United States, shall be removed from Office on Impeachment for, and Conviction of, Treason, Bribery, or other high Crimes and Misdemeanors, or failing to uphold the Articles of this Constitution.

By Marty Piatt, Architect

ARTICLE III – JUDICIAL BRANCH OF GOVERNMENT

Section 1 - Judicial Powers

The Judicial Power of the United States shall be vested in one Supreme Court consisting of twelve Judge Jurists consisting of six men and six women. No single Jurist shall determine the decisive course of any Supreme Court ruling.

The Judge Jurist vested with the greatest ruling seniority serving on the Supreme Court shall assume the role of Chief Justice of the Supreme Court of the United States of America; until such time their Continuance in Office be vacated, the second vested senior Jurist shall assume the role.

The inferior Courts of the Judicial Branch shall consist of Federal District Courts and Appellate Circuit Courts.

The total number of District Courts shall be number equal to twice the number of the several States apportioned to the States determined by the total number of House of Representative members of each of the several States. Each of the several States shall have a minimum of one District Court based upon a minimum of one House of Representatives member.

The number of Appellate Circuit Courts shall equal eleven. Excluding the Supreme Court Chief Justice, each Appellate Circuit Court shall have one presiding Supreme Court Associate Justice.

The Courts shall have Judicial review of all laws enacted by the several sovereign States; the Congress; and the Legislative and Executive Branches of Government.

The Judges, both of the Supreme and inferior Courts, shall hold their Offices during good Behavior; and when deemed necessary by two-thirds vote of the several States, or two-thirds vote of Congress and Executive authority, may be impeached or removed from Federal servitude for failure to uphold the Articles of this Constitution.

Section 2 - Trial by Jury, Original Jurisdiction, Jury Trials

The Judicial power of the United States shall not be construed to extend to any suit in law or equity, commenced or prosecuted against one of the United States by Citizens of another State, or by Citizens or Subjects of any Foreign State. In all Cases affecting Ambassadors, other public Ministers and Consuls, and those in which a State shall be Party, the Supreme Court shall have original Jurisdiction.

In all the other Cases before mentioned, the Supreme Court shall have appellate Jurisdiction, both as to Law and Fact, with such Exceptions, and under such Regulations as the Congress shall make.

The Trial of all Crimes, except in Cases of Impeachment, shall be by Jury; and such Trial shall be held in the State where the said Crimes shall have been committed; but when not committed within any State, the Trial shall be at such Place or Places as the Congress may by Law have directed.

Section 3 – Treason

Treason against the United States shall consist only in levying War against them, or in adhering to their Enemies, or unlawful foreign national Invaders; giving them Aid and Comfort. No Person shall be convicted of Treason unless on the Testimony of two Witnesses to the same overt Act, or on Confession in open Court.

The Congress, as a matter of law, shall have authority to declare the Punishment of Treason, but no Attainder of Treason shall work Corruption of Blood, or Forfeiture except during the Life of the Person attainted.

Section 4 – Compensation

The Judges, both of the Supreme and inferior Courts, shall at stated Times, receive for their Services a Compensation, which shall not be diminished during their Continuance in Office. The Judges shall receive a sole Compensation for their Services, to be ascertained by Law applicable to all those under Federal servitude, and paid out of the Treasury of the United States.

ARTICLE IV – THE STATES

Section 1 - Each State to Honor all others

Full Faith and Credit shall be given in each State to the public Acts, Records, and judicial Proceedings of every other State. And the Congress may by general Laws prescribe the Manner in which such Acts, Records and Proceedings shall be proved, and the Effect thereof.

Section 2 - State citizens, Extradition

The Citizens of each State shall be entitled to all Privileges and Immunities of Citizens in the several States.

A Person charged in any State with Treason, Felony, or other Crime, who shall flee from Justice, and be found in another State, shall on Demand of the executive Authority of the State from which he fled, be delivered up, to be removed to the State having Jurisdiction of the Crime.

No Person held to Service or Labor in one State, under the Laws thereof, escaping into another, shall, in Consequence of any Law or Regulation therein, be discharged from such Service or Labor, but shall be delivered up on Claim of the Party to whom such Service or Labor may be due.

Section 3 - New States

New States may be admitted by the Congress into this Union; but no new State shall be formed or erected within the Jurisdiction of any other State; nor any State be formed by the Junction of two or more States, or Parts of States, without the Consent of the Legislatures of the States concerned.

The Congress shall have Power to dispose of and make all needful Rules and Regulations respecting the Territory or other Property belonging to the United States; and nothing in this Constitution shall be so construed as to Prejudice any Claims of the United States, or of any particular State.

Section 4 – Federal Democratic Government

The United States shall guarantee to every sovereign State in this Union a Federal Democratic form of Government, and shall protect each of them against Invasion; and on Application of the Legislature, or of the Executive (when the Legislature cannot be convened), against domestic Violence.

Section 5 – Repeal of Federal Law

The several sovereign States comprising this Federal Democracy shall have the collective right to repeal any Federal law enacted by Congress whenever two-thirds deem it necessary.

Section 6 – Unlawful Immigration

The several sovereign States may enact laws relating to unlawful immigration not exceeding those uniform Federal Laws of Naturalization and Immigration; and shall be permitted to enforce all such laws preventing unlawful immigration.

ARTICLE V – CONSTITUTIONAL AMENDMENTS

The several State Legislatures, whenever two-thirds deem it necessary, shall propose amending Articles to this Constitution; shall call a Constitutional Convention for proposing amending Articles, which shall be valid to all Intents and Purposes, as Part of this Constitution, when voted upon and ratified by three-fourths of the citizen People of the United States of America.

No amending Article shall abridge, negate, or otherwise undermine any previous enumerated Article of this Constitution hereafter.

The Constitution is not an instrument for the government to restrain the People; it is an instrument for the people to restrain the government; lest it come to dominate our lives and interests.

ARTICLE VI – DEBTS, SUPREMACY, OATHS

All Debts contracted and Engagements entered into, before the Adoption of this Constitution, shall be as valid against the United States under this Constitution.

This Constitution, and the Laws of the United States which shall be made in Pursuance thereof; and all Treaties made, or which shall be made, under the Authority of the United States, shall be the supreme Law of the Land; and the Judges in every State shall be bound thereby, anything in the Constitution or Laws of any State to the Contrary notwithstanding.

The Representatives before mentioned, and the Members of the several State Legislatures, and all executive and judicial Officers, both of the United States and of the several States, shall be bound by Oath or Affirmation, to support this Constitution; but no religious Test shall ever be required as a Qualification to any Office or public Trust under the United States.

ARTICLE VII – CONSTITUTIONAL RATIFICATION

The Ratification of three-quarters of the several States shall be sufficient for the Establishment of this Constitution between the States so ratifying the Same.

ARTICLE VIII – BILL OF RIGHTS

Section 1 - Freedom of Religion, Press, and Expression

Congress shall make no law respecting an establishment of religion, or prohibiting the free exercise thereof; or abridging the freedom of English speech of citizen People, or of the Press; or the right of the People peaceably to assemble, and to petition the Government for a redress of grievances.

Corporations shall not be considered people or persons.

Neither a state nor the Federal Government can set up a church. Neither can pass laws, which aid one religion, aid all religions or prefer one religion to another.

Neither can force nor influence a person to go to or to remain away from church against his will or force him to profess a belief or disbelief in any religion.

The practice of any religion or faith, which poses no threat of harm or death to all non-believers, gentiles, or infidels, may not be abridged.

No person can be punished for entertaining or professing religious beliefs or disbeliefs, for church attendance or non-attendance.

No tax in any amount, large or small, can be levied to support any religious activities or institutions, whatever they may be called, or whatever form they may adopt to teach or practice religion.

Neither a state nor the Federal Government can, openly or secretly, participate in the affairs of any religious organizations or groups. Neither a religious organization nor groups can, openly or secretly, participate in the affairs of any state or the Federal Government; thus creating 'a wall of separation between Church and State'.

Section 2 - Right to Bear Arms

A well-regulated Militia, being necessary to the security of a free State, the right of the people to keep and bear Arms, shall not be infringed.

Section 3 - Quartering of Military Members

No Member of the Military shall, in time of peace be quartered in any house, without the consent of the Owner, nor in time of war, but in a manner to be prescribed by Law.

Section 4 - Search and Seizure

The right of the People to be secure in their persons, houses, papers, effects, and privacy against unreasonable searches and seizures, shall not be violated, and no Warrants shall issue, but upon probable cause, supported by Oath or Affirmation, and specifically describing the place to be searched, and the persons or things to be seized.

By *Marty Piatt, Architect*

Section 5 - Trial and Punishment, Compensation for Takings

No person shall be held to answer for a capital, or otherwise infamous crime, unless on a presentment or indictment of a Grand Jury, except in cases arising in the land or naval forces, or in the Militia, when in actual service in time of War or public danger; nor shall any person be subject for the same offense to be twice put in jeopardy of life or limb; nor shall be compelled in any criminal case to be a witness against himself, nor be deprived of life, liberty, or property, without due process of law; nor shall private property be taken for public use, without just compensation.

Section 6 - Right to Speedy Trial, Confrontation of Witnesses

In all criminal prosecutions, the accused Citizen shall enjoy the right to a speedy and public trial without indefinite detention, by an impartial jury of the State and district wherein the crime shall have been committed, which district shall have been previously ascertained by law, and to be informed of the nature and cause of the accusation; to be confronted with the witnesses against him; to have compulsory process for obtaining witnesses in his favor, and to have the Assistance of Counsel for his defense.

Section 7 - Trial by Jury in Civil Cases

In Suits at common law, where the value in controversy shall exceed twenty dollars, the right of trial by jury shall be preserved, and no fact tried by a jury, shall be otherwise re-examined in any Court of the United States, than according to the rules of the common law.

Section 8 - Cruel and Unusual Punishment

Excessive bail shall not be required, nor excessive fines imposed, nor cruel and unusual punishments inflicted.

Section 9 - Construction of Constitution

The enumeration in the Constitution, of certain rights, shall not be construed to deny or disparage others retained by the People.

Section 10 - Powers of the States and People

The powers not delegated to the United States by the Constitution, nor prohibited by it to the States, are reserved to the States respectively, or to the People.

ARTICLE IX – EQUAL RIGHTS

We hold these truths to be self-evident, that all Men and Woman are created Equal, that they are endowed by their Creator with certain unalienable Rights, which among these are Life, Liberty, and the pursuit of Happiness.

No State shall make or enforce any law, which shall abridge the privileges or immunities of citizens of the United States; nor shall any State deprive any person of life, liberty, or property, without due process of law; nor deny to any person within its jurisdiction the equal protection of the laws.

ARTICLE X – BIRTHRIGHT AND CITIZENSHIP

All Persons born in the United States or in its sovereign territories to Citizens or naturalized Citizens of the Unites States, and subject to the jurisdiction thereof, shall have birthright and are Citizens of the United States and of the State wherein they reside.

Birthright or Citizenship shall not be granted to individuals born to undocumented foreign nationals residing unlawfully having unauthorized residency within the Unites States or its sovereign territories; nor shall those be granted citizenship thereafter.

Immigrants to the United States of America must:

1. Have the means to sustain themselves economically;
2. Not be a financial burden whatsoever receiving no local, State, or Federal aid;
3. Be of economic and social benefit to the country;
4. Be of good character and have no criminal records at all;
5. Be contributors to the general well being of the nation.

By Marty Piatt, Architect

United States Immigration law will ensure that:

1. Immigration authorities will have a record of each foreign visitor or immigrant;
2. Foreign visitors do not violate their visa status;
3. Foreign visitors are banned from interfering in the country's internal politics;
4. Foreign visitors who enter under false pretenses will be imprisoned and/or deported;
5. Foreign visitors violating the terms of their entry shall be imprisoned and/or deported, and shall forever be barred from the United States or receiving U.S. Citizenship;
6. Those who aid in illegal immigration will be fined and/or imprisoned, and permanently deported if illegally residing in the United States.

End.